The Zen of Living and Dying

D0050112

THE ZEN OF LIVING AND DYING

A Practical and Spiritual Guide

PHILIP KAPLEAU

WITHDRAWN

SHAMBHALA
Boston & London
1998

Shambhala Publications, Inc.
Horticultural Hall
300 Massachusetts Avenue
Boston, MA 02115
www.shambhala.com

© 1989, 1998 by The Rochester Zen Center

All rights reserved. No part of this book may be reproduced in any form or by any means, electronic or mechanical, including photocopying, recording, or by any information storage and retrieval system, without permission in writing from the publisher.

Printed in the United States of America
♾ This edition is printed on acid-free paper that meets the American National Standards Institute z39.48 Standard.

Distributed in the United States by Random House, Inc., and in Canada by Random House of Canada Ltd

Library of Congress Cataloging-in-Publication Data

Kapleau, Philip, 1912–
The Zen of living and dying : a practical and spiritual guide/
Philip Kapleau.
p. cm.
Rev. ed. of: The wheel of life and death. 1989.

ISBN-10: 1-57062-198-5

ISBN-13: 978-1-57062-198-7

1. Death. 2. Spiritual life—Zen Buddhism.
3. Death—Religious aspects—Zen Buddhism.
I. Kapleau, Philip, 1912– Wheel of life and death.
II. Title.
BD444.K348 1998
294.3′423—DC21 97-40188
CIP

Even as night darkens the green earth
the wheel turns.
Death follows birth.
Strive as you sleep with every breath,
that you may wake past day, past death!

CONTENTS

PART THREE: KARMA

Editor's Note

The Zen of Living and Dying is a revised and considerably edited version of Philip Kapleau's *The Wheel of Life and Death,* which was originally published in 1989.

ACKNOWLEDGMENTS

NO BOOK is ever the work of one person alone. Behind each completed book are many helping hands. I am exceedingly grateful to the following people for their contributions:

The Ven. Sunyana Graef, who collaborated with me on the "Karma" and "Rebirth" sections. Without her assistance these important subjects would not be covered as completely as I now believe them to be.

The Ven. Mitra Bishop, who acted as my research assistant, typed the first draft of the manuscript, and data processed the whole text.

Geoff Lister, an experienced hospice evaluator, provided detailed information on the structure and functioning of hospices.

Tom Roberts, my longtime friend and senior student, oversaw many aspects of the book, from handling the contract to critiquing *The Zen of Living and Dying.*

Attorney Casey Frank, a good friend and longtime student, compiled the information on the issues of physician-assisted dying, on living wills, and on related topics.

The Ven. Bodhin Kjolhede, abbot of the Rochester Zen Center, Dr. Peter Auhagen, Dr. Christina Auhagen and I had many discussions on death and dying which provided the building blocks for *The Zen of Living and Dying.*

Chris Pulleyn, Ken Kraft, Dr. Mary Wolfe, and Rafe Martin read the manuscript of *The Zen of Living and Dying* and made many useful suggestions.

Doctors Leonard Wheeler, John Sheldon, Maike Otto, and Robert Goldman took time from very busy schedules to share with me their experiences with dying patients.

Nurses Penny Townsend Quill, Carolyn Jaffe, Nathan Hanks,

and Jeffrey Estes graciously answered my numerous questions about terminally ill patients.

Thanks are due Greg Mello for his article on the life of Socrates.

Lastly, I am deeply indebted to Peter Turner, my editor at Shambhala, who did a superb job of editing the original edition of *The Wheel of Life and Death* for republication.

INTRODUCTION

ANYONE RESEARCHING the literature on death and dying confronts a prodigious array of books and articles on these inescapable human experiences. In the past decade their number has ballooned to include controversial suicide manuals, accounts of near-death experiences, and articles on how to execute a living will. This vast literary output obviously feeds a deep human need: the need for answers to the perennial questions "Where did I come from when I was born and where will I go when I die? What meaning has my life, my death?"

To be human is to ask these questions. They reflect our greatest doubts, our deepest alienation from Self. Without answers that satisfy, there remains in the heart a gnawing angst that sours the sweetest of life's experiences. For with the mass of humanity it is still an article of faith that death is the greatest of human misfortunes and that dying is the final and agonizing struggle against extinction. At the same time the incomprehensibility of death, its presumed finality, has awed and terrified men and women since the dawn of consciousness.

Why yet another book on death and dying? And how does this one differ from the rest? Valuable as these numerous studies have been in shaping constructive and compassionate social attitudes toward the fatally ill and in clarifying our ways of thinking about our own life and death, most of them nevertheless lack a spiritual dimension—a religious attitude toward life and death—and practical guidance in what may be called the art and religion of dying.

A spiritual orientation to dying involves, among other things, an understanding and deep acceptance of causation and the continuity of life. It also implies a recognition of the value of rites of passage—funeral services which, when conducted with passion and conviction, help facilitate the smooth transition from this life to future cycles of existence. Many people feel that funerals today are brief, hurried events devoid of true spiritual significance even when conducted by clergy—that they fail to acknowledge the reality of death, loss, and grief.[1]

Sociology professor Robert Fulton and others have noted that over the past generation a tremendous secularization of death has taken place, that now "people die ascetically in aseptic hospitals rather than aesthetically in their homes." The physician has replaced the priest; he is today's magician with the power to extend life; he is our new escort from this vale of tears. For this confusion of values we pay a high price. In his book *Modern Man in Search of a Soul,* Carl Jung (1875–1962) spells out the cost:

> Among all my patients in the second half of life—that is to say, over 35—there has not been one whose problem in the last resort was not that of finding a religious outlook on life. It is safe to say that every one of them fell ill because he had lost that which the living religions of every age have given to their followers, and none of them has been really healed who did not regain his religious outlook.[2]

A spiritual approach to dying need not involve dogmas or creeds or moral absolutes; like the air we breathe, it is inseparable from life. Long ago *The Egyptian Book of the Dead,* the later *Tibetan Book of the Dead,* and the medieval Christian text *The Art of Dying* provided such practical guidance. But these ancient texts have the disadvantage of presenting arcane data couched in terms too esoteric or quaint for many modern readers.

A viable art of dying in our own day could go a long way toward relieving the dehumanized atmosphere of the average hospital death, which has become a tragic sign of our times. Inherently, medical practice expresses deep compassion, but that compassion seems to have gone increasingly astray as the art and religion of dying have become drowned in the science of prolonging life at any cost.

Commenting on the detrimental effect of artificially prolonging life, W. Y. Evans-Wentz in his preface to *The Tibetan Book of the Dead* writes:

> To die in a hospital, probably while under the mind-benumbing influence of some opiate, or else under the stimulation of some drug injected into the body to enable the dying to cling to life as long as possible, cannot but be productive of an undesirable death, as undesirable as that of a shell-shocked soldier on a battlefield. Even as the normal result of the birth-process may be aborted by malpractices, so similarly may the normal result of the death-process be aborted.[3]

And studies have shown that when the mental state of dying patients is not disturbed by sedation or other medication—in other words, when they are fully conscious and capable of responding to their environment with awareness unimpaired—their predominant emotion is not fear but calmness, the more so if they have established belief in the continuity of life.[4]

In fairness to the medical profession it should be said that the practice of thwarting the death process through powerful chemical agents and other means reflects a cultural pattern which not only sees all pain as pointless but also looks upon death as the last great enemy, to be outwitted and subdued at all costs. Death, which ought to be welcomed as natural and inevitable, becomes the Grim Reaper, and dying the terror of all terrors. If modern men and women are again to "preside at their own passing" and not be cheated out of their own death, they must recover their sovereignty as autonomously acting individuals and, while physically active and mentally clear, write the script and set the stage for the drama of their own exit, resisting manipulation by familial and other forces pressing upon them. Remarking on the individual's impotence in the contemporary world to act in this manner, the French historian Phillipe Ariés writes:

> Death in the hospital is no longer the occasion of a ritual ceremony, over which the dying person presides amidst his assembled relatives and friends. Death is a technical phenomenon obtained by a cessation of care, a cessation determined in a more or less avowed way by a decision of the doctor and the hospital team. Indeed, in the majority of cases the dying person has already lost consciousness. Death has been dissected, cut to bits by a series of little steps, which finally makes it impossible to know which step was the real death, the one in which consciousness was lost, or the one in which breathing stopped.[5]

Today dying in the average hospital in America has even less dignity and cohesiveness, I believe it is fair to say, than it had twenty-three years ago, when Ariés' observations were first published. And hospital care itself has become more dehumanized. In part this is due to the stressful conditions under which doctors, nurses, and other hospital personnel are obliged to work. "It is now one of the world's most poorly kept secrets," a national newsmagazine commented recently, "that anxiety, depression, loneliness, and burnout are major factors in the lives of doctors."[6] But there are other reasons. One is the pervasive Western attitude of actively trying to influence events instead of letting them take their own natural course. It is summed up in the expression "Don't just sit there—do something!"

The experience of a doctor friend of mine dramatically illustrates this attitude. One day while he was working as a resident in a large hospital, an elderly lady in a comatose condition was carried into the emergency room, where he was on duty. She had not been in an accident but was dying of a fatal illness. As he began to examine the lady, a senior doctor appeared, took one look at her, and ordered my friend to have her brought quickly into intensive care. "Wait," my friend pleaded. "We both know she's dying. Let me sit with her, hold her hand, and try to comfort her until she dies, which can't be more than an hour or two." Fixing my friend with a withering look, the senior doctor rebuked him with "How can you be so cold and uncaring, Doctor?" and called for an orderly to take the woman to intensive care. "I thought he was uncompassionate," commented my friend, "and he thought I was. How perceptions differ!"

But there is also the good news. The growing hospice movement, dedicated to more personal and sympathetic care of the terminally ill, and the living will movement are hopeful signs of changing attitudes toward death and the dying. Furthermore, changes in the curricula of a number of medical schools in the United States and abroad are focusing not only on treating the dying but on giving them emotional support as well. While the revalidation[7] of the doctrines of karma (the law of cause and effect and of willed action and its fruits on a moral plane) and palingenesis (successive rebirths) have made great strides in the West in recent years, a "lyrical acceptance" by a science-oriented public still seems distant. Nonetheless, many people, convinced that these teachings have substance and meaning and fulfill the yearnings of the heart, have searched among writings of East and West for further knowledge of the revolving phases of life and death. Happily, these individuals have begun to breach the barriers, the intellectual taboos, constructed by the scientific-minded, many of whom find the notion of "rebecoming" unbelievable because it is resistant to proof.

Perhaps the main obstacle to an even wider acceptance of the doctrine of life after death is the difference in philosophical outlook between the cultures of the East and West. "The attitude of Western philosophy is . . . what is *not proved* is to be treated as false," writes Professor P. J. Saher. "The attitude of Eastern philosophy is . . . what is *not proved* may be accepted as true until proved to be false."[8] And yet abundant evidence exists to convince any reasonable mind of the validity of rebirth—a doctrine that needs to be distinguished from both reincarnation and the notion of an afterlife. (See "Rebirth" section, and other passages in this book quoting the psychiatrist Carl Jung, Leo Tolstoy, and other distinguished persons who have written of their past-life experiences.)

Unlike the linear theology of the West, Buddhism, for example, teaches that life and death present the same cyclic continuity observed in all aspects of nature.[9] Buddhism says that the life and death of animate matter is, in each instance, merely the seen aspect of an unending stream of cause and effect which, though appearing to emerge from and sink into the earth at two points, nonetheless has an unseen subterranean existence and appears at other places, in other times, and in other shapes.

The assertion that nothing precedes birth or follows death is largely taken for granted by those who have a here-and-now approach to life. But however widely believed, it is still absurd from an Eastern viewpoint. Such a contention rests on the blind assumption—in its own way an act of faith—that life, of all things in the universe, operates in a vacuum. It asks us to believe that this one phenomenon, the invigoration of supposedly inert matter, springs out of nowhere and just as miraculously disappears without a trace. Most people who hold such views consider themselves "rational," and yet in this question of life and death they deny the principle of the conservation of matter and energy, one of the essential laws of physics, as it applies to the psychic energy of consciousness.

Any explication of the doctrine of karma that ignored rebirth would be as imperfect as a scissors with one blade. Accordingly, much new material, largely from Western sources, on both these subjects has been included in this volume to aid the reader in understanding these subtle yet vital doctrines.

The "Dying" section, besides providing crucial spiritual guidance to the dying and the family, includes detailed instructions on how to conduct meaningful funeral and memorial services and how to relieve the sorrow of grieving relatives during the mourning period. Moreover, I have tried to put into a wider perspective what may be called the practice of daily dying, and I have also provided simple exercises that facilitate the attainment of this highly desirable state. These day-to-day deaths—total immersion to the point of self-transcendence—can through training be perfected and turned into genuine religious experiences. Without the submersion of ego, however, such dyings cannot take place. And so I have found it desirable to deal at length with the nature and source of ego and its role in death and dying; for ultimately a serene or fearful death, like a joyous or painful life, is not unrelated to the subordination or dominance of the ego-I. In the "Dying" section I have also discussed suicide and euthanasia—two subjects which are increasingly claiming the attention of sociologists, psychologists, and religious leaders, given the spectacular rise in self-inflicted death among the elderly as well as the young.

Also presented are meditations on death—exercises to enable the reader to reflect on the omnipresence of the twin phenomena of birth and death. The reader will also find five brief inspirational biographies of people who have faced death uncringingly, even with sublime indifference.

In the Appendixes I have provided information on living wills and the growing hospice movement, do's and don'ts for consoling the bereaved, a checklist of what to do upon someone's death, and instructions on the basics of meditation.

Although *The Zen of Living and Dying* has been divided into four main sections—Death, Dying, Karma, and Rebirth—in reality the life force cannot be divided into categories. These convenient yet artificial divisions really represent movements or expressions of the one nameless "It"; each is part of a larger whole and at the same time the whole itself. When life is truly lived and not conceptualized, such mental constructs as life, death, rebirth evaporate.

The basic aim of this book can be summed up in these words: to help the reader learn to live fully with life at every moment and die serenely with death. Such an affirmative rapport with life and death is possible, however, only if one has discerned that death closes the circle on life just as life prepares the way for death, and that death therefore has a validity and a raison d'être of its own. Such acceptance, moreover, makes it possible to face death courageously and to wisely take from it what it has to offer: a means to replace a worn-out, pain-racked body with a new one and, foremost, a once-in-a lifetime chance to awaken to the true nature of existence. No wonder Socrates inveighed against the notion that death is the greatest of all evils, and Pliny Earle (1809–92) poeticized:

> What is it, then, to die,
> That it should be essential to our happiness?
> It is to throw off all things worldly,

All the dross that man is heir to,
And go forth again clad in the vestment of
immortal life . . .[10]

Beings come and beings go, but the flame of life, the generating impulse animating all existences and underlying the whole of creation, neither comes nor goes; it burns eternally, with no beginning, with no end. Aglow with this enlightened awareness, one can die not like someone being dragged kicking and screaming to the scaffold, but like one about to embark on an enticing adventure. Such an exemplary death, let me emphasize, is causally related to a life artfully lived, a life dedicated to the fulfillment of one's physical, mental, moral, and spiritual potential.

My hope is that this book, if carefully studied, can help the dying person achieve an easy death and even liberate him from painful bondage to birth and death. And it can hearten the living by making them realize that death, like life, is also transitory.

A Note on the Drawings

Wheel: an elemental device that evolved from the circle. The circle symbolizes, among other things, oneness, the indivisibility of all life. Nothing can be added to or subtracted from a circle: it is perfect in itself. In the same way, man in his Essential-nature is whole and complete.

The wheel is one of the principal symbols of Buddhism. The eight-spoked wheel is emblematic of the Noble Eightfold Path leading to enlightenment.

Skull rosary: the skull, which survives the disintegration of the flesh and sinews, symbolizes both the impermanence of the body and the indestructibility of Buddha-nature.

Flame passing from lamp to candle: indicates that dying and death lead to rebirth.

Endless knot: stands for the infinite network of interrelationships among all forms of life.

Phoenix: a mythical bird of great beauty which lived for five hundred years in the desert. It immolated itself on a funeral pyre and then rose from its own ashes in the freshness of youth, living another cycle of years; it represents death and regeneration.

Part One

DEATH

So live that when thy summons comes
To join the innumerable caravan
Which moves to that mysterious realm
Where each shall take his chamber
In the silent halls of death
Thou go not like the quarry slave at night
Scourged to his dungeon
But sustained and soothed by an unfaltering trust
Approach thy grave like one
Who wraps the drapery of his couch about him
And lies down to pleasant dreams.

William Cullen Bryant

1

EXISTENTIAL ASPECTS OF DEATH

What Is Life, What Is Death?

What is life? What is death? To the casual observer the answers may seem obvious: When the heart beats, the blood circulates, the lungs breathe, the brain perceives—that is life. When one eats and sleeps, works, makes love, feels pain and joy, one is alive.

Death, of course, is that condition in which there is a permanent cessation of all the vital functions: respiration ceases, the heart stops beating, the brain no longer reacts to stimuli, and the vital tissues have degenerated beyond any function—in short, one can no longer experience, think, or feel. With death one becomes immobile, a corpse: if buried, fit only for worms to feed on; if cremated, a puff of smoke, then ashes. There is nothing before birth, nothing after death.

But there is another view of the human condition, one that involves what biologist Lyall Watson calls the "Romeo error." This refers to Shakespeare's play *Romeo and Juliet:*

> NURSE: She's dead, deceas'd, she's dead!
> LADY CAPULET: She's dead, she's dead, she's dead!
> CAPULET: Her blood is settled and her joints are stiff;
> Life and these lips have long been separated.

Romeo took their word, and his life . . . but he was wrong.[1]

Or is the error ours? Lyall Watson thinks it is, and he describes our traditional view of death as an error of perception, like Romeo's tragic misunderstanding of Juliet's apparent lifelessness. Commenting on the "death" of Juliet and the actual death of Romeo, Watson writes:

> When Romeo found Juliet pale and lifeless in the tomb and assumed she was dead, she *was* dead. The fact that she later recovered and became more lifelike does not cancel out her death. When Juliet found Romeo lying lifeless with poison in his hand, he too was dead and his death would remain valid even if some quick-witted physician had rushed in from the wings and pumped out his stomach in the nick of time . . .
>
> The Romeo Error is a confusion of life with death and is made so often simply because there is no absolute difference between the two. They are manifestations of the same biological process and differ only in degree.[2]

What we call death is merely a change of state, often temporary and "sometimes 'curable'—death on its own has no clinical, logical, or biological reality and exists only as a construct with validity in interpersonal relationships," as Watson writes. The evidence of biology, psychology, and anthropology points toward the conclusion that life and death exist alongside each other in a constantly changing dynamic relationship. Death, then, does not extinguish the flame of life; it merely changes its form and direction. Put another way, death is not a period but a comma in the story of life, as the writer Vern McLellan noted.

Poets, too, with immaculate perception, have seen into the indivisibility of life and death. Samuel Butler (1835–1902) wrote:

> The dead are often just as living to us as the living are,
> Only we cannot get them to believe it . . .
> To be dead is to be unable to understand that one is alive.

There is a Zen koan that powerfully explores this dynamic of life and death. Like every koan, it points to the nondual One-mind common to all existence. It appears in a book of koans called *The Blue Cliff Record,* a treasure-house of the sayings and doings of some of the wisest of the Zen masters of old. In Zen centers and temples this koan is often assigned to students tormented by the dilemma of life and death. If grappled with, the koan can help dispel this dilemma by revealing that these are not demarcated conditions existing independent of each other but are merely two facets of one natural process, both present at any given moment.

> One day Zen master Dogo,[3] accompanied by his disciple, went to offer his condolences to a bereaved family in the neighborhood of his temple. Tapping the coffin, the disciple said to his teacher, "Alive or dead?"
>
> Master: "I won't say alive, I won't say dead."
>
> Disciple: "Why won't you say?"
>
> Master: "I won't say. I won't say."
>
> On the way back to the temple the following exchange took place:
>
> Disciple: "Teacher, if you don't tell me I'll hit you."
>
> Master: "Strike me if you wish, but I won't say."
>
> Whereupon the student struck his teacher.
>
> Later, after Dogo had passed away, the student went to Sekiso, Dogo's successor, and recounted the whole episode.
>
> Sekiso said, "I won't say alive and I won't say dead."
>
> Upon these words the disciple had a deep realization of the meaning of birth and death.

To understand the deeper implications of the disciple's question, "alive or dead," we need to know what lies behind it. Here is an individual so anguished that he ignores the mourners and doesn't even wait until he and his teacher have returned to the temple, but presses the master for a clear answer. The question of life and death obviously weighs heavily on him. He assumes, of course, that the body in front of him is clinically dead, but since he also believes that we are more than our senses and intellect, he asks, in effect, "Does the life force continue beyond death?"

Sooner or later, all of us, if we are to have true contentment, must face and resolve the same perplexity. Not philosophically but existentially: "Why am *I* on this earth? Where did *I* come from? When I physically pass away, what happens to the energy force I call 'myself'? Do I face total extinction or will I survive in some form or other? Is there a soul substance, independent of my body, that will migrate and reembody itself in a form commensurate with my thoughts and deeds in this life? Or is there perhaps some kind of afterlife, either material or bodyless, in an unknown realm? In short, do I go into nonbeing or a new being?" The query "Is he alive or is he dead?" is really a metaphor for all these questions.

Be aware that several years elapsed between the time the first teacher died and the time the student went to the second master, a period during which he unceasingly meditated and reflected on this gnawing problem. To what end? To free himself of the binding chain of birth and death, for no loftier goal or greater need exists for a human being. To be free from life and death is to be free from the dualistic *restrictions* of life and death. That is, one now lives with absolute freedom because life and death are at once no-life and no-death.[4]

Dogo replies, "I won't say alive and I won't say dead." What else *can* he say? He knows that what we call birth is merely the reverse side of death, as with a door called Entrance from the outside and Exit from the inside. He knows that life and death are mutually dependent, and that you can't desire one without inviting the other. Clutching at life, then, means denying the reality of death.

"Why won't you say? Don't be evasive, teacher. Give me a definite answer," the disciple is demanding. He is crying from the heart. Perhaps this is his first direct encounter with clinical death and he may be thinking, "I see what appears to be death, but where has the life that animated this corpse gone?"

"I won't say! I won't say!" the master persists. "Are you deaf? Can't you hear what I'm telling you?" He too is crying from the heart because of his helplessness to say more. Not even the Buddha could put it differently. If birth is a *temporary* point between what precedes and what follows, and so is death, then at every second there is life, and at every second, death. Which condition is life, which death?

Unable to contain himself any longer, the disciple lashes out at his teacher. "If you don't tell me I'll hit you!" The violence of his words is the measure of his desperation.

Master: "Strike me if you wish, but I won't say. Whether I'm beaten or not, there's no other way to put it."

Later, after Dogo had passed away, the student went to his successor and told him everything that had happened. And once again he hears the old refrain: "I won't say alive and I won't say dead." With that he awakens as if from a deep sleep.

The Masters' Reactions to Death

The Zen masters and other spiritual masters saw life and death as an unbroken continuum, the swinging of an eternal pendulum. Many of them met "the inevitable hour" with a smile and even laughter, often choosing to die in the lotus meditative posture ("death is the supreme liberation") or even while standing. For they saw life steadily and whole; they were unfettered by overinvolvement with any of its parts, death included. It could be said that they had already transcended the self that clings to life. And just as the Zen masters in their moment-to-moment movements are nonverbally teaching their followers how to live, so in their last hours they are teaching them how to die. Thus if they utter any last words, they are not striving for the classy exit line or seeking to express the compacted significance of their life, but are giving their students one last instruction.

Zen Master Takkan

When Zen master Takkan (1573–1645) was dying, his disciples asked him to write a death verse.[5] He demurred at first, saying, "I have no last words." They pleaded with him, so he took up a brush, wrote the character for "dream," and passed away. With this word

Takkan summed up ultimate reality, or absolute Truth, beyond all logic and reason. To realize his meaning of dream is to realize that oneself and everything else are dreamlike, that nothing in the universe is not a dream. Which is to say that all phenomena in the universe are evanescent, illusory, insubstantial. Our bodies are phantomlike, images reflected in the water. Or as a philosopher wrote, "Waking life is a dream controlled."[6]

Takkan often spoke of "Dream Zen." In one of his *One Hundred Dream Poems* he wrote that "right is a dream; wrong too is a dream." So, too, for him life is a dream and death is also a dream. Heaven and earth and all things under the sun are a dream. This is the same as saying there is no dream at all.

For Ikkyū Sōjun, a Zen master of fifteenth-century Japan, life and death were also dreams, as witness this verse of his:

Born like a dream
In this dream of a world
How easy in mind I am,
I who will fade away
Like the morning dew.

One prays for the life of tomorrow
Ephemeral life though it be.
This is the habit of mind
That passed away yesterday.

The Original-nature
Means non-birth, non-distinction.
Then know that illusion
Is birth, death, rebirth.[7]

The perception of life as a dream is by no means confined to the Zen masters. Leo Tolstoy (1828–1910), the Russian novelist and social philosopher, has much to say about dreams and past lives in a letter published two years before his death:

> Now our whole life, from birth unto death, with all its dreams, is it not in its turn also a dream, which we take

> as the real life, the reality of which we do not doubt only because we do not know of the other more real life? . . . The dreams of our present life are the environment in which we work out the impressions, thoughts, feelings of a former life . . . As we live through thousands of dreams in our present life, so is our present life only one of many thousands of such lives which we enter from the other, more real life . . . and then return after death. Our life is but one of the dreams of that more real life, and so it is endlessly, until the very last one, the very real life—the life of God . . . I wish you would understand me; I am not playing, not inventing this: I believe in it, I see it without doubt.[8]

Zen Master Taji

As Zen master Taji (1889–1953) approached death, his senior disciples assembled at his bedside. One of them, remembering the master was fond of a certain kind of cake, had spent half a day searching the pastry shops of Tokyo for this confection, which he now presented to him. With a wan smile the dying master accepted a piece of the cake and slowly began munching it. As he grew weaker, his disciples inquired whether he had any final words for them.

"Yes," the master replied.

The disciples leaned forward eagerly so as not to miss a word. "Please tell us!"

"My, but this cake is delicious!" And with that he slipped away.[9]

Zen Master Tung-shan Liang-chieh

When Zen master Tung-shan Liang-chieh (807–69), the first patriarch of the Sōtō Zen sect in China, was dying, a monk said to him, "Master, your four elements[10] are out of harmony, but is there anyone who is never ill?"

"There is," replied Tung-shan.

"Does that one look at you?" asked the monk.

"It is my function to look at him," answered Tung-shan.

"How about when you yourself look at him?" asked the monk.

"At that moment I see no illness," replied Tung-shan. So saying, he passed away.

The "one," of course, is our Essential-nature personified. It is not subject to birth or death. It is neither being nor nothingness, neither emptiness nor form-and-color. Nor is it something that feels pain or joy. It is beyond all sickness.

Zen Master Hui-neng

On the eighth of July, Zen master Hui-neng (638–713), the sixth Chinese patriarch of Zen, announced to his monks, "Gather around me. I have decided to leave this world in the eighth month."

When the monks heard this, many of them wept openly.

"For whom are you crying?" the master asked. "Are you worrying about me because you think I don't know where I'm going? If I didn't know, I wouldn't be able to leave you this way. What you are really crying about is that *you* don't know where I'm going. If you actually knew, you couldn't possibly cry, because True-nature is without birth or death, without going or coming . . ."[11]

How is it that the masters can regard death so lightly? Only because they know what whether we are killed or die naturally, death has no more substantiality than the antics of puppets in a film. Or that it is no more real than the cutting of air with a knife, or the bursting of bubbles, which reappear no matter how often they are broken.[12] Moreover, the masters know they will be reborn through affinity with a father and a mother when their karma relations so impel them.

Chuang-tzu

Chuang-tzu, the Chinese Taoist sage of the fourth century B.C., was visited after the death of his wife by his friend Hui-tzu, who came to express his condolences. The latter arrived to find the master sitting on the ground with his legs spread wide apart. The widower was singing away and whacking out a tune on the back of a wooden bowl. "You've lived all these years with your loving wife and watched your eldest boy grow to manhood. For you not to shed a tear over her remains," exclaimed Hui-tzu, "would have been bad enough. But singing and drumming away on a bowl—this is just too much!"

"Not so," the master replied. "I am a normal man and grieved when she died. But then I remembered that she had existed before this birth. At that time she was without a body. Eventually, matter was added to that spirit and, taking form, she was born. It is clear to me that the same process of change which brought my wife to birth eventually brought her to death, in a way as natural as the progression of the seasons. Winter follows autumn. Summer follows spring. To wail and groan while my wife is sleeping peacefully in the great chamber between heaven and earth would be to deny these natural laws, of which I cannot claim ignorance. So I refrain.[13]

Satsujo

When Satsujo, a deeply enlightened woman, lost her granddaughter, she could not contain her grief. An old man from the neighborhood came and admonished her, "Why are you wailing so much? If people hear this they'll all say, 'Why does the old lady who was enlightened under the famous Zen master Hakuin mourn her granddaughter so much?' You ought to lighten up a bit." Satsujo glared at her neighbor and scolded him, "You bald-headed idiot, what do you know? My tears and weeping are better for my granddaughter than incense, flowers, and lamps!"[14]

Incense and flowers are *symbolic* offerings to the memory of her granddaughter. They are outward forms for her inward grief. Offerings are a way of relating concretely to the dead through objects. But Satsujo, as a deeply enlightened woman who has seen into the nonduality of life and death, doesn't need to enlist such aids to reach her granddaughter. Her tears, which express her deep love for her granddaughter, have the power to bridge the land of the living and the land of the dead.

Being enlightened doesn't mean you have no feelings, that you are cold and unemotional. On the contrary, it means that you are able to express your feelings freely and spontaneously. This point is illustrated by an old Zen story. A young novice became disenchanted with Zen when he heard that a revered master had screamed in pain as he was being murdered by thieves. The young man contemplated leaving Zen training, feeling that if the old master screamed in the face of death, Zen itself must be a fraud. However, before he was able to leave, another teacher taught him something of what Zen is all about and removed his misconceptions.

"Fool!" exclaimed the teacher. "The object of Zen is not to kill all feelings and become numb to pain and fear.[15] The object of Zen is to free oneself to scream loudly and fully when it is time to scream."[16]

Zen Master Soyen Shaku

Another story concerns a well-known Zen master of recent times, Soyen Shaku (1859–1919), who was the abbot of a large Zen monastery in Kamakura, Japan.[17] It was the abbot's custom to take a walk through the town early each morning with his attendant. On one such occasion he heard wailing coming from a house. Going inside to investigate, the abbot inquired, "Why is everyone crying?" He was told, "We are mourning the death of our child." Immediately the abbot took a seat among the family and began loudly weeping and wailing with them. On the way back to the temple the attendant asked the master, "Do you know those people?" "No," replied the abbot. "Then why did you cry with them?" "To share their sorrow," responded the abbot.

To many readers this story may seem bizarre. Yet a true Zen master is nothing if not compassionate. To rejoice with those who rejoice and to cry with those who sorrow would be most natural for such a person even if the grieving family were total strangers to him.

Zen Master Nan-chuan

A reaction to death with a twist involves Zen master Nan-chuan. When he died, one of his senior disciples stood in front of the master's coffin and gave a loud laugh. A priest, who was also a student of the late master, reproached him, saying, "Wasn't he your teacher? Why do you laugh when you should be grieving for him?"

The disciple replied, "If you can say an appropriate word that fulfills the Buddha's teaching, I will grieve." The priest stood mute. Deploring this, the disciple said, "Alas, our teacher has truly gone," and he wept loudly. The significance of this last statement is crucial to understanding the whole dialogue.

An appropriate word is any live, spontaneous word or action charged with the force of one's whole being. The admired live word is the gut word, concrete and vibrant with feeling. The dead word is the explanatory word, dry and lifeless, issuing from the head. The first unifies, the second separates. Now, the important thing is not to wobble but to respond at once. The same idea is expressed in the folk saying "He who hesitates is lost."

The senior disciple wants to test the priest, so he deliberately laughs in front of the master's coffin to see what kind of response it will evoke. The latter fails the test by scolding the disciple for laughing instead of weeping. Whereupon the disciple baits another "trap" with the words "If you can say an appropriate word, I will grieve." Unable to respond, the priest stands mute. There is a place for silence, of course, but this isn't it.

What Is "Birth and Death"?

In Sanskrit the realm of birth and death is called *saṃsāra:* the mundane phenomenal world of toil and struggle; of impermanence; of the transformation which all phenomena, including our thoughts and feelings, are ceaselessly undergoing in accordance with the law of causation. Birth and death can be compared to the waves on the ocean. The rise of a wave is one birth; the fall, one death. The size of each is conditioned in part by the force of the previous one, the force itself being generated by air currents, ground swells, rain, the moon, and perhaps other elements. This process infinitely repeated is birth-death-rebirth—the wheel of existence. The other side is that in our *Essential*-nature there is no coming or going, no birth, no change, no death. The problem, then, is how to transcend birth and death and find the place where there is no birth and no death. According to Zen master Dōgen, that place is the very realm of birth and death.

We can speak of two kinds of birth and death: momentary and "regular." Momentary birth and death—that is, momentary creation and destruction—takes place every millionth of a second, or at some such phenomenal speed, as old cells die and new ones come into being. So we can say that a new self is constantly being born, and that a man of sixty is not the same as, yet not different from, the person he was at thirty or at ten. Living is thus dying, and dying living. In fact, with every inhalation we are being reborn and with each exhalation we are dying.

You can compare birth to the appearance of clouds in the sky, and death to their breaking up and scattering in all directions. Although a cloudy and a clear sky can be described as different conditions, the sky is unaffected. Or, to change the metaphor, our True-essence is like a mirror, which reflects different phenomena. These phenomena have a limited existence in time and space and in that sense are ultimately unreal. But the mirror itself is permanent and real—only in terms of this simile, of course—since it projects varying images without being marked by them. Similarly, True-mind embraces all phenomena without being affected by them.

By training ourselves to live fully with life and to die wholly with death at *every* moment, we are able to transcend both, going beyond even the dualistic distinctions of transcendence and non-transcendence, subjective and objective. (See "Daily Dying.") Our life, as someone said, is not a mystery to be solved but a reality to be lived.

Upon death, what happens to the force, the energy, that created and sustained the physical organs and bodily functions? Does this energy have an objective aspect? What can we *understand* about that realm where consciousness has not yet divided itself into subject and object? Nothing at all. The world we see is a reconstruction made by the limited instruments of our intellect and five senses. It follows, then, that whatever you understand intellectually is only an *aspect* of truth. What is beyond understanding—uncognizable—is the *whole* truth. From the absolute standpoint of Original-nature, then, the terms "subjective" and "objective" have no validity. That is why we can say that life is no-life and death no-death.

Actually, we can't say whether anything exists or doesn't exist, simply because nothing has an enduring life of its own; all forms are empty of a self-substance, and nothing is the same from moment to moment. Everything is in flux, constantly forming, dependent upon causes and conditions, disintegrating, and reforming again. It's like a film. We get the impression that people are moving or acting in it, but it's all an illusion. The actions are real enough in terms of the film—they're not a hallucination—but otherwise they are unreal.

Speaking of the identity of contraries, the sage Chuang-tzu says, "The sage knows nothing of the distinction between subjective and objective. From the standpoint of the Way, all things are One. People guided by the criteria of their own mind see only the contradiction, the manifoldness, the difference; the sage sees the many disappearing in the One . . ."[18]

That this notion of the identity of contraries is not simply a product of the oriental mind can be seen in these words of the Greek philosopher Heraclitus: "Listen, not to me but to reason, and confess the true wisdom that 'All things are One, All is One,' the divided and undivided, the begotten and the unbegotten, the mortal and the immortal, reason and eternity, father and son, God and justice . . . The beginning and the end are one. Life and death, sleeping and waking, youth and age are identical." By seeing inaction in action and action in inaction, immobility in motion and motion in immobility, and the like, we arrive at the true state of things, their Thusness.

The Force of the Universe

The power or force or energy of the universe animates all existences. It cannot be named, for to name it is to limit it and it is beyond all categories and limitations. But if we must give the nameless a name—and we need to if we want to speak about it—we may provisionally call it True- or Essential-nature. "It" also relates to the flow of cause and effect, that is, the generation and disintegration of phenomena according to causes and conditions. Simply put, all phenomena are transformations of True- or Essential-nature. In other words, everything by its very nature is subject to the process of infinite transformation—this is its True-nature.[19] Now, you may ask, what is True-nature grounded in? *Shunyata,* a Sanskrit word that is usually translated as "the Void," or "no-thing-ness." This *shunyata,* though, is not mere emptiness or a negative cipher. It is alive, dynamic, devoid of mass, beyond individuality or personality—the womb of all phenomena.

This True-nature cannot be separated from our physical bodies. An early sage sang:

> The corpse is here,
> Where is the man?
> Truly, I know
> The spirit is not in this bag of skin.

However, Ta-hui, a great Zen adept, refuted the heretical notion that spirit exists apart from flesh:

> This corpse as it is is the man [woman]
> The spirit is the bag of skin.
> The bag of skin is the spirit.

The implications of this latter are far-reaching. We cannot repudiate the material world of form in favor of an opposing world of spirit or soul—or vice versa—without setting up a duality that inherently does not exist. The basis of the material world is the spiritual, and the world of form in turn influences and is inseparable from the spiritual realm. Or to put it another way, since the spiritual is the power or force that pervades and underlies everything material, what happens in the physical world depends primarily on spirit—that is, Mind.

In his book *Modern Man in Search of a Soul,* Carl Jung confirms the identity of spirit and body:

> But if we can reconcile ourselves with the mysterious truth that spirit is the living body seen from within, and the body the outer manifestation of the living spirit—the

> two being really one—then we can understand why it is that the attempt to transcend the present level of consciousness must give its due to the body. We shall also see that belief in the body cannot tolerate an outlook that denies the body in the name of the spirit.[20]

We see evidence of the role of the body in the attitude of those American families who, in the Vietnam War, lost sons or brothers or husbands or fathers whose remains were never found or who in one way or another were never accounted for by the military authorities. As you know, our government has been under pressure over the years from many American families to get Vietnam to repatriate the remains of their loved ones in spite of a long lapse of time. Equally significant is an agreement signed by Vietnam and France in which the former agreed to exhume and repatriate the remains of French soldiers who died in Vietnam after 1939.[21] Why all this concern for remains? My perception is that, at some level of their being, the American and French families feel that the remains embody the *substance* of the missing loved ones.

What is involved here, I feel, is the need for families to come to grips with unresolved emotions that have smoldered for a long time. For this purpose you need a body, or at least some portion of it. Because the destruction of the loved one took place in a remote country under chaotic wartime conditions, and with much suffering, the need to repossess the remains, and honor them in a formal ceremony becomes compelling. In reverencing the remains as relics, the family reaffirms its link with the departed and reassures its members of their love for and fidelity to the memory of the departed. The intuitions of the families must tell them that spirit cannot be abstracted from body.

Why Do We Fear Death?

Not all cultures fear death and therefore deny it, as ours does. Lyall Watson insists there is absolutely no evidence to suggest that fear is a natural and inevitable part of our dying behavior. "On the contrary," he writes, "in cultures where death is dealt with more openly and seen as part of the living process there is no fear of death . . ." He also says that he does not know of a single organism "that manifests a natural fear of death itself . . . When terminal patients have had enough time, or have been given enough of the right kind of help to conquer their fears and accept the inevitability of dying, they often experience feelings of peace and contentment . . ."[22]

Socrates in a striking passage implies that fear of death is *unnatural* because it is grounded in the egoistic notion that one knows what one does not know: "To fear death, gentlemen, is nothing other than to think oneself wise when one is not; for it is to think one knows what one does not know. No man knows whether death may not even turn out to be the greatest of blessings for a human being; and yet people fear it as if they knew for certain that it is the greatest of evils."[23]

Why, then, in the developed Western nations is the fear of death so widespread? What are the causes and how can they be overcome? Some have their genesis in the unprecedented violence of our time and its explosions into intermittent warfare; others can be traced to the ongoing threat of nuclear annihilation and the destruction of all life as we now know it. Generally, the fear of death can be broken down into the specific fears of pain, loneliness, abandonment, mutilation, and loss of self, however self is defined. No doubt it also has a nonrational dimension, like the fear of the dark and the fear of the unknown. But it has deep psychological roots as well. These are set forth by the French psychotherapist Ignace Lepp in his book *Death and Its Mysteries.*[24] Since his observations are perceptive, I will try to summarize them and also indicate what I believe to be the root cause of the fear of death from a Buddhist perspective.

Lepp feels that the fear of death, which he distinguishes from a paralyzing anxiety about death, is normal and actually increases our joy in living. (Lepp also distinguishes the fear of death from the fear of *dying.*) He observes that if human existence obeyed the laws of logic, we could expect to find that those who live most intensely and love life most passionately would fear death the most, and that those who find life a painful burden would welcome death.

But his research shows that the opposite is usually true. He cites examples of people in France during World War II who "vegetated more than they lived"; these people were the most afraid and the first to run for the shelters during air raids.

Lepp then goes on to point out that there are human beings who aren't afraid of their own death but of the death of others, particularly those they love or depend on. Furthermore, he makes the pertinent observation that sometimes we experience an agonizing fear of another's death because we see in that person's death a harbinger or reminder of our own mortality.

An aspect of our fear of death which is relatively recent in origin, and which Lepp treats in his book, is a fear of collective death. Since the fifties, with the onset of the insane race for nuclear superiority, the fear of collective death has become pervasive. Lepp finds it psychologically significant that the fear of death by thermonuclear war or accident is greatest in those countries that have the largest number of these frightful weapons. Today, the stronger and richer a nation is, the greater is its insecurity. Lepp feels this is a partial explanation of the disarray of our time, which is expressed in crime, vandalism, and eroticism, and in the accelerated pace of life. Even modern music and dance seem to express the despair of a humanity that no longer believes in its own future.

Ultimately, Lepp argues, the neurotic fear of death is closely related to a person's sense of individuality; the more one is conscious of oneself as an individual rather than as a member of a group, the greater is the fear of death. For Lepp the principal cause of the fear of death, at least in the West, seems to be the excessive individualism of modern people. In the older civilizations of the East, relatively little importance is given to individual destiny. In the prosperous countries of the West we live more exclusively for ourselves, and our sense of self-identity is more developed.

What is Lepp's prescription for overcoming the fear of death? After identifying alcohol, narcotics, and the frenzied pursuit of pleasure in today's society as so many efforts to dispel this fear, he surveys the various philosophic approaches of the West and finds them all sadly lacking. Finally he concludes, "It is my conviction that an intense love of life is the best and perhaps only effective antidote against the fear of death."[25]

With his emphasis on individuality, Lepp, I feel, hints at the cause of the dread of death without directly pinpointing its roots. This fear, to put it more precisely, seems to me to be *grounded* in a strong sense of the "I"—an attachment to a finite self—and the feeling that death may bring about its dissolution. Death is feared because it is seen as the end of our existence; it precipitates us into oblivion.

How, it may be asked, can an intense love of life develop when one's "fiery energies" are constantly focused on the assertion of the ego-I—a stance our individualistic society actively encourages? In those cultures which equate human perfection with the loss of ego, death is not the tragedy it is felt to be in societies such as our own which worship at the altar of the finite self. So long as we associate Mind with brain and see the brain only as part of the body, we will be terrified at the thought that one day we will disintegrate and become a nothing—a zero.

Speaking of the fear of death, the philosopher Horace Kallen writes, "There are persons who shape their lives by the fear of death, and persons who shape their lives by the joy of life. The former live dying, the latter die living. Whenever I die, I intend to die living."[26] As a way of life, Kallen's philosophy is admirable. But like Lepp, he doesn't tell us how our puffed-up egos, the bar to the cultivation of that joy, can be deflated.

Understandably, Lepp, as a psychotherapist, employs the methods of his profession in dealing with the death anxiety, which he feels is neurotic (although the *fear* of death, he says, is not). He goes on to say that "a neurotic fear of death is most often the expression of a general anxiety whose real causes are unconscious and originate with the trauma of adolescence, childhood, or birth." However, a serious illness or the death of a loved one can cause the fear to blossom into consciousness. Coping with this neurotic fear may require isolating childhood or adolescent traumas that have crystallized into repressions, obsessions, depressions, phobias, or other psychological conflicts, all of which are a bar to a healthy, joyous rapport with life.

Moreover, straightening out a convoluted psyche can be a long and laborious process requiring many years' treatment, with results not always favorable. It can also be expensive. If the root cause of the fear or anxiety about death, namely a full-blown sense of I, is not dealt with, such apprehensions, I believe, cannot truly be dispelled. Still, if the fear of death can be saddled to an aspiration for awakening, it can spur one toward enlightenment.

The ultimate aim of the psychotherapist, presumably, is to adjust a patient to the norms of society so that he or she can function freely within them. But since those norms themselves reflect a neurotic state—one that views reality from the false standpoint of self and other instead of as a nondual whole—the patient's inner vision, even when freed of neurotic restraints, is still myopic. And so while psychologically well-adjusted individuals may want to cultivate an intense love of life, they are unable to do so for the reasons indicated; inevitably they end up chasing shadows—shadows of hope as well as of fear.

From a Buddhist perspective, the key to dispelling the fear of death is the loosening of the fetters of the ego. We loosen these fetters every time we forgo indulging our own desires but rather support the group effort, whether that group be our own family, fellow workers, friends, neighbors, or even one's country. But equally important, we must stop despising or adoring our personal self, neither retreating from life nor pushing at it. Every horizontalizing of the mast of I is a step in the direction of whittling down ego and thus the fear of death.

Part of this process is cultivating a certain quality of meekness. When Christ said, "The meek shall inherit the earth," he wasn't referring to the spineless and the obsequious, but to those with forbearance and humility, those not overly proud or self-assertive. *Meekness* does not translate as weakness. In the original sense of the word, *meekness* means self-surrender—giving up all self-seeking. In the words of the philosopher Moses Maimonides, "No crown carries such royalty with it as doeth humility."[27] But as we know, modesty can also be the worst form of vanity: "You can have no greater sign of a confirmed pride than when you think you are humble enough."[28]

To effect a complete and authentic transformation, we need to sidestep the twin evils of a mock, prideful humility on the one hand and compulsive self-assertion on the other. It is only from this purified state that it is possible to awaken to the realization of who and what we are.

Ego

When we talk about the ego, it is important to be precise because it's a word with many shades of meaning. The ego-I can be defined as the sense of oneself as an isolated being set apart from other selves—in other words, the unshakable belief that "*I* am here and the world stands outside me." But this notion of oneself as a discrete individual is a fiction produced by our senses and bifurcating intellect. Modern psychology, I understand, views ego somewhat differently. It attaches importance to the ego because it sees it as relating to our self-image, that is, to understanding ourselves as a particular organism that experiences the external world through our senses. In this view, consciousness is inconceivable without an ego. If there is no ego, there is nobody to be conscious of anything. And so the ego is said to be indispensable to the consciousness process with which it is identified.

We are talking here about what may be called the individual empirical consciousness, a level of awareness tied to the five senses and the discriminating intellect. The image of ourselves that grows out of our time-and-sense-bound consciousness is, in an ultimate sense, unreal. In fact, all of our self-limiting activities grow out of this false picture of ourselves. As a result of this false picture, we postulate a dualistic world of self and other, of things separated and isolated, of pain and struggle, birth and death, killing and being killed. This picture is untrue because it barely scratches the surface. It is like looking at the one-eighth of an iceberg above the water and refusing to acknowledge the seven-eighths underneath. For if we could see beyond the ever-changing forms into the underlying reality, we would realize that fundamentally there is nothing but harmony and unity and that this perfection is no different from the phenomenal world of incessant change and transformation. But our vision is limited and our intuitions weak.

Now ego, that shadowy, phantomlike figure with insatiable desires and a lust for dominance, sits astride the senses like some oriental potentate. Or, to change the simile, ego is like a magician carrying up his sleeve the deadly tricks of greed, anger, and wrong thinking. Worse, he is quite capable of rationalizing his actions with an air of sweet reasonableness. This wily and slippery conjurer deludes us into believing we can enjoy the delights of the senses without pain only by delivering ourselves into his hands.

Of the many devices employed by ego to keep us in his power, none is more effective than language. The English language is so structured that it demands the repeated use of the personal pronoun "I" for grammatical nicety and presumed clarity. Actually this "I" is no more than a figure of speech, a convenient convention, but we talk and act as though it were real and true. Listen to any conversation and see how the stress invariably falls on the "I"—"*I* said . . . ," "*I* did . . . ," "*I* like . . . ," "*I* hate . . ." All this plays into the hands of ego, strengthening our servitude and enlarging our sufferings, for the more we postulate this I the more we are exposed to ego's never-ending demands.

Our relative mind of ego, aided by language, deceives us in other ways. It constantly tempts us into distinctions, comparisons, and judgments which take us further and further from the concrete and the real into the realm of the speculative and the abstract. Take the case of an individual walking along who suddenly hears the sound of a bell. Immediately his discriminating mind evaluates it as beautiful or jarring, or distinguishes it as a church bell or some other kind. Ideas associated with a similar sound heard in the past may also intrude, and these are analyzed and compared. With each such judgment the experience of pure hearing becomes fainter and fainter, until one no longer hears the sound but hears only his *thoughts* about it.

Let us now examine the source of ego from the standpoint of the nine consciousnesses of Buddhist psychology. The first five are the root-consciousnesses of seeing, hearing, tasting, touching, and smelling. The sixth consciousness is the conceptual faculty that distinguishes and classifies the data of the senses and is what we call the intellect. The seventh root-consciousness is the seat of the persistent I-awareness and is the source of our value judgments, egoistic opinions, self-centeredness, and illusory notions, all of which give rise to actions that accord with them. The eighth is the repository, or storehouse, consciousness, where the seeds of all mental activity and sense experiences are recorded moment after moment. This consciousness, which persists even after death, retains vestiges of awareness of previous existences and the seeds of new karmic causes. Also to be found on this eighth level are certain memories of the prebirth condition—feelings of floating or flying, of freedom, of an oceanic oneness with all things. These sensations often occur in dreams and are usually accompanied by a sense of tremendous well-being. To those sensitively attuned to them, such vestigial memories of the prebirth period can give a hint of the freedom of the state we miscall death.

The ninth level is the pure, formless Self-consciousness—our True-nature. It is related to the eighth level so intimately that there is almost no difference between the two. It can be compared to a limitless ocean, in which each individual life is a wave on the surface. (See Diagram 1.)

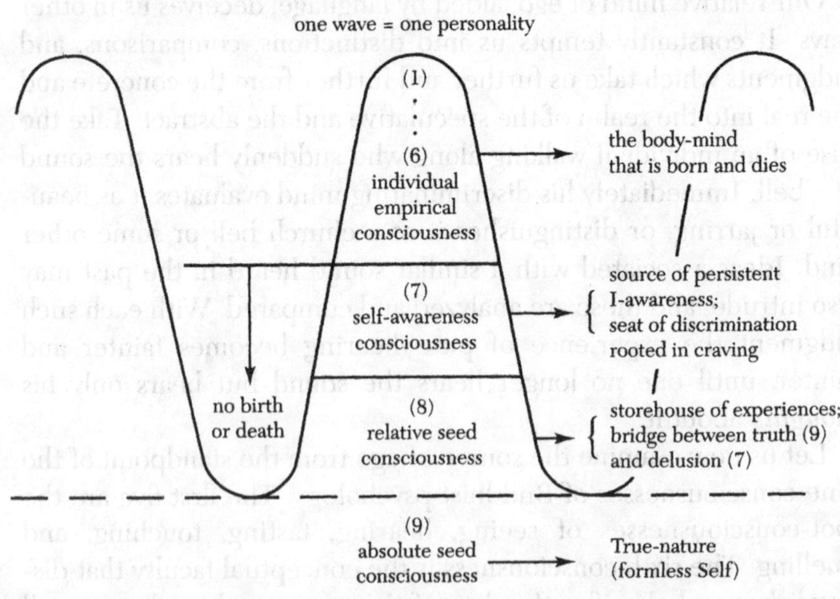

DIAGRAM 1: *The Nine Levels of Consciousness*

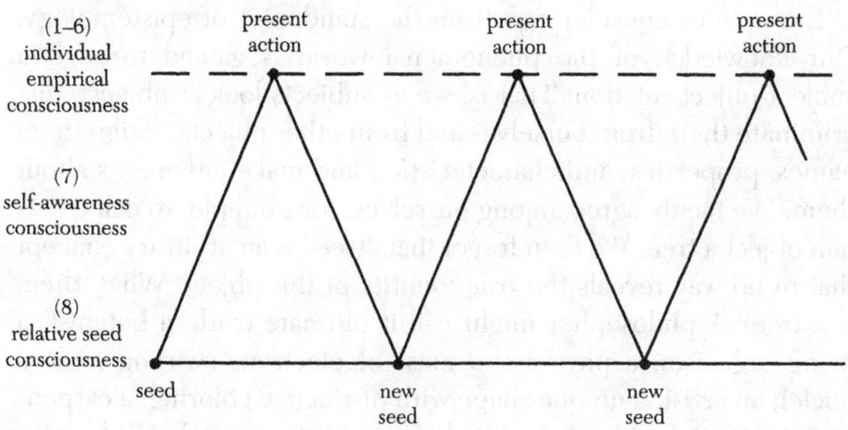

DIAGRAM 2: *Cause and Effect and the Levels of Consciousness*

In a sense, the eighth level is the basis of personality and character since it continuously seeds new actions, giving rise to different thoughts and varying behavior. (See also Diagram 2.) These thoughts and behavior patterns in turn change the quality of the repository consciousness as they are instantaneously impressed upon it to become new seeds of action. Karma (which will be discussed in detail later) develops as the ever accumulating seed experiences, in response to causes and conditions, blossom forth as new actions—which are not only effects but also causes of seeds. This process, even while it is fragmented, is continuous and endless.[29]

Strictly speaking, ego itself cannot be said to survive death. However, the seventh level of consciousness, the former abode of the I-awareness, does persist. It can be likened to a blank sheet of paper—flypaper—lying in wait for the ego's return. In fact, it is the ego-serving desire for a body, and all that that implies, that is the propelling force behind rebirth. Or, stated another way, rebirth is the inevitable consequence of our not having attained total liberation in the preceding life. (See "Rebirth" section.) Thus the unending cycle of birth-living-dying-death-rebirth continues unbroken, driven by the volition, instincts, and habit patterns born of craving, anger, and delusion—driven by, in a word, ego. The physical body is, as it were, a composite or crystallization of our deluded, ego-based thoughts.

Let us now consider ego from the standpoint of epistemology. Our knowledge of the phenomenal world is gained through a subject-object relation. That is, we as subjects look at objects, discriminate them from ourselves and from other objects, assign them names, properties, and characteristics, and make judgments about them. We tacitly agree among ourselves, for example, to call a certain object a tree. We then forget that "tree" is an arbitrary concept that in no way reveals the true identity of this object. What, then, is a tree? A philosopher might call it ultimate truth; a botanist, a living organism; a physicist, a mass of electrons swirling around nuclei; an artist, a unique shape with distinctive coloring; a carpenter, a potential table. To a dog, however, it is a urinal. All descriptions or analyses are but a looking from one side at that which has infinite dimensions. The essential quality of the tree is more than anything that can be said about it.

Similarly, we tinker with time by dividing it into past, present, and future, and into years, months, days, and so forth. This is convenient, but we need to remember that this "slicing" is artificial and arbitrary—the product of our discriminating mind, which discerns only the surface of things. Timelessness is unaccounted for. Thus we conceive a world that is conceptual, limited, and far removed from the actual. Because we view objects as from a distance, we do not have an all-embracing, direct, intuitive awareness of them. And since we have not penetrated them to their core, our knowledge of them is limited and one-sided.

At the center of this process is the ego-self. Because it stands apart from all other selves, it considers itself the unique center of things. In reality it is merely an objectified self and not the true, living, unconditioned Self, which underlies and unifies all existence. This latter cannot be objectified or be known through reason or conceptualization, for it is inconceivable and unimaginable. It is the elusive, unnameable actor always behind the scenes. Thus all attempts to know our original Self through intellection and imagination are doomed to failure.

Actually there is no personal self: the entire universe is the Self. Not knowing we are this majestic Self, we imagine ourselves to be no more than this puny body, just a speck in the universe. Thus we mistakenly postulate an other, imagine a gulf between self and other where none exists, and then exalt ourselves and put down others. This is the basic delusion of sentient beings.

Our estrangement from the real Self is reflected in the unsatisfactory quality of our life—the pain, the existential anxiety, the unfulfillment. This human predicament can be compared to a wheel not running true on its axle and thus grinding. Fragmented and frustrated, we long for wholeness and freedom.

We are split off from our true Self in yet another way. Even as we exist in time and space, in a world that is finite, impermanent, and material, *simultaneously* we inhabit a world that is infinite, eternal, and formless. Owing to our bifurcating intellect, which divides and separates, we are alienated from our Essential-mind. This Mind cannot be perceived until we are in an awakened state. Thus we are the flawed children of Mother Earth and Father Spirit. Living in our temporary home, the biosphere, with its pain, its beauty, its joy, we are estranged from our permanent abode, the viable Void.

This brings us to a consideration of intellect and its relation to ego. It should be remembered that the illusion of ego—of one's own separate existence as an enduring reality, set off against the rest of the universe—may be seen as the root cause of the problems of life and death: fearful clinging to life and terror of a death which appears to be the annihilation of one's life. The discriminating intellect is perhaps the foremost instrument of the ego in perpetuating this illusion. In Western psychology, I understand, intellect is usually considered the last faculty to develop in a child. Actually, intellect exists in a rudimentary state even in the embryo. With intellect's further unfolding, our perception of the world as it really is becomes distorted. I touched on this earlier. Now let me expand on it. Conditioned as we are to filter all perceptions through the intellect, which in turn conveys them to the seventh level of consciousness (where the sense of an ego-I takes hold), we find irresistible the belief that each of us is a discrete and separate entity. As the persistent ego-I awareness develops and strengthens over time, it becomes more and more solidified through the intellect, affecting in turn our perception of the world.

The net result is that we begin to think and act as though we were separated entities confronted by a world external to us. In the unconscious, the idea of I, or selfhood, becomes fixed, and from this arise such thought patterns as "I hate this, I love that; I need this, I don't want that; this is mine, that's yours." Nourished by this fodder, the ego-I comes to dominate the personality, attacking whatever threatens its position and grasping at anything which will enlarge its power. Antagonism, greed, and alienation, culminating in suffering, are the inevitable consequences of this circular process. The ego-I, or small self, can be compared to a tumor: in one sense it is foreign to the body; in another, it was produced by it. Or, to change the metaphor: "Far from being a door to the abundant life, the ego is a strangulated hernia. The more it swells, the tighter it shuts off that circulation of compassion with the rest of life on which man's health depends absolutely, [and] the more pain is bound to rise."[30]

In spite of all this, the ego, this wily creature, is not to be despised; for when his machinations become unbearably painful, there arises within us an irresistible longing for freedom from the restriction and pain, and a desire to transcend these sufferings so as to attain inward peace and wisdom.

Ego performs yet another valuable function. Behind all creative endeavors—whether it be designing a spacecraft, creating a work of art, or uncovering an unknown law of nature—lies the desire, conscious or unconscious, for Self-knowledge. And the propelling force behind this desire is ego—the wish of the self to undertake these activities. We can also say with Ernest Becker that ego represents a natural urge by the life force itself toward an expansion of experience, toward more life.

For those of the highest spiritual attainment the ego is transmuted into a selfless-I. Because the body still exists, however, the pull toward the reinvigoration of an ego-I continues. For this reason even spiritual masters must be on guard against falling into habit patterns that favor the reassertion of ego. Only one who is free from the slightest thought of self can be said to be truly egoless and therefore Buddhalike. For such a one no thoughts of the body remain. In this state it is possible to go to one's death without the slightest trace of sorrow, rancor, or fear. Dying for such an individual is no different from living, living is another form of dying, and both at base are seen as unreal.

Buddhahood is latent in each of us. After all, the Buddha himself was once no different from you and me. But we do need to strive to get out of ourselves, to "get lost," to immerse ourselves totally in whatever confronts us. In losing ourselves we gain a relationship to something greater than the self:

> Bravely let go your hold
> On the edge of the precipice
> And die to the small self.
> Then what is naturally revealed
> Is the True-nature in which
> There is neither life nor death.

This vivid image of a precipice is a metaphor for the varied circumstances, more painful on the whole than joyous, of our life. Most of us are, metaphorically speaking, hanging by the skin of our teeth from a precipice. At any moment we may fall and be dashed to bits on the jagged rocks below. Dying to the I means freeing oneself from attachments, from *clinging*—to people, to wants, to hopes, to fantasies, even to ideals ("poisoning the real with the ideal," in D. H. Lawrence's seminal phrase), and, above all, to one's sufferings. We need to stop clutching at the momentary aspects of life and let go of our preconceived notions of how things should or should not be. Only then can we be reawakened to a wholly new world—greater, freer, and more beautiful than the old, ego-dominated one. Kierkegaard sums it up superbly:

> To let go is to lose your foothold temporarily.
> Not to let go is to lose your foothold forever.

While Kierkegaard may overdramatize, he nevertheless captures a profound truth. The process of dying is as important for life as the process of being born. It is only because we identify the process of dying with the dissolution of the body that we arrive at our one-sided and negative conception of death.

A death-dealing blow to the I is at the same time a life-giving action. In Zen this is called the Great Death and the Great Renewal. To die the Great Death is to transcend life and death and achieve utter freedom. It makes the prospect of physical death secondary and unimportant. Zen master Bunan put it this way:

> Die while alive
> And be thoroughly dead.
> Then do what you will,
> All is good.

When a master was told by a prospective student, "I would like to learn Zen from you," the master asked, "Are you prepared to die?" The student replied, "I came here to learn Zen, not to die." "If you can't die you will never learn Zen," responded the master.

The true spiritual heroes in all the religious traditions have been those who did not hesitate to leap, hands high in the air, into the abyss of fire confronting them, into the ever burning flames of their own primordial nature.[31] With this leap of faith, all delusive feelings and perceptions perish with the ego-root and one is reborn into a luminous world of true freedom. Only such a revived one can sing:

> He who dies
> Before he dies
> Does not die
> When he dies.[32]

Now, none of this is said with the purpose of romanticizing death. The point is really to strip death of the tragic solemnity, the denial and fear, with which we surround it so that when our time to slip off comes, we won't tremble with fear. Our stubborn denial of death, as I said earlier, betrays a deep-seated fear of life. Life, let me emphasize, is our main concern, not death. To the awakened, our world is enchanting, filled with wonder and awe. It teems with endless diversity. The marvels of nature are a delight to the eye, the ear, the nose. Human and other creatures, plants, trees, rivers, rocks, insects, anthills—all palpitate with life. Every single thing shines with its own light. Every single thing sings out the glory of creation. Existence is a marvelous thing.

We are all flowers
blossoming
in a blooming universe.[33]

Facing Death Fearlessly

There hasn't been a culture or civilization in history, I think it is fair to say—whether it be that of aborigine tribes in Australia or the Greek culture at its zenith—that has not bestowed its highest accolades on those men and women who faced death unflinchingly, with courage and dignity. When they knew they had to die, these heroes didn't rage against it. They conquered death by their supreme indifference to it or—and this amounts to the same thing—their total concurrence in it, robbing it of its power to sting and thus gaining true immortality. Think of Christ and Socrates, of Thomas More and Joan of Arc, and of the Zen masters and the Buddha—how inspiring their lives and deaths! And how equally inspiring the lives of innumerable ordinary men and women who calmly looked death in the face. The last tribute we owe life is a dignified death.

A dignified, or "good," death is one in which there is no railing or struggling against imminent death—above all, a death without sadness, without regret, without apprehension, without bitterness, without terror. It is dying freely, naturally, like falling asleep, not clinging to or clutching at life, just "going with the flow"—not "flow" or "letting go" in a psychological sense, but in the transcendent sense of the "eternal yea," of yielding to an inner, mysterious force that takes over when all self-striving ceases. This can be seen in the following example:

> When Zen master Tung-shan felt it was time for him to go, he had his head shaved, took a bath, put on his robe, rang the bell to bid farewell to the community, and sat up till he breathed no more. To all appearances he

> had died. Thereupon the whole community burst out crying grievously as little children do at the death of their mother. Suddenly the master opened his eyes and said to the weeping monks, "We monks are supposed to be detached from all things transitory. In this consists true spiritual life. To live is to work, to die is to rest. What is the use of groaning and moaning?" He then ordered a "stupidity-purifying" meal for the whole community. After the meal he said to them, "Please make no fuss over me! Be calm as befits a family of monks! Generally speaking, when anyone is at the point of going, he has no use for noise and commotion." Thereupon he returned to the Abbot's room, where he sat up as in meditation till he passed away.[34]

Zen masters aside, not all ordinary people die in pain. But it is possible to go with the flow even if one is in deep pain. Let me illustrate this with another story. As a Zen master lay dying he cried out in pain. Upset by his cries, one of his students said, "Master! Why are you calling out like that?" The master responded, "My crying in pain is no different from my laughing in joy." Like these masters, if you train yourself to become one with your daily life, you will be able to go with the flow whatever the circumstances of your death—or life.

2

MEDITATIONS ON DEATH

A good death
does honor to a whole life.
PETRARCH

MEDITATIONS ON DEATH are a means of purifying the mind in order to gain a crucial revelation of the meaning and significance of life and death. As such, death meditations have been regarded as an indispensable element in a wide array of cultures: the Egyptian and Indian, the Chinese and Japanese, the Hellenic and Roman, the Hebrew and Islamic, in both their ancient and modern forms. Because of death's general unfathomableness and the dread and terror it inspires in most people, the conquest of death, or deathlessness, has a central place in the teachings of all religions. Unless this fear and terror is replaced by comfort and hope, a tranquil mind state is impossible. The unwillingness to think of death is itself a kind of death, for the poignancy of life is inseparable from the knowledge of its inevitable decay.

Death meditations may strike some as a morbid preoccupation, a falling in love with death rather than with life. Yet the deep acceptance of death as the teacher of life divests these reflections of any macabre quality. The purpose of death meditations is to instill in the meditator the confidence to walk unafraid with the ever-present prospect of death, for one never knows when it may come and take us. The denial of death, so common in our culture, inevitably strengthens the fear of it and underscores what Socrates said about the unexamined life not being worth living. Actually, pondering and meditating on death is part of the religious practices of every major tradition. There are some orders of Christian monks and nuns, for example, who live with their simple coffins always in sight and who even turn a spadeful of earth daily from the place that is to eventually serve as their grave. By contrast, some people strongly feel that thinking about their demise will only hasten it—a not uncommon form of denial.

Those who are strongly repelled by the thought of confronting their own demise even in a symbolic way—as well as those who have suffered from mental illness, particularly depressive disorders, and those who are psychologically fragile—are cautioned to avoid the more intense type of death meditations described here. To undertake them under these circumstances could result in an increase in fear and anxiety rather than a lessening of them. Children, too, should not attempt these exercises.

In his book *Inventing the American Way of Death,* the historian James Farrell (1830–1920) makes a vital point about the denial of death in American society:

> Keeping death out of mind cuts people off from an important fact of their physical, mental, and spiritual existence. If knowing that we will die is part of what makes us human, then forgetting that we will die threatens our humanity. In the same way, the denial of death in American society also cuts people off from our common humanity, keeping them at such a distance from the deaths of others that they cannot grieve or mourn except in the culturally prescribed "way" . . .[35]

Plato in his *Phaidon* insists that "they are the true votaries of knowledge who practice nothing else but how to die or to meet death."[36] Masao Abe elaborates on this: "For Plato . . . to philosophize is nothing other than precisely to practice dying while living.

It is to live through dying, to practice dying while living. Herein is the way of the philosopher for Plato—the way in which death is overcome."[37]

The Buddha was equally emphatic about the value of such meditation: "Of all footprints, that of the elephant is supreme. Similarly, of all mindfulness meditations, that on death is supreme."

As well, Marcus Aurelius (A.D. 121–180), the Roman emperor and Stoic philosopher, wrote, "The constant recollection of death is the test of human conduct."[38]

Meditation that totally involves body and mind takes us beyond the senses, beyond our thoughts and feelings, into a transcendent state. But death meditations are valuable not only for that reason. When they are fueled by the primal terror of death, they can break through the psychological armor encasing us and evoke what may be called the "questioning mind," the prerequisite for genuine transformation.

Understandably the various religions have cultivated forms of death meditation appropriate to their basic spiritual aims. The methods of these religions have been preserved in both the written and oral traditions of the different cultures. *The Egyptian Book of the Dead, The Tibetan Book of the Dead,* and the medieval text *The Art of Dying* are perhaps the best known. The material that follows is drawn partly from these writings, but also from the various Buddhist traditions, with which I am most familiar. These meditations on death are intended to help the student confront the reality of his own finitude in a concrete way and thereby gain an intense awareness of his own eventual death, and with it a greater appreciation of life.

Generally, meditations on death can be divided into philosophic reflections and experiential aspects. The philosophic portions, consisting of ancient writings by prominent masters, are still taught in many monasteries and spiritual centers in both the West and the East as a theoretical basis for the practices themselves. For the so-called practical, I have drawn upon the oral teachings handed down by masters in the various traditions. Also included are specific methods of meditation transmitted to me by my own teachers during my fifteen years of training in Asia, thirteen of them in Japanese

Zen monasteries and temples. In addition, I have added methods of practice congenial to Western students. Where any of the practices are inextricably entwined with their native cultures, I have sought to put them in the context of our own Western culture.

Reflections on Death: Eight Points of View

These death meditations are abstracted from the *Visuddhimagga*, by Buddhaghosa (fifth century A.D.), a highly respected Buddhist monk-teacher. To enable the meditator to come to grips with the reality of his own death, the text instructs him to reflect on death from the following eight points of view:

1. death as having the appearance of an executioner, that is, as though a murderer were standing in front of one ready to strike one down
2. death as the ruin of all success
3. death as the inevitable end for all persons: just as it strikes down the great and mighty, so will it strike us down also
4. death as the result of "sharing the body with many": a reflection on the infinite number of factors, both internal and external, that can cause death
5. death as lying near at hand
6. death as "signless," that is, nothing about it can be predicted or known in advance
7. death as the certain end of a lifespan that is short at best; and
8. death as a constant phenomenon, occurring at every moment.[39]

I will elaborate on only one of these eight points, the third, and will briefly touch on some of the others, leaving it to the reader to supply his own examples illustrating the substance of each of the other points. Reflecting on these points is indispensable preparation for meditation on the word *death*, the core of the practice, which we will discuss a little later. We all know that we cannot escape death, but intellectual recognition is one thing, experiential awareness another. This is the great value of symbolically confronting death through these meditations.

Meditation on the Inevitability of Death

The third point concerns death as the end for everyone. In this practice one is instructed to reflect on the deaths of about seven accomplished individuals who have had worldly success, fame, and power and yet could not avert death. They might be past figures or contemporary. For example, one might think of Julius Caesar in this line from *Hamlet*:

> Imperious Caesar dead and turn'd to clay
> Might stop a hole to keep the wind away.

One can reflect, "Caesar was the most powerful man of his day, his armies had conquered most of the known world, his wealth was enormous—yet death eventually struck him down and returned him to dust. How can *I* hope to escape the same end?" One should remind oneself that the powerful and the weak, the sage and the fool, the generous and the stingy, the most honored of men (an Einstein, for example) and the most miserable beggar—the same fate awaits them all, and us too: death. In the grave we are all equal. Similarly, one can reflect on the violent deaths of tyrants such as Hitler and Mussolini. Both dictators had absolute power over the lives of millions of people, yet their ultimate fate, too, was death.

Reflecting on the Eight Points

One may ponder these eight views while sitting, standing, lying down, or walking, or when one is riding in a car, a bus, a plane, or a train. It is helpful to memorize them or to write them on a small card to keep for reference. They can be elaborated or modified as one sees fit. That is, one may supply more personally meaningful metaphors or may relate these eight points to one's own life experiences. Their value, however, lies in retaining their essential formulations as reference points and reflecting on them.

In connection with these reflections, and as an adjunct to them, one needs to remind oneself again and again of how fortunate one is to have the rare privilege—the good karma—of being born a human being in this lifetime, and that the deepest purpose of human life is to awaken to the meaning of birth and death.

It is inadvisable to perform these exercises at random. Rather, begin with one exercise and continue to meditate on it until it has sunk deeply into your consciousness, after which you can go on to the next practice, working with it in the same manner.

Meditating on the Word *Death*

The *Visuddhimagga* defines death as "the cutting off of the life force for the length of one existence." The meditator is instructed to retire to a quiet, solitary place and focus his mind on the thought "Death will take place, the life force will be cut off," or simply to meditate on the word *death*. The practice seems outwardly simple, yet to develop an ongoing mindfulness of death is actually quite difficult. This is due to what Freud in his essay on death called "our attitude towards death"—that while we airily proclaim that death is the fate of all of us, actually we act as though an exception will be made in our case.[40] Implicit in Buddhaghosa's treatise is his conviction that only constant mindfulness of death and frequent meditation on it will dislodge this deep-seated belief.

If early in life one works at dispelling this subconscious belief that "Somehow death will spare *me*," and reflects on the ever-present possibility of death, life takes on new meaning and direction. The uncertainty of when death may come makes us value each moment and frees us from the illusion, common to the young, that we have an infinite amount of time to accomplish things. The conviction that death may strike at any time enables us to focus on what is meaningful and to discard the nonessentials on which we expend so much precious time. The realization that the grave is our common destiny arouses compassion for the least among us; this is not unlike people's experiences in European bomb shelters during World War II, where strangers, made intimate by sharing the possibility of immediate death, gave of themselves to help others in ways rarely seen in more ordinary times. And not the least, it encourages us to live each day as though it were the last.

This is attested to by many people, among them the distinguished psychologist Abraham Maslow, who suffered a near-fatal heart attack and afterward wrote a letter about it to a friend: "The confrontation with death—and the reprieve from it—makes everything look so precious, so sacred, so beautiful, that I feel more strongly than ever the impulse to love it, to embrace it, and to let myself be overwhelmed by it. My river has never looked so beautiful . . ."[41]

Let us now focus on the meditation itself. Masters of old advise, "Stick the word *death* on your forehead and keep it there." In the beginning it is effective to harmonize the inhalations and exhalations with the soft vocalization of the word *death.* Later the word may be uttered only on the exhalation. One need not visualize the word itself, unless picturing it helps keep it in mind. The mind should be fully concentrated on the meaning of the word *death*; care should be taken to avoid a mechanical repetition of it.

Meditation on a Death Koan

Zen master Hakuin (1686–1764) said:

> If you should have the desire to see into your own nature, you should first investigate the word *death.* If you want to know how to investigate the word *death,* then at all times while walking, standing, sitting, or reclining, without despising activity, without being caught up in quietude, merely investigate the koan: "After I am dead and cremated, where has the 'true person of no rank' gone?" [Or, in other words, "After I'm dead, where am I?"]
>
> Among all the teachings and instructions, the word *death* has the most unpleasant and disgusting connotations. Yet if you once suddenly penetrate this "death" koan, [you will find that] there is no more felicitous teaching than this instruction that serves as the key to

> the realm in which birth and death are transcended, where the place in which you stand is the Diamond indestructible, and where you have become a divine immortal, unaging and undying. The word *death* is the vital essential that you must first determine for yourself.[42]

Meditation on the Transitory Nature of Life

In all earnestness tell yourself, "The most important task facing me as a human being is to transcend the ceaseless cycle of births, deaths, and rebirths, to awaken to the true meaning of my life and death." To arouse this determination, one must be deeply aware of the evanescent nature of life: that we are born in the morning and die in the evening; that the friend we saw yesterday is no longer with us today. Most of us see impermanence in the life of another but do not relate it to our own body. Seriously tell yourself, "Even though I live to be seventy or eighty, death will surely catch up with *me.*" But even this is putting it too mildly. Think of what might happen to you tonight or tomorrow. You might be killed in a plane or car crash, or be caught in an avalanche, flood, or earthquake. Or you could be tortured or shot by terrorists. Or, closer to home, you might discover that you have a life-threatening disease.

A Meditation on Death Using Beads

Many years ago in Burma I stayed at the home of a businessman with a spiritual outlook on life. He meditated every day, and to judge from his serene, radiant countenance and deep contentment (he was sixty-five at the time), his meditations, though informal, were most effective. This is how he performed them: Every morning he rose at five and seated himself, with his feet firmly on the ground, on a park bench overlooking a brook that flowed through his property. He told me he made it a point not to slouch or lean back, but to sit erect. In his right hand he held a long string of smooth beads, which he rubbed one at a time while he visualized each member of his family, then his friends, and lastly those about whom he had harbored unkind thoughts. All these people he then embraced mentally, directing thoughts of loving kindness toward them. This exercise over, he began concentrating on the word *death,* more or less in the manner outlined above, fingering each bead as he focused on the word. This type of meditation is suitable for beginners and advanced students alike.

The Day of the Dead in Mexico

The skull, which survives the disintegration of the flesh and sinews, is a symbol of both the impermanence of the body and the indestructibility of our Essential-nature. This seeming disparity has parallel religious and social significance. It can be seen most vividly on the Day of the Dead in Mexico. Throughout the country on November 2, *calaveras* ("living" skeletons) rise up from their sepulchral abodes, magically called back to life for a brief day in a symbolic mingling of life and death. These whimsical memento mori can be seen merrily playing musical instruments, engaging in trades they practiced in their earthly existence, or taking part in such social activities as weddings and dances. They are striking reminders of the fleeting nature of earthly existence and the vanity of human desires. Calaveras are actually another form of meditation on death and, as such, are more personal and real since they are objectifications of departed parents or grandparents or children. They forge a link between animate and inanimate existence, thus helping to preserve the chain of continuity of the family.

On the days leading up to the Day of the Dead, families welcome back the departed with food and drink, song and merriment. If Grandfather José was fond of tamales during his earthly existence, a plate of them is placed in front of his photograph on an altar set up for the occasion in his family's house. And on homemade altars in other homes, families place special cakes inscribed with the names of their departed, yellow flowers (associated with the dead), and candles—offerings made not to death but to the "returning dead." On the final night of the festival, José's family joins other families in a candlelight vigil at the local cemetery to "light his way (and that of the other 'returning dead') back" to the grave.

These rites are a symbolic way of bringing "alive," if only for a few days, the loved one who is gone. As Antonio Rodriguez has written, "So great is the faith of the Indian in this magical rite that he does not have to see the absent loved one on that day of communion between two forms of life that are so disparate in order to feel his presence. The father, mother, child, brother or sister is there in spirit, almost physically, and it is they who are being celebrated."[43]

Death is teased and made to dance and merrily cavort in these calaveras. The Grim Reaper is unmasked and revealed to be a jolly fellow underneath his macabre exterior. Death is thus seen for what it is, a temporary point between what has been and what will be, and not as the black hole of oblivion. As an old Mexican refrain sings:

> Get used to dying
> before death arrives,
> for the dead can only live
> and the living can only die.[44]

Mexicans from all walks of life participate in Day of the Dead festivities to one degree or another, but in certain small towns and villages, the celebrations seem to be more widespread. It must not be supposed that Mexicans are enamored of death, or view with joy, for example, the demise of a loved one, simply because they surround themselves during these days with the symbols of death in their dance, costumes, music, and folk art. Quite the contrary. Death is given its due—as in other countries, the death of a loved one is a sad, tearful event—but death is not denied or glossed over or hidden away. In fact, the very presence of such elaborate festivities proclaims that the living still love the ever-present dead.

Other cultures have similar celebrations, though perhaps not so vivid as the Mexican. In Japan, for example, on the Buddhist holiday of O-bon, when the spirits of the dead are said to return to their ancestral homes, similar scenes take place, usually in the villages. In Europe in the medieval period the Dance of Death served the same function, and perhaps still does in certain countries. But in the United States and Canada, Halloween, a children's festival peopled by goblins and ghosts and shorn of all religious significance, has largely supplanted All Souls' Day, the Christian equivalent of the Day of the Dead. Many churches, however, still perform services and prayers for the dead, and many people place commemorative messages and verses in the newspapers.

Matters of Worldly Anxieties

Lastly, this advice from a Zen master is worth heeding:

> Matters of worldly anxieties are like the links of a chain joined together continuously without a break . . . If you don't exert yourself to struggle with them, then as time goes on, with you unknowing and unawares, they will have entered deeply into you. Finally, on the last day of your life, you won't be able to do anything about them.
>
> If you want to avoid going wrong when you face the end of your life, from now on whenever you do anything, don't let yourself slip. If you go wrong in your present doings, it will be impossible not to go wrong when you are facing death.[45]

3

FACING DEATH

Death never takes the wise man
by surprise.
He is always ready to go.
JOHN DE LA FONTAINE

MOST OF THE following accounts sum up the lives and deaths of people in history who have faced death with lofty serenity. These people include the Greek philosopher Socrates, a monk of old, the Indian sage Ramana Maharshi, and the Buddha himself. Also included are two contemporary people who died of cancer—one unperturbed, the other terror-stricken. Except for this last account, all these passings exemplify a theme of this book: that a calm, accepting death, so desirable and yet so rare, is the outcome of a life artfully lived—"the actualization of the fierce energies of the life processes," a life characterized by enlightened awareness and a resolute acceptance of death whether as a natural process or as an event imposed from the outside.

Notwithstanding, we know that in every culture and civilization throughout history, ordinary, heroic individuals, many of whom lacked a spiritual orientation—a practiced belief in either God, karma, rebirth, or the life of the spirit—have faced their own death without a qualm. A number have bravely died as martyrs, condemned to death for their convictions, for their actions in defending religious, political, or social freedoms in the face of brutal repression and injustice, or simply because they belonged to a certain ethnic group. More commonly, countless soldiers in wartime have courageously faced death. The same is true of civilians. And of course there have been those admirable women and men who, though suffering from a fatal illness or disability, have uncringingly looked death in the face.

In the history of America one thinks of Nathan Hale and the words he uttered as he was about to be hanged by the British as an American spy: "I only regret that I have but one life to give for my country." If he actually did speak these words, can we infer from them that he faced death with utter equanimity? In World War II, members of Japanese kamikaze squads often wrote home, "As I go into my last battle, how happy am I to be able to sacrifice myself until my seventh lifetime[46] for the glory of the emperor and the honor of Japan!" Were these lofty sentiments inspired by a heroic patriotism or did they conceal a deep fear or neurosis?

Stated more concretely, did all these courageous individuals somehow manage to overcome their fears, or were they fearless? And if the latter, was it perhaps because of an inability to imagine their own death? In other words, how consummate was their seemingly composed acceptance of death? We can't say, for we know so little of their lives. We do, though, know much more about the life and the manner of death of those whose brief biographies follow.

Socrates (470?–399 B.C.)

Socrates, the Greek philosopher of Athens, is one of the best-known models in the West of a solitary hero who moved as freely into death as he walked through life, with utter serenity and fearlessness. From Plato's dialogues we learn that this "wisest of men" was completely unintimidated by death, and where one would expect despair and anxiety in his last hours, he is full of peace and loving wisdom. His only concerns are to comfort those who have come to comfort him, and to set an example of how to die a laudable death.[47] From what source came the wisdom that inspired such serenity? To get an answer to this question, let us briefly examine some significant milestones in Socrates' life: that of soldier and philosopher; his trial, sentencing, and imprisonment; the extraordinary scene preceding his drinking the hemlock poison decreed by his captors, and its fatal aftermath.

Very little is known of Socrates' early life, since Plato—our principal source of information about Socrates—was with him for only the last ten years of his life. We do know that Socrates was an Athenian soldier distinguished by his courage, endurance, and presence of mind in battle. When nominated for military honors, he demurred, giving the honors instead to his superior, whose life he had saved. Once, while on campaign, Socrates amazed his fellow soldiers by standing rapt and intent for twenty-four straight hours; Plato implies that such "rapts" were not an uncommon occurrence. In later life Socrates showed conspicuous courage in defending the constitutional rights of an accused group against an angry and confused assembly, and on another occasion he defied a murderous group of tyrants at the risk of his life.

Socrates trained himself so that all his needs were satisfied with the smallest means, but he was no ascetic in his youth. Plato says that Socrates "knew how to want and how to abound." His temperament was a happy one, marked by a peaceful outlook, a gentleness toward his interlocutors, and a sense of ironic humor that was famous even in his day. At the same time he spared no one from his candid observations and piercing logic, and this quality, along with his Olympian detachment, unsettled and probably angered many people in Athens.

Socrates felt a divine mission to seek truth and to uncover all pretensions to wisdom, a mission given him by the oracle at Delphi. Although a private man in the sense that he never sought public office, he identified strongly with his fellow Athenians and cared deeply for their spiritual welfare. He urged people to discover and live by fundamental values, and he likened himself to a gadfly to the state, a *true* statesman because he attended to what was really best for the people rather than what was merely popular.

The formal indictment against Socrates was made on charges of heresy and of corrupting the youth of Athens. For these charges the prosecution urged the death penalty. In his defense Socrates turned the tables on his accusers and, without attacking them, put all Athens on trial. He was convicted by a narrow margin and asked to name an alternate penalty—exile might have been a possibility. Instead, he suggested that he ought to be supported by the state in return for his services. The judges, used to more humble supplication, angrily sentenced Socrates to death by an even greater margin.

During the time between the sentencing and the execution, Crito, who was one of Socrates' oldest friends, urged Socrates to escape and provided the means to do so. Socrates refused, saying that, among other reasons, while the decision was wrong, the court was a duly constituted one and should be obeyed. In this, as at the trial, he showed himself to be a true citizen, more upright and discerning than his accusers, the court, or his friends. The trial, the prison scene with Crito, and the manner of Socrates' death—quoted later from Plato's *Phaedo*—have stirred the hearts and minds of people for twenty-four centuries with their dignity, calm, and clarity of insight.

How could Socrates face death so courageously? The simplest answer is that he was used to dying. He had died to his personal interests in battle, as he states in the *Apology*; he had died in his "rapts," when he would forget his body in contemplation; he had died to pleasure often in his search for wisdom, a search conducted in poverty and simplicity; and he had died emotionally and intellectually to his old self many times in his process of spiritual growth, both in discourse and in silence. In a very real sense, then, he was in the habit of dying every day, and the manner of his death was the proof of his sincerity in all that had come before. In the *Phaedo* Socrates is quoted as saying, "Then in fact, Simmias, those who rightly love wisdom are practicing dying, and death to them is the least terrible thing in the world."

Obviously, then, Socrates felt in his bones that death was no punishment or evil. A good man can never be harmed by a bad, he said; virtue transcended temporal power completely. After death, Socrates believed, life continues; the *true* judgment then occurs, with judges unblinded by any mortal veils and thus able to apprehend, penetrate, and intimately know the soul of the newly dead.

The reward of the truly virtuous and undistracted votary of wisdom is to go where he can converse with and test the gods and the ancient heroes and worthies. This was Socrates' unshaken faith.

At the same time, reason told him that death was an unknown, and since unknown, a possible good. To debase himself prior to death was a known evil, one that could impair his spiritual progress after death. He saw no reason to desire a known evil, possibly a great one, instead of a possible good. For other men, this kind of thinking does not penetrate very deeply into the mind and heart. For Socrates, his intellect, emotions, and spiritual life were all of a piece; he had trained himself to live by the highest lights he was aware of, and thus he narrowed the gap between knowing, doing, and being.

While Socrates was unable to turn the tide of Athenian decline, his words and actions have been of immense influence in forming what is valuable in Western civilization. And in this sense Socrates still lives today. He is always waiting to test us, and his trial is going on right now, as all of us choose between the good, as much as we may know it, and the expedient—between the genuine search for value and the hollow conventionalities that are all around us.

Plato's Account of the Last Hours of Socrates

Crito made a sign to the servant, who was standing by; he went out and returned with the jailer, who was carrying the cup of poison. Socrates said, "You, my good friend, who are experienced in these matters, shall give me directions how I am to proceed."

The jailer answered, "You have only to walk about until your legs are heavy, and then to lie down, and the poison will act." At the same time he handed the cup to Socrates, who in the easiest and gentlest manner, without the least fear or change of color or feature, looking directly at the jailer, took the cup and said: "What do you say about making a libation out of this cup to any god? May I or not?"

The man answered, "We only prepare, Socrates, just so much as we deem enough."

"I understand," Socrates said, "but I may and must ask the gods to prosper my journey from this to the other world—and so be it according to my prayer."

Then raising the cup to his lips, quite readily and cheerfully he drank off the poison. And hitherto most of us had been able to control our sorrow, but now when we saw him drinking and saw too that he had finished the draught, we could no longer forbear, and in spite of myself my own tears were flowing fast; so that I covered my face and wept, not for him but at the thought of my own calamity in having to part from such a friend. Nor was I the first; for Crito, when he found himself unable to restrain his tears, had got up, and I [Plato] followed; and at that moment Apollodorus, who had been weeping all the time, broke out in a loud and passionate cry which made cowards of us all.

Socrates alone retained his calmness. "What is this strange outcry?" he asked. "I sent away the women mainly in order that they might not misbehave in this way, for I have been told that a man should die in peace. Be quiet, then, and have patience."

When we heard his words we were ashamed and refrained our tears. Socrates walked about until his legs began to fail, and then he lay on his back, according to directions. The man who gave him the poison looked at Socrates' feet and legs now and then. After a while he pressed Socrates' foot hard and asked him if he could feel anything. Socrates said, "No." Then he pressed higher and higher on Socrates' legs and showed us that they were cold and stiff. Socrates felt them himself and said, "When the poison reaches the heart, that will be the end."

He was beginning to grow cold about the groin when he uncovered his face, for he had covered himself up, and said—they were his last words—"Crito, I owe a cock to Asclepius; will you remember to pay the debt?"

"The debt shall be paid," said Crito. "Is there anything else?"

There was no answer to this question, but in a minute or two a movement was heard, and the attendants uncovered him. His eyes were set, and Crito closed his eyes and mouth.

Duncan Phyfe (1895–1985)

The hero of the previous biography was a charismatic figure, a stalwart individual who challenged the political, social, and religious ideologies of his time and as a consequence suffered execution at the hands of the state. Duncan Phyfe, the subject of the present biography, was no such mover and shaker—he was Everyman. He merits a place in this book by reason of his having lived an ordinary life extraordinarily well, thus preparing the way for a beautiful death, with no regrets. At a time when so many of his contemporaries, overcome by fears of a painful death, prefer to die by their own hand and not by God's, so to say, Duncan Phyfe's death stands out in marked contrast. Neither death nor life held terrors for him, for he was in love with life and accepting of death. Until he died, in his own bed at the age of ninety, he wavered not the slightest in his conviction that death was not the end but the springboard to yet another life.

The circumstances of Duncan Phyfe's outer life give scarcely a hint of the rich spirituality that developed within him in his later years. Born in 1895 in Cold Spring, New York, the nephew of the famous furniture maker Duncan Phyfe, he served in World War I in France as an ambulance driver and was decorated by the French. Later he became a sound engineer. After installing sound systems in South Africa, he returned to the United States to work for RCA, where he invented the speaker that attaches to cars in drive-in theaters.

He married twice and had two children, a daughter and a son. After he retired in the early sixties, he and his wife traveled all over the United States in an Airstream trailer, finally settling in San Diego, California. A Christian but not a churchgoer, in San Diego he became interested in a sect of Christianity that believed the Kingdom of God is here on earth. He had been born and baptized in the Methodist church, but he left it when he became an adult because, in his own words, "I did not find in it the basic truths I was looking for."

Upon his wife's passing he went to live in a trailer in Santa Fe, New Mexico. His zest for adventure and joy in living led him, in his eighties, to buy a motor scooter on which he zipped around Santa Fe. About this time he was "discovered" by a group of idealistic New Age artists and writers who had been drawn to this Shangri-la of the Southwest by its promise of greater personal freedom and the chance to make a name for themselves in the arts. But artistic and personal success were slow in coming; meanwhile they had to struggle to eke out a living. They were sheep who needed a shepherd, and in Duncan Phyfe they found one. He became their benefactor, father confessor, and spiritual mentor; at the same time he was nourished by their freewheeling spirits and youthful enthusiasms. He had always gravitated toward younger people rather than people of his own age because of his youthful outlook on life. "I never felt I was getting old," he said. "I love people, and my greatest joy was giving them joy."

With characteristic energy and thoroughness, Duncan devoted himself to helping his newfound friends become acclimated to the rarefied atmosphere of Santa Fe. But he did not confuse his priorities. When they lacked groceries, he did not give them the pap of heaven but edible kitchen stuff; he knew that the rumblings of an empty stomach will drown out the sounds of the most eloquently spoken spiritual truths. Similarly, when their roofs leaked and the wiring in their run-down quarters wouldn't work, he didn't pray to God to help his young friends acquire the wherewithal to make the necessary repairs; instead, he made them himself at his own expense. Mechanically talented, he constantly made his skills available to them. Despite his advanced age, he was ever ready to chauffeur a young friend around town or to baby-sit for those with small children.

My first meeting with this remarkable man took place at the home of his son and daughter-in-law. He was in bed with cancer of the gallbladder and liver. Earlier he had been operated on and was told his cancer was terminal. His cheerfulness and lucidity—he was ninety at the time—belied the fatal character of his illness.

As we talked, he sat propped up in a double bed in a comfortable room containing a large stereo set that he himself had built. In addition to Duncan, in the room were his writer friend who had introduced me to him; my assistant, who was taping our talk; and I. Duncan seemed entirely at ease, making no effort to sound profound or holy.

"Duncan, what do you feel the purpose of your life to be?"

"To prepare myself for the doors beyond."

His friend interrupted to ask, "Might not part of your purpose here also be to give light and joy to other people?"

"That is so. A great desire of mine has been to give light to those who are seeking it—to give it to them to the best of my ability and the best of my understanding—that is, to give them fundamental truths. There are so many dimensions of consciousness besides this three-dimensional time set we are boxed into."

"I understand that death might come to you at any time. How do you feel about that?" I asked. His reply startled me:

"I think that's wonderful."

"You really aren't afraid?" I pressed him.

"No, I have no trauma about it whatsoever. I am at peace with the world and with my Creator. What more could I ask?"

To determine the source of his serenity and confidence, I asked him what he thought would happen to him after he died. Unhesitatingly he replied, "All the most wonderful things one could conceive of. Death is nothing but an ongoing expansion of life, to which there is no limit."

Again I asked, "No doubt in your mind that you will be reborn in one form or another according to your karma?"

"Not the slightest."

"Has this belief or awareness given you great peace of mind?"

"Yes, it has." There was no mistaking the sincerity of his words or the peace of soul he radiated.

At one point I asked whether he was having physical or mental pain. "No, not really. It is just that I hate to part from dear friends. But I know I will go beyond what you might call this present 'vale of tears.'" Questioned whether this life had really been a vale of tears for him, he said he had used the term merely as a figure of speech—that after all, there was so much pain in the world today: wars and other violence. "But if you look around, you can also see some beautiful spots of love in this world," he added. Earlier, in fact, he had insisted that everything boils down to one word—love. "It holds the world together and is the source of divine Mind." That could have sounded trite but for the radiance that shone in his face as he uttered that one word "love." He looked positively beatific.

Another time I asked him why he thought most people were afraid to die.

"I suppose it's a revulsion against what they take to be eternal oblivion. Most people want to continue on—not necessarily in this life but to go on and on and not feel that this is all there is; and if it is all there is, why did it ever start? Most people who are afraid of dying," he continued, "feel that death is the end, a closed thing."

"Duncan, can you honestly say that you face the prospect of death without fear or dread—willingly?" Raising himself higher in the bed and looking me straight in the eye, he answered—"Willingly." No one could doubt the conviction behind his words.

Duncan Phyfe died August 12, 1985, some three weeks after our interview. His son and daughter-in-law, who were with him, said that during the last few days of his life he was semiconscious, responding mainly with smiling eyes. Strongly evident was his love for everyone and his eagerness for the unknown ahead. Said his son, "It was almost a euphoria. He wanted to go." In fact, about a week before he died he had asked, somewhat impatiently, "Why doesn't God come and take me?"

For the last six hours he was calm and unconscious. He died curled up in the fetal position.

He was loved by many.

Leah (1933–87)

The following narrative by a psychotherapist describes how his friend and colleague Leah (not her real name) died. It has been included here to illustrate a painful, panic-stricken death—a classic example of someone who, by her own admission, had not prepared herself for dying.

Leah was diagnosed with ovarian cancer at age fifty-two. Her initial reaction to the doctor's report was brief: "I don't have a good feeling about this." She quickly made up her mind to fight the cancer on all levels. But despite chemotherapy and radiation, with their usual side effects, the cancer kept spreading and she was in pain more often. Doctors were running out of alternative treatments.

We talked about how the mind worked to deny things. She would say, "When I'm in pain, all I want to do is accept that I'm dying and be prepared for it . . . But then the pain subsides and I find myself looking through the newspaper to see if there's a sale on dresses."

A month before she died, Leah was hospitalized for the last time. She had deteriorated fairly rapidly, and death became an any-day-now proposition. She lost more and more of her physical functioning and there were fewer and fewer choices about what to do with her time. The simplest act required her complete attention, if not someone's assistance.

On the last evening, I was at her bedside, as was her daughter, Gail, along with a friend of Gail's. I had met Gail only once, the previous night, and she now told me that the doctor had said, "Tonight will probably be the night." Leah was wearing an oxygen mask. She was very weak, barely talking.

Leah had said before that she liked hearing others talk even if she couldn't participate directly. So Gail and her friend reminisced about their childhood. At one point Gail mentioned that her mother had always liked the sound of her friend's laughter, and her friend asked Leah, "Want to hear a joke?" In her clearest, most energetic act of the evening, Leah took off the oxygen mask and said, "What is it?" Gail's friend told the joke and we all laughed, with Leah smiling a little-girl smile. She became a little more animated, complaining about the incompetent nurses, praising the good ones, and joking about "the crazy one who was only interested in [her] bowel movements." She knew she was being entertaining, and we laughed quite a lot.

After a little while Gail's friend left. Then Leah said she wanted a priest to come and give her the last rites. Although Leah was actually Jewish, she grew up in Europe during the Second World War, and her mother, unable to take care of her, put her in a nunnery at age five. She often said that the nuns were her real mothers.

I went to call the priest. When I returned there was a noticeable change. Leah was quieter. I held her hand and was quiet with her. Gail sat on the other side of the bed and held her other hand. The priest came. Leah had her eyes closed and didn't appear to notice him. Her daughter asked, "Do you want to see the priest?" Leah opened her eyes and looked. She said, "Not yet," and pulled her body back as much as she could. She began to look agitated. The priest asked her if she was Catholic, and she explained a little about her background, saying she wanted the blessings of both the Catholic and Jewish faiths. She told the priest that in her most desperate moments of pain and despair, she saw Jesus and called on him for help.

The priest began to administer the last rites. His voice was so low while he was saying the prayers that we couldn't really hear him. Gail and I stepped out into the hall while he heard Leah's final confession. We both were dismayed that in this critical moment his ability to transmit any kind of spiritual inspiration seemed nonexistent. He called us back in, completed the ritual, and left. Gail asked her mother if she felt any better for having seen him, but she didn't answer.

Leah was quiet now for longer periods, but with a growing sense of mental agitation. I could feel it very clearly. Not knowing what to say or do, I held her hand and began to focus my own mind as I had learned to do in meditation. I could feel her mind very clearly, feel the fright starting to build. The more I was able to let go of anything arising in my mind, the more I could "touch" her, and her agitation subsided.

This period of relative quiet was interrupted after thirty or forty minutes by a tremendous upsurge of terror. Leah was starting to panic. She said, "I'm frightened!" and began to shake. I focused my own mind more intensely, and from time to time I could feel it having an effect, but more and more she was on her own. She started to call to God with great intensity, over and over. For days she had barely been able to talk above a whisper; now she cried out to God, and to us she begged, "Help me! Help me! I want to get back to the peace I was feeling!" The terror began to come in waves over her, and her whole body shook. She began hallucinating, talking in a fragmented, disconnected way about images she alone saw. She would speak for long periods in French, her native language, and would call out, "*Peur! Peur!*" (Fear! Fear!)

She asked us to help her sit up, and without real help she sat up herself for the first time in a week. I have never seen such terror.

Gail said to me from the other side of the bed, "You really die alone . . . She had a hard life and she's having a hard death." How much of our lives is spent in the illusion that we can avoid the results of our actions; we believe this until the hour of our death, when there's no escape from the fruits of what we've sown in our life. Helplessly I watched Leah as she was swept along by a stark and relentless river of everything that was unresolved in her life. She took off her oxygen mask and said to me, "You've been so impressed with me. You thought I was dealing with my death, but I did nothing to prepare for this!" She put the mask back on, still very agitated, and withdrew into herself. Suddenly, almost violently, she took the mask off again and said in desperation, "I want to die but I can't get out!" She pointed to her chest and made a motion with her hands as if to tear it open. Gail and I took turns fanning her to keep her cool. She became weaker and quieter, and what she said was not lucid.

Leah had been quiet and seemingly far away for at least half an hour when, at 2 A.M., I decided to go home. Gail, too, went to lie down in the lounge for some much needed rest, and she asked a nurse to wake her if anything happened. Leah had once said she wanted to be alone at the moment of death because she felt it would be easier for her—that she would find it less painful to let go if others weren't present.

Leah died, alone, sometime within the next hour.

SENG-CHAO (384–414)

An example of remarkable composure in the face of death is that of the Buddhist monk Seng-chao. An exceptionally talented writer and a religious genius, he wrote many philosophical treatises and religious tracts. The emperor, hearing of his abilities, ordered him to leave the monastery and return to lay life to serve as the imperial secretary. Seng-chao refused, and as a result he was condemned to die by decapitation. He was only thirty. He appealed to the emperor for a week's reprieve in order to complete a book on metaphysics titled *Treatise on the Jewel Treasure.* It was granted. When the work was finished, he calmly submitted to the execution. At the point of death he composed the following verse:

> The four elements[48] essentially have no master.
> The five *skandhas*[49] are fundamentally void.
> When the naked sword cuts off my head
> It will be like cutting a spring breeze.

Admirable as Seng-chao's sublime indifference to death is, one cannot but speculate that in a previous existence he had killed someone and was therefore expiating that karma in this life. For the moral law of cause and effect decrees that violence to another never goes unpunished. As a Buddhist, Seng-chao must have known this. He may even have considered his untimely death atonement for a past capital offense.

Sri Ramana Maharshi (1879–1950)

The manner of dying of Sri Ramana Maharshi, one of modern India's most revered religious figures, is reminiscent of that of the Zen masters, whose teachings his own closely resembled. He was honored as much for his wisdom as for the exemplary character of his life. When asked where he would go upon his death, he replied, "They say that I am dying, but I am not going away. Where could I go? I am here . . ."[50]

Here follows a fuller account of the death scene of this remarkable sage:

> On Thursday, April 13, a doctor brought Sri Bhagavan [Maharshi] a palliative to relieve the congestion in the

> lungs, but he refused it. "It is not necessary, everything will come right within two days," [insisted the Maharshi, who was dying of cancer.] . . .
>
> At about sunset Sri Bhagavan told his attendants to sit him up. They knew already that every movement, every touch, was painful, but he told them not to worry about that. He sat with one of the attendants supporting his head. A doctor began to give him oxygen, but with a wave of his right hand he motioned him away . . .
>
> Unexpectedly a group of devotees sitting on the veranda outside the hall began singing "Arunachala-Siva."[51] On hearing it, Sri Bhagavan's eyes opened and shone. He gave a brief smile of indescribable tenderness. From the outer edges of his eyes tears of bliss rolled down. One more deep breath, and no more. There was no struggle, no spasm, no other sign of death: only that the next breath did not come.[52]

Gautama the Buddha (563–483 B.C.)

Lastly, as an example of a quintessential approach to death among the masters, let us now consider the *parinirvāna* of Gautama the Buddha. The Sanskrit word *nirvāṇa* literally means extinction: the unconditioned state beyond birth and death that is reached after all ignorance and craving have been extinguished and all karma, which is the cause of rebirth, has been dissolved. The term *parinirvāṇa,* used only in reference to the Buddha, means complete extinction, the state of perfect freedom from bondage reached by Gautama Buddha at the time of his utter passing away.

To set the stage for the final act of the drama of Gautama's earthly life, let us trace the significant events of his final days. A good starting point is his last preaching tour. Tradition tells us that when he came to the town of Pava, in northern India, he halted at the mango grove of Chunda, a pious follower and worker in metal, who invited the Master and his monks to dine at his house the following day. The meal consisted of sweet rice, cake, and mushrooms. Stricken with grievous pains as a result of eating the mushrooms—which, it turned out, were poisonous—the Buddha, mindful and self-possessed, nonetheless bore the pains without complaint. When they abated somewhat, he said to Ānanda, his faithful attendant, "Let us go on to Kushinagara." They had not gone far when the Master turned aside from the path to the foot of a tree and said, "Ānanda, fold my robe in four and spread it out for me. I am weary and must rest awhile."

And then he spoke to Ānanda concerning Chunda the smith, saying that none should impute the least blame to Chunda because the Master died after receiving the last meal at his hands. "On the contrary," said the Buddha, "there are two offerings of food which are supremely precious: that which is given before the Tathagata[53] attains to Perfect Insight, and the other before his utter passing away. Good karma has redounded to Chunda the smith; therefore let him not feel any remorse.

"Come, Ānanda, let us continue our journey to the sala grove of the Mallas."

When they got there he said, "Spread out for me the couch, with its head to the north, between the twin sala trees. I am weary, Ānanda, and would like to lie down." He laid himself down on his right side, with one leg resting on the other. Then he told Ānanda that his utter passing away would take place at the third watch of that night.

The texts tell us that the Buddha first passed through the four stages of rapture. Rising from the fourth stage, he entered the successive stages of the infinity of space; the infinity of thought; emptiness; the realm between consciousness and unconsciousness; and the realm where the consciousness of both sensations and ideas has wholly passed away.

Now it seemed to Ānanda that the Master *had* passed away; but he entered again into every stage in *reverse* order until he reached the second stage of rapture, and then he passed into the third and fourth stages of rapture. And passing out of the last stage of rapture he immediately expired.

Earlier, when many of the Buddha's followers were weeping at his announcement that he would soon pass away, he reprimanded them for grieving when they should be rejoicing:

> In this hour of joy it is not proper to grieve. Your despair is quite inappropriate, and you should regain your composure. The goal, so hard to win, which for many aeons I have wished for, now at last is no longer far away. When that is won, no earth or water, fire, wind or ether is present; unchanging bliss beyond all objects of the senses, a peace which none can take away, the highest thing there is; and when you hear of that and know that no becoming mars it and nothing ever there can pass away—how, then, is there room for grief in your minds? At Gaya,[54] at the time when I won enlightenment, I got rid of the causes of becoming, which are nothing but a gang of harmful vipers; now the hour comes near when I get rid also of this body, the dwelling place of the acts accumulated in the past. Now that at last this body, which harbors so much ill, is on its way out; now that at last the frightful dangers of becoming are about to be extinct; now that at last I emerge from the vast and endless suffering—is this the time for you to grieve? . .[55]

By ordinary reckoning the Buddha lived to the venerable age of eighty; he had been teaching and preaching for forty-five years since his supreme enlightenment at the age of thirty-five.

PART TWO

DYING

You have to learn to do everything, even to die.

GERTRUDE STEIN

Learn to die and thou shalt live,
for there shall none learn to live
that hath not learned to die.

THE BOOK OF THE CRAFT OF DYING

Since dying has become fashionable, no one's life is safe anymore.

JEWISH PROVERB

4

THE DYING PERSON AND DEATH

The Process of Dying

IN A BOX in a corner, a very dark corner of the mind of each of us, is a voice. The voice says, "I am going to die. One day I am going to die."

We tend not to venture near that corner. We rarely listen to that voice. Sometimes it speaks to us so clearly and emphatically that we have to listen. When we're sick, when we narrowly escape harm, when someone we know dies, we hear it speaking to us. We hear it more frequently as we age, as our bodies fail, as our cumulative experience of death increases. Sometimes the voice emits a powerful, powerful scream that shakes us mercilessly. When someone we love dies, the voice tells us that our life is forever altered, that there is no going back.

The voice reminds us that we are, like everyone else who ever lived, mortal, expendable. How we react to this voice, how we try to block it out, determines how we live our lives.[1]

If we are to die with a measure of peace, we must have some understanding of who or what it is that dies. Most people believe they are a body and a mind, an I, an ego, a self, a soul, identified by the name Tom or Mary. But "body" is only a name for a combination of changing elements, and "mind" a name for a succession of thoughts. Without thinking too much about it, we believe that the psychophysical combination called Tom or Mary is the real person. But this is true only in a conventional sense. Actually:

> There is no doer but the deed
> There is no experience but the experiencer
> Constituent parts alone roll on.[2]

Everything mental or physical is in a state of change; nothing is stable or static. If we reflect on this carefully, we will see that there is no person who dies, only a *process* of dying. Just as moving is a process and walking is a process, so dying is a process. By refusing to identify our True-self with our actions, we are able to grasp the fact that all life is just a process.

Many people know this quote from Woody Allen: "I don't mind dying. I just don't want to be there when it happens." These words are more than just funny: a deep truth is concealed in them. If you "don't want to be there" when dying, learn how to merge with dying, so that *you* "disappear," transcending body and mind. Rid yourself of the thinking that distinguishes death from dying, self from other, and similar antagonistic opposites. Who remains then to say or think, "I'm dying"? In this highly desirable condition there can be no clinging to life, no railing against death.

This merging with dying is a meditative state, but one that occurs in a more everyday fashion. Suppose, for example, you are at an art gallery where a number of high-quality paintings are being exhibited. You look around and suddenly you are "grabbed" by one of them. You take in the entire picture in one fell swoop. Irresistibly it draws you into itself. Your reflective mind now begins to analyze the painting. "The colors are rich, the forms pleasing, the relationships intimate"—all this is the functioning of your analytical mind. But you have not yet merged with the painting. You gaze and gaze at it, going deeper and deeper, losing yourself in it. The picture engulfs you. Time and space disappear. You are no longer you, a subject separate from the painting as object; your mind and body have merged with the painting—you have entered its heart. This state defies description. Tears begin to well up, yet you aren't aware of them. You are one with the painting.

This state of total immersion, or *samadhi* to use the Buddhist term, is a quality of being in which one is no longer aware of oneself as a subject separate from a person, thing, or activity as an object. It is a state of intense yet effortless concentration, of heightened and expanded awareness. Limited, or positive, samadhi is partial unity with an object or action.

There are degrees of samadhi. Let us say you are absorbed in watching a gorgeous sunset. That is positive samadhi. You start with an object and then transcend it. Absolute samadhi, on the other hand, is objectless. Since there is no subject-object awareness to begin with, this state is not entered into in relation to anything. The concentrative power developed through certain kinds of objectless meditation makes it possible for one to reach the uncommon state of absolute samadhi. But upon entering that condition, one has no self-conscious awareness of being in it. States of absolute samadhi are of much longer and deeper duration than those of positive samadhi. In positive samadhi one often experiences blissful feelings. In absolute samadhi, on the other hand, no thoughts or feelings arise. This "no-thoughting" is not an insensibility or trancelike condition in the negative sense. Human thought is awareness in motion; samadhi is awareness at rest. Samadhi and enlightenment can be said to be identical from the view of our intrinsic wisdom mind. But seen from the developing stages leading to awakening, absolute samadhi and enlightenment are different.

All the senses—and the intellect as well—can be vehicles for positive samadhi. Hearing music, looking at a painting, engaging in a sport, pondering a subject, even engaging in sex—all these can be the means of attaining the *temporary* state of positive samadhi. "Temporary" is an important distinction, for one enters and leaves positive samadhi with relative ease. The more you cultivate oneness in your life, the easier it becomes to achieve positive samadhi.

Daily Dying

The truth about dying is that we actually experience it every day of our lives. Were you ever rejected by someone you deeply loved? At the time, didn't you feel as though a part of you had died? And how did you feel when someone very close to you passed away?

Didn't part of you die with him or her? There are so many little dyings every day, aren't there? These daily dyings are the price we pay for a commitment to any relationship.

Disruptions of human relationships occur regularly throughout life. They include loss of parents, death of a mate, divorce, death of family members, death of close friends. Because we attach ourselves to forms, letting go is not easy. The more we cling to people and things, the more we experience pain at our loss of them. We meet change with resistance and fear and therefore try to avoid it. Change produces the greatest stress for most people. The standard rating scale for stress shows that virtually all major stress grows out of recent transitions, such as sickness, moving from one city to another, divorce, change of job, change in health, change in economic status. But at the top of the list is death. Death alone is the only change over which we have no control. All seasons of life—infancy, adolescence, middle age, old age—inevitably involve human loss. But these "deaths" are also precursors to a new life, for if we merge with the sorrow—not standing outside it—suddenly the pain, the suffering, disappears; and it is followed by a heightened awareness, a liberating joy. From such dyings emerges the unshakable knowledge that loss and gain, good and bad, cannot reach our innermost being. These daily deaths, then, are resurrections. No one need wonder what it means to die, for everyone at one time or another has had intimations of his or her own mortality. But because the picture of death painted by our culture is tinted in such gloomy colors, we shrink from it, often in terror, and pretend it can't happen to us. As Robert Samuelson wittily observed, "We Americans are great optimists. No one has yet devised a preventive for death, but we keep looking."

To be reborn hourly and daily in this life, we need to die—to give of ourselves wholly to the demands of the moment, so that we utterly "disappear." Thoughts of past, present, or future, of life and death, of this world and the next, are transcended in the superabundance of the now. Time and timelessness coalesce: this is the moment of eternity. Thus our every act is a matter either of giving life or taking it away. If we perform each act with total absorption, we give life to our life. If we do things half-heartedly, we kill that life.

Jacques Lusseyran, a blind French Resistance leader who survived a Nazi death camp, pinpoints how to achieve such a transcendent relation to life and death:

> Memories are too tender, too close to fear. They consume energy. We had to live in the present; each moment had to be absorbed for all that was in it to satisfy the hunger for life . . . Don't hoard. Eat the food right away, greedily, mouthful after mouthful, as if each crumb were all the food in the world. When a ray of sunshine comes, open out, absorb it to the depths of your being. Never think that an hour earlier you were cold and that an hour later you will be cold again. Just enjoy.
>
> Latch on to the passing minute. Shut off the workings of memory and hope. The amazing thing is that no anguish held out against this treatment for very long. Take away from suffering its double drumbeat of resonance, memory, and fear. Suffering may persist, but already it is relieved by half. Throw yourself into each moment as if it were the only one that really existed. Work and work hard.[3]

We die because we are alive. Living means birth and death. Creating and destroying signify life. The evidence of our having lived is the fact that we die.[4] Dying to (that is, total immersion in) the task at hand—whether one is working on an assembly line, engaging in a sport, dancing, playing chess, mountain climbing, or singing—paradoxically leads to a heightened sense of awareness, a peak state in which there is a feeling of invigoration and relaxed awareness coupled with a rapturous joy.[5]

We are not, of course, speaking here of those who are understandably fearful of a long and painful illness and the great financial burden it will impose on their family. And yet essentially the problem is the same for all: how to live fully with life while alive and die serenely with death when dying, free from anxiety and other worrisome emotions. In the end the quality of our death, like the quality of our life, is a matter of an unbridled (pain-producing) ego or a restrained (peaceful) one.

In order to have a peaceful death you have to start *now*. The first step is to begin a spiritual practice. Beware of substituting reading for actual practice, for it is easy to be enticed away from practice by the sirens of literature, psychology, philosophy, and the like. The reading of certain books can provide a compass and a map, but they are no substitute for personal experience. The good book, to paraphrase Emerson, is the one that gets you onto the meditation mat (or chair).

Painful memories, bothersome feelings, and other "incomplete business" once lodged in your unconscious will surface to consciousness as your mind becomes quieted and deeper levels are attained. As you continue to meditate regularly and are aware and alert in your daily doings, the disruptive elements in your life will lose their hold over you and eventually disappear. Too, you will experience greater clarity in your life as a whole, and this will reflect itself in peace and tranquillity when your dying hour is at hand. In this connection a middle-aged woman wrote me, "If on my deathbed I can look at my life knowing I struggled with my [spiritual] practice but had not reached full awakening, I would still have more peace of mind than if I never tried anything at all."

We Die as We Have Lived

For the way we die reflects the way we have lived. A good death puts the stamp on a good life. "Just as a well spent day brings happy sleep, so a life well used brings happy death."[6] But if we have lived a life of emotional turmoil and conflict, or a selfish and inane existence, our dying will be troubled and painful. Instead of seeking ways to prolong our lives through medical technology, we would better serve ourselves and society by dedicating ourselves to improving the spiritual and moral quality of what life we have.

The mental agony of facing death for one who has lived a troubled and alienated life is vividly portrayed by Tolstoy in his moving story "The Death of Ivan Ilyich." In the story, Tolstoy describes the unbearable spiritual suffering of the dying Ilyich, who in a moment of truth understands that in itself death is not frightening. Rather, what evokes the greatest pain is the type of life he has led—the knowledge that his life has been sinful, not in the commonly accepted moral sense but in relation to the inner voice, what we might call conscience. Put simply, he feels that his life was useless and ill spent. And as he approaches death, the only real relief comes to him in those rare moments when he follows the promptings of his inner voice and not popularly accepted opinions and customs.

Significantly, many who survived cruel oppression and the utmost loss of freedom in slave-labor and concentration camps affirm that it was not imprisonment itself, and all that that implied, that was frightening; rather, it was recollection of the life they had led prior to arrest. In his well-known book *The Gulag Archipelago*, Solzhenitsyn more than once attests that mental suffering was greatest when he and his fellow prisoners reflected on the unwholesome aspects of their life prior to prison, "about sinning with respect to one's own soul—which meant sinning with respect to other people as well."[7]

Survival and the Inner Voice

To these cases may be added another group of men and women who did not die passively but survived life-threatening circumstances because they listened to and followed a mysterious inner voice. Among them is Jacques Lusseyran, mentioned earlier. When only nineteen he was seized by the Gestapo, along with five of his coworkers in the Resistance movement, and condemned to death "for subversive acts against the German occupation authorities." During the 180 days he was incarcerated, he was ceaselessly interrogated. Then, instead of executing him, the Gestapo inexplicably shipped him and his companions to the notorious Buchenwald death camp in central Germany. In his book *And There Was Light* Lusseyran writes that of the two thousand Frenchmen who were shipped off with him in cattle cars to Buchenwald at the end of January 1944, about thirty survived, he among them.

What enabled Lusseyran, blind and virtually defenseless, to survive? Chiefly it was his refusal to submit to fear and despair—a refusal buttressed by a strong faith in God that neither hunger, constant cold, oppressive labor, nor sickness could diminish:

> Have I said that death was already there? . . . Sickness and pain, yes, but not death. Quite the opposite—life, and that was the unbelievable thing that had taken possession of me. I had never lived so fully before. There were names which I mumbled from the depths of my astonishment. No, my lips did not speak them, but they had their own song: Providence, the Guardian Angel, Jesus Christ, God . . . There was one thing left which I could do, not refuse God's help, the breath He was blowing upon me. There was the one battle I had to fight, hard and wonderful all at once: not to let my body be taken by fear. For fear kills and joy maintains life. Also I could try to show other people how to go about holding on to life. I could turn toward them the flow of light and joy which had grown so abundant in me . . . From that time on they stopped stealing my bread or my soup . . . Hundreds of people confided in me. The men were determined to talk. They spoke to me in French, in Russian, in German, in Polish. I did the best I could to understand them all. That is how I lived, how I survived . . .[8]

Lusseyran's response to his imprisonment coincides with those of Solzhenitsyn and other sensitive Russian writers who were imprisoned in labor camps in the Soviet Union and who have written books about their experiences. Some of these books are analyzed and commented on by Mihajlo Mihajlov in his article "Mystical Experiences of the Labor Camps":

> All the authors agree that arrest, prison, and camp—simply to say the loss of freedom—have formed the most profound and significant experiences of their lives . . . Although they underwent the most extreme spiritual and physical suffering during their imprisonment, they also experienced a fulfilling happiness undreamed of by people outside the prison walls . . . Those having gone through the most adverse circumstances, which threatened both soul and body, unanimously affirmed that those who have sacrificed their souls to save their body

> have lost both; while for those who were prepared to sacrifice their body to save their soul, some kind of strange and mysterious law, eluding understanding, preserved both . . . Life experience has revealed to us that deep in the human soul is an unfamiliar force which is stronger than all the external forces of enslavement and death . . .[9]

Should One Struggle Against Death?

Now, a question that frequently comes up for one struggling with a terminal illness is, "Should I fight against death or surrender to it?" From what I have seen, read, and been told by doctors and nurses, that problem is eventually resolved by the patients themselves in a natural manner. It is true that in the beginning, patients are confused and often distraught. Their minds are filled with conflicting thoughts and emotions. On the one hand, there are feelings of denial, guilt, fear, depression, loneliness, apathy, and despair; on the other hand, there is the desire, often desperate, to prolong their life. And always there is the pain to cope with—physical and mental. Some terminally ill patients I have been with feel they are letting their family down if they don't struggle against their illness. Others in chronic pain often oscillate between fight and flight, especially when the pain is associated with symptoms of deterioration, such as loss of appetite and weight and increasing physical dependence. The message from the body is clear: "Unless a miracle occurs, you can't survive for long." The patient knows she is on a collision course with death. Still, if she becomes convinced that what we miscall death is not the black void of extinction but merely a transitional stage, it is unlikely she will clutch at life or surrender to death out of deep despair.

Dying Well

How individuals respond to a fatal illness—in other words, how they die—depends of course on their personality and their values, but mostly on the quality of their faith and spiritual awareness. And these latter qualities can be developed through training, as the seventh Dalai Lama points out: "In order to die well, with the joy and confidence of being within the white rays of spiritual awareness, it is essential to begin readying yourself now. Familiarize yourself with the profundities of the scriptures." Few in our culture, though, whether priests or scientists, seem willing to believe that dying well can be an achievement. Many magazine articles and books tell us how to live, but few tell us how to die. Most focus on the loss, the tragedy, the pain.

To die artfully is to die thinking of nothing, wishing for nothing, wanting to understand nothing, clinging to nothing—just fading away like clouds in the sky. That is the acme of artful dying; such an accomplishment, though, presupposes considerable spiritual insight. To be able to die thinking of nothing implies that, through meditation and other spiritual practices, you have gained control over your wayward thoughts and a high degree of mastery over your emotions. To die wishing for nothing assumes you have realized that fundamentally you are whole and complete and therefore lack nothing. To die wanting to understand nothing means you have perceived that all things, including your thoughts, feelings, and perceptions, are impermanent, arising when certain causes and conditions bring them into being and passing away with the emergence of new causal factors. To die clinging to nothing means you have realized that nothing is really ours, neither body nor mind nor life itself—and that therefore death is a letting go of that which we never really owned in the first place. As he lay dying, the mystical philosopher Plotinus (A.D. 205?–270) spoke cryptically of the "that":

> I am making my last effort to return
> that which is divine in me
> to that which is divine in the universe.

Two Different Ways of Dying

Let me tell you about two people with whom I was acquainted who died in totally different ways; you may draw your own conclusions as to their relative merits.

Peter (not his real name) was a man in his late thirties with a lovely wife and two young children. He led an active life, traveled extensively, engaged in many sports, and had friends in all walks of life. Then he suddenly, or so it seemed, came down with a particularly malignant form of bone cancer. Chemotherapy was prescribed. At first he responded to it, but then he grew worse as the disease entrenched itself in his bones. He took to his bed and began to lose weight rapidly as his appetite evaporated. At this point a new experimental drug was tried. If it worked, Peter's doctor told him, he might go into remission and add six months or more to his life. At first the new drug did seem to help, for with the aid of a walker Peter could get out of bed to go to the bathroom. Soon, however, the excruciating pain returned, a pain so severe that stronger and stronger pain-suppressing drugs had to be prescribed along with more powerful sleeping pills.

Peter was a fighter and he fought his disease with both fists. He would not accept the judgment that his cancer had marked him for an early death. He had much to live for: two young children whom he adored and who needed him as much as he needed them. The new drug, unfortunately, neither alleviated the pain nor gave him added vitality. At this point several cancer specialists were consulted. They recommended yet another experimental drug. When this new drug failed to produce any lasting improvement, Peter fell into a deep depression. More than once he lamented, "Have I led such an evil life that I deserve this terrible pain and suffering?" Still Peter fought on. There were additional drugs, and with each new one his hope again soared. However, his wife and friends, moved by his continuing pain and mental agony, urged, "Let go! . . . let go! . . . it's all right. Why prolong your suffering?" It was as though they understood what Peter did not understand, that "there was wisdom in knowing when to die with the least inconvenience to others and distress to oneself, and that much medical progress only prolonged life for a few uncomfortable months to the greater glory of the patient's doctor."[10]

But Peter wouldn't give up. "If I can get six months more through these drugs," he insisted, "I'll have that much more time with my kids." So he battled his cancer even as it was literally killing him. His condition steadily worsened. A priest was called and Peter was given last rites. Miraculously, he again rallied and pulled himself out of death's grasp, to everyone's amazement.

At this point, at his wife's urging, I visited Peter, whom I knew. I spoke to him about what he might expect in the intermediate state after decease, and I gave him several simple mantras for later use. Since Peter was still conscious, I recited the mantras slowly to him and he repeated them after me. Although he rehearsed these procedures with me, I felt that his heart was not in them: not because he didn't believe in the continuity of life—he did and had read much about it—but because of his unwillingness to come to grips with his own death. One week after I saw him he died in his wife's arms, heavily sedated and semiconscious. Some eight months had elapsed from the time he had been stricken with his fatal illness to the time of his death.

What did Peter gain from his fierce struggle with his cancer? He may have added several months to his life. If so, he paid a high price for it. He shriveled to a mere husk of a man; he suffered such excruciating and unremitting pain that he was unable to handle a visit from his children. Moreover, the effect of his pain and struggle on his wife and parents was such that it left them exhausted and depressed. Was the trade-off worth it? Granted that it is a tricky business for a doctor to predict how long a patient with a life-threatening illness may live, was the doctor justified in feeding Peter's hopes by holding out to him the possibility of added months of life with each new drug? "Many new therapies have severe side effects—some even shorten life," says Dr. Robert J. Temple, director of the Food and Drug Administration's Office of Drug Research and Review.[11] When none of the drugs proved to be the "magic bullet" Peter hoped for, he suffered a relapse and his anguish and depression deepened. Perhaps even worse, since his focus was on extending his life and not confronting his imminent death, he made little effort to prepare himself psychologically. When the moment came for him to exit from what had become for him and his family a vale of tears, he could not, as we have seen, do so with consciousness unimpaired.

Now let me tell you about another kind of dying.

Grace (not her real name) was a middle-aged woman with grown children. She was diagnosed as having a large, malignant tumor that required surgery. While in the hospital she became aware of how strong was the fear of death and dying among the other patients. Seeing and hearing of these fears of others, she thought, "How can I help people who are afraid of death? I have met death already in a car accident in which I came close to being killed, and

I lost my fear of death with that experience. I know that in helping other people I will be helping myself."

Although her surgeon removed the large tumor, it came back, having metastasized. Eight months later she had further surgery. Shortly after that I made her acquaintance via a videotape in which she was interviewed at her home by the director of the Life Center for Attitudinal Healing[12] in Santa Fe, New Mexico, of which she had become a member. Asked whether she was having any pain, she told the interviewer that while she had some, only occasionally did she take painkillers; she had found that doing hatha yoga, which made her mind peaceful, enabled her to dispense with painkillers most of the time.

Told by her oncologist that her particular cancer was resistant to radiation and chemotherapy, she chose alternative therapies. One was diet. Another was acupuncture treatments, which, she said, "seems to do something for the endorphins, which are that part of the brain which helps to combat or reduce pain and heightens energy levels." Even with acupuncture, the pain she did experience was real enough, and in mentioning it to her doctor she quoted this amusing though pertinent limerick:

> There was a young fellow of Deale
> Who said, "Although pain isn't real,
> When I sit on a pin and it punctures my skin,
> I dislike what I think that I feel."

To cope with her cancer and the pain it generated, Grace also resorted to meditation and visualization. The methods of visualization were detailed in a series of tapes she had obtained from Dr. O. Carl Simonton's Cancer Counseling and Research Center in Texas. The procedure was to visualize the immune system and then to imagine white blood cells searching through the body to attack the cancer cells. Another method she used, also recommended on the tapes, was to visualize white dogs consuming the cancer cells. Sometimes she did the first, sometimes the second. She felt that through these techniques the tumor had reduced somewhat. And by using guided imagery—imagining a burning sensation, for example, to be the tingle of a cool shower on a hot day—she was able to distract herself from the pain.

Unfortunately, at this time her mother died and Grace began

going downhill. It wasn't just the grief occasioned by her mother's death, she explained, but also the fact of knowing she had a fatal illness. "When people learn for the first time that they have a life-threatening illness, it often comes as a shock and there's a lot of anger connected with it. Some feel this anger more than others, and they ask, 'Why should this happen to me?'"

Grace went on to make clear that she herself never felt this anger. Still, she did say that it was a mystery why one person would contract a serious illness and not another, or why one person in a bad car accident might become a quadriplegic while another in the same accident emerged unhurt. "We don't know why these things happen," she told the interviewer, "so I did think, 'Why me?' Nevertheless it is a challenge to learn how to cope with an affliction. Having worked in the medical field for many years, I took an interest in my illness as if it were something out of a book."

Grace felt that an enthusiastic rapport with all aspects of life helped alleviate illness, because it took one's thoughts off oneself. She also spoke of the value of music. In her room in the hospital, she often sang with the occupant of the bed next to hers. Grace also felt strongly that with a sense of humor and a lively attitude, one could do much to help lessen the pain of one's illness. In this connection she spoke of the value of laughter—citing the book *The Anatomy of an Illness* by Norman Cousins, in which Cousins described his experience of curing himself of a serious illness by using laughter, among other methods. Laughter, according to Cousins, actually changes body chemistry.

When asked whether she herself was using laughter, she replied, "Oh, definitely." When her daughters visited her in the hospital, she said, "We all just cracked up and laughed our heads off about all sorts of things. You go on being you no matter what is happening to your body. The illness may be attached to you somewhere, but it is not you. Even though you can't have a hike up the mountains, you can go on having fun in many ways."

She went on to say, "You know, there is really no security in good health, because at any point you may become ill. We [the seriously ill] are in a way no different from a healthy person in that our security should be in a spiritual life. We need to deal with the bad things as a way of learning and growing, and find a way to turn them around, to sort of leap over or grow out of them."

When asked whether she and others in her support group at the Life Center for Attitudinal Healing ever talked about death, she replied, "Yes, we talk about death a lot, and some people are very frightened about that experience. Of course, when you have a malignancy, there is always the question of death and you have to face it. And so I asked myself, 'What is good preparation for death?' and I came to the conclusion that it was the same as good preparation for life.

"Many people seem to feel that death will be the end of them totally, the end of everything, the end of seeing their loved ones. They think it is just a huge, blank abyss. A lot of us don't believe that at all."

In response to the question "What do you believe?" she answered, "I believe in life after life. I think that death is going through another door. I am sure of it. The times when I have been faced with death there has been a sort of prerecognition of what I was going through, and it was something wonderful. There was the feeling of 'This is it. This is it, and it's going to be just wonderful.' "

Grace died in the summer of 1984.

Two to three weeks before her death she wasn't taking anything but liquids. The evening before she died one of her daughters sat with her and held her hand. She reported that her mother lay there peacefully and then said, "You know, I'm ready to go into a dark room and close the door."

Later that evening Grace's daughters had a delightful conversation with their mother, after which she said, "I'm going to take a nap now." She never awoke from it. The next morning, around eight, one of her daughters, who was sitting beside her bed knitting, reported hearing the death rattle.

Grace's attitude toward her life-threatening illness was admirable. Many people with a belief only in life after death find that this alone can guide them well through dying to death. However—and this was the case with Grace—ignorance of the nature and significance of karma produced painful questioning. Had she understood the relation of karma to sickness, she would never have asked, "Why me?" when she learned she had a malignant tumor.

5

THE DILEMMA OF PAIN

Oh, it is real. It is the only real thing.
Pain. So let us name the truth, like men.
We are born to joy that joy may become pain.
We are born to hope that hope may become pain.
We are born to love that love may become pain.
We are born to pain that pain may become more
Pain, and from that inexhaustible superflux
We may give others pain as our prime definition.

ROBERT PENN WARREN

NO DISCUSSION of dying would be complete without talking about the dilemma of pain. We will consider two manifestations of pain: first, the pain inherent in the life process—in birth, "minor" sickness, old age, death, and other incidents of life; and second, pain arising from an injury, a serious sickness, or a life-threatening illness—cancer, let us say. In the course of this discussion we will also consider pain and suffering not as an abstract fact but as the teacher of life. Thus, we will discuss how we can learn from pain as well as how we can bring it to an end, or at least minimize it.

Here I am using the terms "pain" and "suffering" interchangeably, though, strictly speaking, they are not quite the same; suffering, it has been said, is the "psychic component of pain endured." The term the Buddha used for "suffering" was *dukkha*, a word of greater depth and complexity than is implied by the bald translation "suffering." We get a sense of the deep meaning of dukkha when we understand that the word was used to describe a wheel not running true on its axle, or a bone slipped out of its socket. Because life is out of joint, there is friction and pain. Dukkha, then, implies pain, grief, affliction, distress, or frustration. It also refers to impermanence, to a lack of wholeness or perfection.

Existential Pain

The Four Noble Truths of Suffering

Having a rational mind of the highest order,[13] the Buddha analyzed the specific life dislocations that give rise to pain, and like a good physician—he was in fact called the Great Physician—he prescribed the remedy. This diagnosis he called the Four Noble Truths—convictions about life which came to him in the course of his six-year quest for enlightenment. (They are called noble because adherence to them exalts life.) His teaching, then, went beyond the simple observation of facts. He penetrated the causes of suffering and showed how they could be overcome.

The first of these truths affirms the fact of the universality of suffering—not suffering as a theoretical problem but suffering as a part of what it means to be alive: "The [First] Noble Truth of Suffering is this: Birth is suffering; aging is suffering; sickness is suffering; death is suffering; sorrow and lamentation, pain, grief, and despair are suffering; association with the unpleasant is suffering; disassociation from the pleasant is suffering; not to get what one wants is suffering—in brief, the five aggregates[14] of attachment are suffering.[15]

To this may be added the afflictions and mental woes to which children are subject and which are as hard or often harder to bear than the catastrophes awaiting them later in life. Sensible men and women know that illness may strike them at any time, while the middle-aged often look forward to old age with the fear of protracted illness, the fear of being unloved and unwanted, and the fear of "the final agony"—death. Moreover, for countless numbers of people there is the suffering caused by cold, hunger, or near starvation. Nor can we ignore the painful struggles of so many to survive earthquakes, typhoons, floods, fires, pestilences, and epidemics, not to mention wars, slavery, and terrorism. With good reason the Chinese describe life as "a bitter sea of suffering."

Although the Buddha's message has been called pessimistic and life-denying by some, actually it is neither. "That Buddha gave his life to demonstrating how well-being might be attained," writes Huston Smith, "is . . . proof that his basic optimism was maintained in the face of the most unromantic recognition that the affairs of men and society are in the most imperfect state imaginable, a state of misery bordering on complete chaos."[16] Buddha, for example, recognized that there are great joys in family life, in pleasures of the senses, in mental well-being, and in many other ordinary human experiences. In a well-known Buddhist scripture, the *Dhammapada,* there is a section on happiness which includes the following: "Let us live happily, then, we who possess Nothing.[17] Let us dwell feeding on happiness like the shining gods . . . Health is the greatest of gifts, contentment is the greatest wealth; trust is the best of relationships. Awakening[18] is the highest happiness.[19]

And yet when we feel happy and at the same time know that happiness doesn't last forever—that in itself is a source of grief. The fleeting nature of happiness only emphasizes the ubiquity of suffering.

"The [Second] Noble Truth of the Origin of Suffering is this: It is this thirst [craving] which produces re-existence and re-becoming, bound up with passionate greed. It finds fresh delight now here and now there, namely, thirst for existence and becoming; and thirst for nonexistence [self-annihilation]."[20]

The term Buddha used to describe the origin of life's pain or dislocation was *tanha,* a word usually translated as "craving," "thirst for," or, more commonly, "desire." He did not condemn all desires, for he knew there are those that are life-enhancing and those that lead to suffering. The desire to improve oneself mentally, physically, and morally, for example, is surely worthwhile. The desire to help others without thought of personal gain is likewise commendable. Even more meritorious is the desire for spiritual liberation, or awakening.

It is the desires that arise from ego, strengthen it, and cause pain that are harmful. In the words of the scholar John Blofeld:

> The cause of all our sufferings and rebirths is—if we are compelled to state it rather inadequately in one word—desire, which, like many other Buddhist terms, is a word used to connote both itself and its own opposite, in this case aversion. It is because, in our ignorance, we cling to some things and abhor others that we have to revolve endlessly in samsara's round; for desire and aversion lead us to think in such dualistic categories as self and other, existence and non-existence, good and bad, desirable and repulsive, and all the rest. We fail to see that this vast universe, with its beauty and its horror, is a creation of our own minds—existing in that Mind with which our minds are in truth identical. However, if we are willing to accept this as at least a working hypothesis; if we begin training ourselves to refrain from desire and aversion and from every other kind of dualistic thought and behavior; if we withdraw from the realm of appearances into the secret place of the heart and surrender our so-called and previously cherished "selves" to its stillness, then mental creations will gradually lose their power to afflict or disturb us. Whereat our minds will become like polished mirrors, reflecting every detail of the passing show and yet remaining unstained, perfectly unaltered by reflections of things, whether beautiful or hideous.[21]

What lies at the root of all sorrow, then, is the delusory notion of an ego-I—that "I am here, and what is not me is out there"—and the concomitant dualism of self and other. These in turn lead to craving for things to satisfy the imperious demands of the ego-I, and clinging to those things as though they were substantial and enduring instead of in a state of change and decay. We build the house of our life on sand, the grains fall apart and the house crumbles.

"The [Third] Noble Truth of the Cessation of Suffering is this: It is the complete cessation of that very thirst, giving it up, renouncing it, emancipating oneself from it, detaching oneself from it."[22] This truth logically follows from the second one. If the cause of life's pain is exalting the ego-I and thirsting for the objects that sustain it, the cure lies in getting rid of this craving. If we can get out of our cocoon of personal wants and desires and shift our focus to the greater expanse of life outside us (yet of which we are a part), our conflicts and frustrations, and the pain arising from them, will subside. The way to accomplish this, says Buddha, is through the Noble Eightfold Path: "The [Fourth] Noble Truth of the Path Leading to the Cessation of Suffering is this: It is simply the Noble Eightfold Path, namely right view; right thought; right speech; right action; right livelihood; right effort; right mindfulness; right concentration."[23]

The Cessation of Suffering

What Buddha's treatment amounts to is a therapy, a practice, a training for life itself. This intentional way of living he called a path. A path, we must not forget, needs to be walked, not talked about. What the Buddha is proposing here is a rigorous system designed to release the individual from the repressions imposed by blind impulse, ignorance of self, and craving. An entire course from starting line to winning post is mapped. By long and patient discipline the Eightfold Path intends nothing less than to remake the total man and leave him a different being, a person cured of life's crippling disabilities.[24] As Buddha tells us, "Happiness he who seeks may win if he practices."

This practice involves more than just sitting on a mat or in a chair and trying to calm and concentrate the mind. Among other things, it means becoming *completely* absorbed in *whatever* you do, whether it be meditating, eating, sleeping, walking your dog, or doing your income tax. It also means learning to be mindful and self-possessed in every situation. Training, then, in the widest sense means being aware and alert at all times and cultivating a mind state free from gratuitous judgments, discriminations, preconceptions, and emotional colorations. When we are full of things to do, places to go, wants to be satisfied, how can we become absorbed in each moment? "Simplify, simplify, simplify!" urges Thoreau.

The Essence of Life Is Change

Craving or clinging to things or people inevitably leads to suffering. Why? Because impermanence is a law of life, so sooner or later we must part from what we try to hold onto, and this parting is painful. The nature and consequences of this clinging are well stated by the German master Lama Anagarika Govinda:

> The very essence of life is change, while the essence of clinging is to retain, to stabilize, to prevent change. That is why change appears to us as suffering. If we did not regard objects or states of existence from the standpoint of possession or selfish enjoyment, we should not feel in the least troubled by their change or even by their disappearance; on the contrary we enjoy change in many cases, either because disagreeable states or objects are removed or because it provides us with new experiences or reveals to us a deeper insight in the nature of things and greater possibilities of emancipation . . . It is therefore not the "world" or its transitions which is the cause of suffering but our attitude towards it, our clinging to it, our thirst, our ignorance.[25]

The Implications of the Eightfold Path

The import of the Noble Eightfold Path is this: to overcome pain and suffering and find deep contentment and joy in life, there must be an awakening. The precondition of an awakening is a life of ethical behavior, meditation, and nonattachment. To this must be added a seeing into one's True-nature and with it the True-nature of everything. Because one cannot progress on the road to enlightenment unless his mind is free of the inner disturbance which thoughtless and wanton behavior produces, a lifestyle based on decent behavior is the foundation of spiritual realization.

Degrees of Awakening

There are, of course, degrees of awakening. One may perceive dimly or may see with great clarity; the gradations are many and subtle. When we truly perceive that the Essential-nature of the phenomenal world is void of any enduring substance, we cease clinging to that world, for it becomes clear that it is illusory—as illusory as the antics of puppets on a stage. And death, too, is seen as having no more substantiality than the movements of these puppets.

Buddha's awakening was so profound that people often asked him "*Who* are you?" implying "To what order of being do you belong?"

"Are you a god?" they asked.

"No."

"An angel?"

"No."

"A saint?"

"No."

"Then what are you?"

"I am awake," answered the Buddha, and that in fact is the meaning of the word *buddha* (from the Sanskrit root *budh,* meaning "to wake up, "to know").

The following example conveys to some extent the mind state that awakening evokes. Take a person blind from birth who gradually begins to recover his sight. At first he can see very vaguely and darkly and only objects close to him. As his sight improves, he is able to distinguish things at a yard or so, then at ten yards, then at a hundred yards, then even a thousand yards. At each of these stages the phenomenal world he has been seeing is the same, but the differences in the clarity and accuracy of his views of that world are as great as the difference between cheese and chalk. The world hasn't changed—only his vision of it has. This *seeing* has been called "the hazy moon of enlightenment."

With awakening you realize that up to now you've been looking at the world as though "through a glass darkly." Now, for the first time, you see things as they really are: you find the world awash with beauty and delights of the senses that you never imagined existed. Of course, the quality of the seeing depends on whether your awakening was shallow or deep. But surprise and wonder are evident even in a relatively mild awakening.

Now, being fully awake does not mean you don't ever feel pain. Even the Buddha felt pain and sadness, and felt them deeply, but he didn't cling to these emotions.

The unawakened, the deluded, go through life "in a daze and a doze." Being on the whole discontented with their lot, they are unhappy most of the time. Random, irrelevant thoughts carom through their minds all day long. So when they look they don't really see; when they listen they don't really hear. What does come through is mostly the rustle of their own thoughts, not the rhythms and melodies of life.

Physical Pain

We have discussed existential pain—the pain of life itself. What about physical pain? What of the suffering inherent in a disease such as cancer of the bone? Or serious injury in an automobile accident?

Dr. Cicely Saunders, medical director of St. Christopher's Hospice near London, has over the years developed the concept of total pain. The idea behind this concept is that pain arises not simply from a physical stimulus, but through a complex interaction of many factors, some of which are illustrated in Diagram 3: "Total Pain." Most people, when asked to describe their pain, are at a loss. Pain is a physical sensation very much colored by emotional states, spiritual condition, cultural conditioning, fear of the disease causing the pain, fear of the death that may result, and the perception of one's condition relative to the cause of the pain. In addition, perception of one's total life circumstances, how one learned to

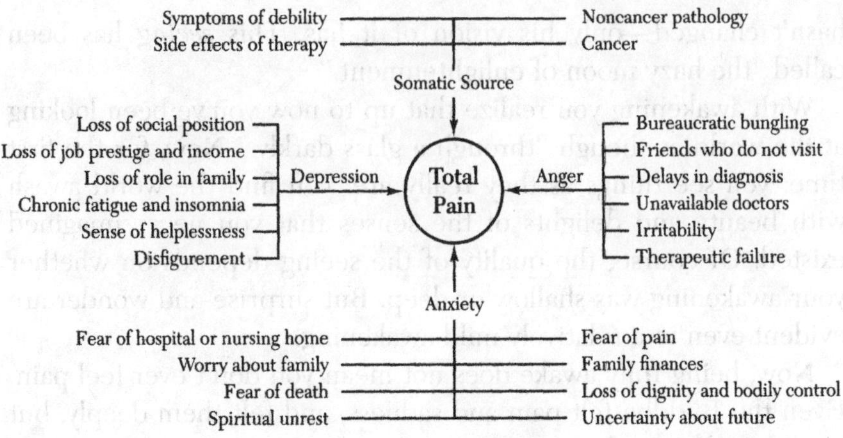

DIAGRAM 3: *Total Pain.*
(From Robert G. Twycross and Sylvia A. Lack, *Symptom Control in Far Advanced Cancer: Pain Relief*)

relate to pain as a child, fatigue, and even the degree of distraction from the pain at any given moment influence the sensation. Studies have shown that music, white noise, hypnosis, or a distraction of attention will raise the threshold of pain, while fear, stress, and fatigue will greatly lower it. "Every sufferer of chronic pain has learned to force himself to concentrate on activities that become so absorbing that pain is not felt or is greatly diminished . . . People who suffer severe pain after brachial plexus lesions report that the most effective way to reduce their pain is to absorb themselves in their work."[26]

The tighter the sense of self as a being separate from other beings, the more one feels physical as well as existential pain. In this sense there is no boundary between the two.

Acute Pain and Chronic Pain

Acute pain has the advantage of being finite—that is, one knows that, terrible though it may be, it will not continue forever. Chronic pain, on the other hand, can go on and on and on, even to the end of life—and many who suffer from it do wish the end of life were just around the corner. According to Dr. Robert Twycross, a British expert on pain, chronic pain is often due to an incomplete understanding of the source or sources of the patient's pain by his or her doctor; for physical pain can arise from much more than the specific tumor, incision, lacerations, or illness of the patient. Bedsores, constipation, anxiety, exhaustion, changes in posture or in the use of limbs in response to pain, and more will cause pain. Friends, family, doctors, and nurses interacting with the patient can, by their attitudes and responses to the patient alone, help alleviate pain. Sir David Smithers, director of the department of radiotherapy of a British hospital, made it a rule that his resident physician should visit terminally ill patients each day. However brilliant a doctor may be at clinical pharmacology, "if he has no time for chat, he knows nothing about terminal care. In this context, chat means 'patient chat' while the doctor listens. Although demanding of both time and emotion, the benefits are considerable."[27]

Pain Control

The value of pain control in raising the consciousness of the dying patient and making him or her comfortable is emphasized in a tape made under the auspices of St. Christopher's Hospice:

> The last few weeks before death . . . there are so many things which need to be said, practical arrangements to be made. If during this period the patient is distracted by chronic pain, dulled by heavy sedation, or uncomfortable because of dry mouth, bedsores or constipation, then a vital opportunity is going to be missed. The doctor caring for the dying patient is no longer looking for a cure or even a means of keeping the disease in check. His medical skill is directed towards controlling a constantly changing kaleidoscope of symptoms. But if the doctor can raise the level of a person's consciousness above the immediate preoccupation with their own body, this will give them the opportunity to end their lives in comfort, at one with themselves and their family.[28]

There are many paths available for control of pain that allow the patient to remain clearheaded. It is not within the scope of this book to study them in depth, but they include (besides thoughtfully prescribed drugs) hypnosis, behavior modification techniques, acupuncture, relaxation techniques, psychiatric counseling, and meditation. Each person's pain is individual, based on his or her life experience and expectations as well as on all the other factors mentioned earlier, and so no universal prescription can be made to end or mitigate it.

It can be said, however, that relieving existential pain will also significantly relieve physical pain. And physical pain can have the great benefit of pushing a person beyond complacency to search for ultimate Truth.

One's Attitude Toward Pain

Pain can be life's greatest teacher. Some kinds of pain are so all-consuming that one's sense of separation, one's ideas of who one is, one's clinging to all manner of things, disappear into that primordial fire of pain; nothing else exists. During that eternal moment, something imperceptible happens, and when the pain retreats or disappears, one is not the same person anymore. This is possible only if there is no separation from the pain—no fighting, no resisting, no hating, just "Owwwwwwwwwwww!"

But if one thinks, "Oh, my God! This horrible pain! It's terrible! I've never been in such pain!" one remains an isolated, small self, whipped around by one's own desire to be something other than what one is at that moment.

Although it is true that absorbing yourself in anything that takes your mind off your own body will make you less aware of pain, meditation is especially effective for this purpose. There are, of course, many kinds of meditation. Strictly speaking, meditation involves putting something into the mind—either an image or a sacred word that is visualized, or a concept that is thought about or reflected on, or both. To the degree that one approaches a condition of samadhi—that is, absorption to the point of self-forgetfulness—one loses awareness even of one's body, let alone of pain.

A very effective practice for attaining samadhi is meditation on a fundamental problem that grips one, such as "Where did I come from when I was born, and where will I go when I die?" or "The great spiritual masters say that each of us, that all existence, is inherently flawless. Why, then, am I in pain now, and why is there so much pain and suffering in the world?" To resolve the contradiction between the truth of the statement of the masters and what appears to our senses to be just the opposite, one must struggle with this spiritual problem. And of course there must also be present the conviction that one can find answers.

Meditation to relieve pain can be carried on whether one is bedridden or not, but if one is not forced to lie in bed, sitting upright is the most effective way to meditate.

6

SUICIDE AND EUTHANASIA

SUICIDE AND EUTHANASIA are the biting sides of death and dying. The former, it seems, has become more prevalent, especially among teenagers and the elderly; the latter has become more and more a topic of serious inquiry as technical advances allow people who once would have died to remain "alive" in conditions where they are hardly living. The newspapers and newsmagazines are full of stories of elderly people who—finding themselves with painful terminal illness, frightened of the specter of being completely incapacitated and having to be cared for by others, or just plain fed up with trying to live a restricted life in a deteriorating body with a fading mind—decide to "leave it all behind," sometimes with the help of friends.

Those of you who followed the Vietnam War are no doubt aware of another kind of suicide: that of monks and nuns immolating themselves. They did this in an attempt to halt the terrible killing and destruction in Vietnam by bringing it to world attention. For these monks and nuns it was an attempt to trade one life for many. There are other contemporary stories of people sacrificing themselves for the sake of others.

Suicide

What we call suicide is defined as "the intentional taking of one's own life; to kill (oneself)."[29] Often a high degree of ego is involved in suicide. Venturing to kill oneself is frequently a statement of rage, the result of "a desire to make someone feel sorry for either not doing anything to stop the [suicide] or for causing it in the first place."[30] The act of self-destruction is the suicide's supreme gesture of defiance, a symbolic thumbing of his nose at society—the society that at the same time he is dramatically accusing of having failed him rather than he it. It has been found that many suicidal persons are really ambivalent about ending their life; they seek to make a statement through their attempts at killing themselves, rather than to succeed necessarily with the killing.[31]

There is also a type of death that is called subintentional suicide. A person who constantly takes chances with his life by putting himself in risky situations—such as abusing drugs or habitually driving fast and recklessly—is an example. "The subintentioned death is one in which the person plays some partial, covert, subliminal, or unconscious role in hastening his own demise."[32] This, too, comes from an egotistic position.

Of course, not every person who commits suicide does so for selfish reasons. One such person was Zen master Yamamoto. At the time of his death he was the abbot of a large and respected monastery in Japan. Having grown old—he was ninety-six at the time, if I remember correctly—he was almost completely deaf and blind. No longer able to actively teach his students, he made an announcement that it was time for him to take his leave, and that he would die at the start of the new year. He then stopped eating. The monks in his temple reminded him that the New Year period was the busiest time at the temple, and that for him to die then would be most inconvenient. "I see," he said, and he resumed eating until the early summer, when he again stopped eating and then one day toppled over and quietly slipped away.

It's worth noting that this master simply abstained from taking nourishment. One might say that he didn't act to continue his life. Yet he didn't act aggressively to kill himself either. His was more a letting go. There was no self-pity, no family to leave behind in shock, just an acknowledgment that his usefulness had ended and that it was time to move on.

A doctor friend of mine who works in cancer wards told me, "You know, when I make my rounds in the hospital, chronically ill, elderly patients will often say to me, 'Doctor, please give me something to end this misery!' and I tell them, 'I don't have to give you anything; all you need do is stop eating.' But you know, I've never known one who did." When I asked him why they didn't, he said, "What these patients really wanted was someone to give them an easy way out—to take the responsibility for their own living and dying off themselves and put it on the physician."

Ordinary people want to die because they are suffering great mental or physical pain and don't want to endure it anymore. That is understandable—nobody wants to needlessly bear great pain. Such pain is terribly debilitating. On the other hand, according to experts on physical pain, no one need be in great pain these days from, say, a terminal illness, because of the advances in diagnosis and techniques for controlling pain.

Too, pain and suffering have the potential for bringing about significant spiritual change in a person. Not only this, but the manner in which pain is endured can have a great moral effect upon those privileged to be attending such a person. There are many stories of people who are physically handicapped to an extreme by illness or accident, yet have a positive and practical outlook on life and do not consider killing themselves an option. Magdalena Cintron, age sixty-nine, has a reputation as a cheerful, kind, and giving person despite being in constant pain as a result of paralysis. She has lived in a room in a hospital in Rochester, New York, for four years:

> She cannot leave, even to attend religious services in the hospital chapel, because she's connected by a hose to a respirator, a machine that breathes for her, pumping in measured amounts of air every minute of every day.
>
> She is also almost completely paralyzed, only able to

shrug her shoulders a bit and slightly shift her legs. She must be fed, bathed, turned, lifted and dressed by nurses and therapists, carefully, so her breathing tube isn't disconnected. Her hands and feet are bundled in gauze, to prevent sores or bruises as she is moved.

And yet when questioned, Magdalena Cintron says she has never thought of asking that her machine be shut off.

"No! Because then I couldn't breathe," she explains, looking slightly surprised at the question. "I am used to it, in a way," she adds, her voice hoarse and barely audible, an effect of being on the respirator.[33]

If an individual wants to take his life for purely unselfish reasons—that is, he doesn't want to impose an intolerable financial and emotional burden on his family and friends because of his irreversible illness—certainly the karmic consequences of putting an end to his life would be diminished. (See "Karma" section.)

Suicide and Religious Belief

Over the centuries various religious faiths have taken every conceivable view of suicide, from recommending it to resolutely and uncompromisingly opposing it. There have been civilizations where the suicide of a wife or servant following the death of a husband or master was expected—as in the Hindu concept of *sati,* where the wife throws herself upon her deceased husband's funeral pyre. St. Augustine, it is reported, felt that suicide for whatever reason is a crime because "suicide is an act which precludes the possibility of repentance, and . . . it is a form of homicide, and therefore a violation of the sixth commandment ["Thou shalt not kill"], not justified by any of the exceptions, general or special to that commandment."[34] Orthodox Protestantism has been just as forceful: "Indeed, its rejection of the doctrine of purgatory makes it still more uncompromising in condemnation of suicide and less hopeful with regard to the future destiny of suicides."[35] Judaism too has repudiated self-destruction in no uncertain terms.

Buddhism is emphatic in its opposition to suicide, chiefly because it holds that only with a human body-mind can one become enlightened and thereby dispel the ignorance that is the root source of suffering. One of the canonical texts quotes the Buddha to this effect: "[Moreover,] a monk who preaches suicide, who says: 'Do away with this wretched life, full of suffering and sin; death is better,' in fact preaches murder, is a murderer, is no longer a monk."[36] Buddhism also teaches that a person cannot avoid by suicide the sufferings which are the result of his former evil deeds—nor can he by killing himself arrive more rapidly at the results of his good deeds. (See "Karma" section.)

"The strong Buddhist objection to suicide," writes Ananda K. Coomaraswamy, internationally known scholar, "is based on the very proper ground that . . . something more powerful than a dose of poison [is needed] to destroy the illusion of I and Mine. To accomplish that requires the untiring effort of a strong will."[37]

It is important here to distinguish between the canonical doctrines of a religion—in this case those concerning suicide—and their violation by misguided followers who have a perverted understanding of them. It is true that ignorant or disturbed Buddhist monks have immolated themselves. But followers of other major religions—Christianity and Islam in particular—have also sacrificed their lives for what they felt were valid religious reasons.

EUTHANASIA

Originally the Greek word *euthanasia* meant "painless, happy death." A secondary meaning is "the act of putting to death painlessly a person suffering from an incurable and painful disease or condition."[38] Increasingly it is being used as a synonym for "mercy killing." It can involve an action that will end life—such as removing the feeding tube from a comatose patient or the respirator from one who cannot otherwise breathe. It can consist of nonaction—that is, not resuscitating a person who has a heart attack or respiratory arrest. Or it can be the painless killing of infants born without limbs or badly deformed.

Some people believe there is a moral distinction between active euthanasia (removing a feeding tube from a comatose woman) and passive euthanasia (not resuscitating a terminal patient if he has, say, a heart attack). As I understand it, the latter has become generally acceptable legally, that is, a patient's basic right to make moral choices, in this case to refuse life-sustaining treatment: "Cardiopulmonary resuscitation, surgery, antibiotics, and even food and water, can be stopped . . . Hospitals routinely allow mentally competent adult patients to refuse life-sustaining treatment such as chemotherapy."[39] It has also become widely accepted that food and water can be withdrawn, although in some states termination of all other treatments must occur first, and clear, written directions to withhold food and water are required.

As for removing the feeding tube from a comatose person, there have been many authoritative cases where legal decisions have allowed such action: "The majority [of justices deciding in a Massachusetts court case to remove the feeding tube from a comatose man], deeming feeding tubes too 'intrusive,' declared that medical advances require a distinction between death as traditionally conceived and 'death in which the body lives in some fashion but the brain (or a significant part of it) does not.' "[40]

So in a purely legal sense, neither of these cases is murder, though the karmic consequences are something else again. On the other hand, there are cases of desperately sick people who despaired of life, and because their entreaties to "pull the plug" on them were refused by either the hospital authorities or a judge, they continued to live and later were grateful to be alive and well. The following story is a case in point:

> "If I ever become so ill that only machines can keep me alive," Jacqueline Cole, 44, told her husband, Presbyterian Minister Harry Cole, "I want you to pull the plug."
>
> Last spring Cole suffered a cerebral hemorrhage and fell into a coma. Her husband waited forty-one days for her to recover, then asked Maryland Judge John Carroll Byrnes to order doctors to let the comatose woman die. Byrnes said no, it was too soon to give up hope.
>
> Six days later Jacqueline Cole awoke, smiled, and re-

> turned her husband's joyous kiss. "Miracles can and do occur," said the happy minister. "I guess we've muddied the waters surrounding the question of a person's right to die."[41]

However, this story can also lead to the "tyranny of the anecdote." If we base our decisions on extreme cases, it becomes very difficult to analyze these issues. First, there is no *medical* opinion of what state of consciousness Jacqueline enjoyed during the "coma," so we don't know how to accurately compare her experience to others. Second, we do not know what level of functioning life she enjoyed after awakening. The sad reality is that extremely few people return to a functional life after a lengthy loss of consciousness.[42]

What are the attitudes of the religions on euthanasia?

> The Catholic church does not require its members to accept any life-preserving treatment if it would prolong the dying process . . . However, the church says "comfort" care must continue, including food and water. Thus . . . if a patient were in a permanent coma, a respirator could be shut off but feeding could not be withdrawn.
>
> Judaism . . . also condemns any form of active euthanasia but allows the refusal of life supports if they only would prolong the act of dying.
>
> The Lutheran church sees euthanasia as murder or suicide, but allows Christians to "let nature take its course" when they are dying. In other words, dying Lutherans can refuse resuscitation or artificial life supports . . .
>
> Strictly speaking, most black churches favor continuing all treatment—even the [use of] respirators for comatose patients—because of their feeling that every human life, "even life on the border," is in the hands of God . . .[43]

James Rachels, in his book *The End of Life: Euthanasia and Morality*, sees an inherent contradiction in this last contention: "If it is for God alone to decide when we shall live and when we shall die, then we 'play God' just as much when we cure people as when we kill them."[44]

Buddhism holds that because death is not the end, suffering does not cease thereupon, but continues until the karma that created the suffering has played itself out; thus, it is pointless to kill oneself—or aid another to do so—in order to escape.

The Hospice and Euthanasia

In part because of their success in fostering growth in life's final stage, and in part because of their success in the control of symptoms, hospices take away much of the energy from the debate about euthanasia. One strong-minded patient at St. Christopher's hospice told author Sandol Stoddard, "Hospices should be everywhere. All this talk about euthanasia is absolute nonsense. Well-meaning, of course, and I do sympathize, but the fact is, you don't have to kill people to make them comfortable."[45] British hospice director Dr. Richard Lamerton put it this way:

> If anyone really wants euthanasia, he must have pretty poor doctors and nurses. It is not that the question of euthanasia is right or wrong, desirable or repugnant, practical or unworkable. It is just that it is irrelevant. We as doctors have a duty so to care for our patients that they never ask to be killed off . . . Dying is still a part of living. *In this period a man may learn some of his life's most important lessons.*[46] (emphasis added)

7

TO THE TERMINALLY ILL

When a man lies dying
he does not die from the disease alone.
He dies from his whole life.

CHARLES PEGUY

DURING A LIFE-THREATENING illness it is vital that you maintain warm and intimate relations with friends and family members. At the very least, you need a trusted friend in whom you can confide your fears and hopes. Such warm and abiding relationships help stave off the sense of isolation that is strongly felt at this time and help establish an appropriate atmosphere whether you are at home, in a hospital, or in a nursing home.

THE VALUE OF REPENTANCE

Through repentance you can empty your mind of guilt feelings, which often come up with great force at this time, ease your worries and fears, and find peace of mind. Try repeating the following verse:

All evil actions committed by me
since time immemorial,
stemming from greed, anger, and ignorance,
arising from body, speech, and mind,
I now repent having committed.[47]

Repentance is not simply a way of expressing regret for past transgressions. If done earnestly, it is a way of casting out forever the residue of feelings still weighing on the heart. It is unlikely, however, that one recital will eliminate all guilt feelings. The verse, therefore, should be repeated again and again. As an old Jewish saying has it, "You have only to repent the last day of your life, and since you don't know what day that is, you must repent every day."

Keeping Your Mind Clear

If you are suffering intense pain, it is well to ask your doctor or nurse to ease it with drugs that do not render you unconscious or semiconscious. Those who are not used to taking drugs and are sensitive to them should beware of heavy drugs—especially painkillers, most of which contain narcotics. Such drugs can induce a respiratory arrest or affect one's mental condition. A patient should not hesitate to ask his nurse whether a painkiller about to be administered could trigger an adverse reaction. Or else a family member can ask. It is common knowledge that in most American hospitals the experience of death is clouded by drugs. When drugs are necessary to relieve pain, there is no alternative, but *heavy* sedatives, tranquilizers, and painkilling drugs are also used for purposes of patient management. Therefore make every effort to avoid them.

Breathing to Dispel Anxiety

Should you find yourself becoming anxious or tense, the following breathing exercise can bring relief, particularly if you also regularly engage in the breathing exercises described in "Meditations for the Dying Person."

An effective way to arrest the rise of anxiety is to take three long, deep, full breaths, relaxing with each breath, and concentrating only on the breath. In this breathing, expand the abdomen, allowing it to naturally rise with the in-breath and fall with the outbreath. Your eyes may be open or closed.

The Mind at the Moment of Death

Your mind state at the time you draw your last breath is crucial, for upon this hinges the subsequent direction and embodiment of the life force. Only with a disciplined and spiritually prepared mind can you hope to resist the pull of old patterns of craving and clinging as your final energies are slipping away. The impulses of thought, feeling, and perception all gather together in this last breath with great potency and can thwart the attainment of a higher level of consciousness and even enlightenment itself. (See "Karma" and "Rebirth" sections.)

Verses on the Faith Mind

To prepare yourself for the culminating moment, you would do well to read, or have read to you, a sacred text or favorite prayer. Among spiritual literature, the *Verses on the Faith Mind*[48] has been handed down as one of the most efficacious texts for the liberation of mind from painful bondage to birth and death. It contains the wisdom taught by all fully enlightened ones. The following is the substance of these verses:

The Way is perfect like vast space,
where there's no lack and no excess.
Awakening is to go beyond
both emptiness as well as form.
All changes in this empty world
seem real because of ignorance.

The Great Way is without limit,
beyond the easy and the hard.
Just let go now of clinging mind,
and all things are just as they are.
In essence nothing goes or stays.

To seek Great Mind with thinking mind
is certainly a grave mistake.
If mind does not discriminate,
all things are as they are, as One.

To the Terminally Ill

When all is seen with "equal mind,"
to our Self-nature we return.

With single mind one with the Way,
all ego-centered strivings cease;
doubts and confusion disappear,
and so true faith pervades our life.
There is no thing that clings to us,
and nothing that is left behind.
In this true world of emptiness
both self and other are no more.

The Way's beyond all space, all time,
one instant is ten thousand years.
Not only here, not only there,
truth's right before your very eyes.
One thing is all, all things are one—
know this and all's whole and complete.

When faith and mind are not separate,
and not separate are mind and faith,
this is beyond all words, all thought.
For here there is no yesterday,
no tomorrow,
no today.

To prepare yourself through the *Verses on the Faith Mind* means to reflect upon them daily and to try to perceive their inner meaning with your intuitive consciousness. At the time of sinking into the death coma, intellect ceases to function; thus if the truths of these verses have penetrated the deepest strata of consciousness, they will be available as a guide.

Biblical Prayers

Should you feel more comfortable with a prayer directed toward God, try reading, or having read to you, either the Twenty-third Psalm or the following prayer:

Our bodily senses fail us, yea mislead us, when we seek to grasp the abiding realities of life and its deeper meanings;

Teach us, O God, to trust the promptings of our heart which strive to wrest from death its prey.

Make keen that inner-sense, which reveals us to ourselves,

To glimpse that in ourselves which is beyond death's reach.

Grant us the intuition to discern in the complexities of our being that innermost self, of which the body is only the instrument and outward symbol;

And the insight to realize that, as the melody survives the lute and the meaning the written symbol, so the soul survives the body.[49]

The Twenty-third Psalm

The Lord is my shepherd,
I shall not want;
He maketh me to lie down in green pastures.
He leadeth me beside still waters,
He restoreth my soul.
He leadeth me in paths of righteousness
For his name's sake.
Yea, though I walk through the valley
Of the shadow of death,
I shall fear no evil.
For thou art with me;
Thy rod and thy staff,
They comfort me.
Thou preparest a table before me
In the presence of mine enemies;
Thou anointest my head with oil,
My cup runneth over.
Surely goodness and mercy shall follow me
All the days of my life;

And I shall dwell in the house of the Lord
Forever.[50]

Reflections on Death

While your mind is unclouded and you are relatively free of pain, reflect on what the spiritually enlightened masters teach about preparation for the process of dying. Understand that just as you were born into this world at your karmic hour, so will you die when your karma decrees it. You have passed through these same shadows many times, though you may not remember, and have experienced many rebirths. While you must enter the kingdom of death alone with your karma of good and evil, there is no cause for trembling. Enlightened ones in all realms of existence wait to guide you. They will not abandon you. They have no other purpose than to release you from the sufferings of recurring birth and death.

Who Are the Great Enlightened Ones?

Who are these fully awakened ones and why should you believe in them? They are those exalted beings who through complete awakening are able to manifest their innate perfection and love; they are those "in whom all spiritual and psychic faculties have come to a state of perfect harmony, and whose consciousness encompasses the infinity of the universe."[51]

Although we all possess the seeds of great love and compassion, without the light of the enlightened ones' wisdom and the waters of their compassion these seeds would never sprout. Or, to change the metaphor, just as a receiver tuned to a specific wavelength can pick up broadcasts thousands of miles distant, so can we receive the boundless aid of the fully enlightened ones if only we open ourselves to their compassion. This is the basis of the responsive communion between these supremely awakened ones and ordinary human beings. For the deepest level of communication is not communication but communion, as Thomas Merton pointed out. Such communion is beyond words and concepts.

This might sound like channeling or communicating with spirits of the dead. The two, however, are not at all the same. Receiving aid from enlightened ones does not mean having some long-dead entity take over the body, speaking and acting through it in order to give guidance to oneself and others. That sort of thing has nothing to do with the world of true spirituality; it belongs to the occult.

In what manner, then, do we open ourselves to the compassion of the enlightened? By having faith in their existence, by grasping the hand being offered us. Unless we cry out for help we can't be heard. In William James' penetrating sentence, "All religion begins with the cry 'Help!'"

Is this hard to accept? Ask yourself, "What happens to the unique consciousness force of the Buddhas and Christs after the disintegration of their bodies?" Science tells us that no energy is destroyed, and the qualities that these saviors embodied—overwhelming love and compassion—are therefore still available to us.

The reality of life is far more complex and all-encompassing than we dare to imagine. As the Eastern religions have long held, and as such scientists as David Bohm and neurophysiologist Karl Pribram (both of whom see the universe as a hologram in which each of the components contains the whole) confirm, the material world is an illusion fabricated by our limited senses, which give us an incomplete, and therefore a false, picture of the true nature of reality.

As I said earlier in this workshop, quoting the Buddha, each one of us is not simply a part of the universe; we are each the whole. Our faith, then, is this: that we can awaken to our intrinsic wholeness.

Meditations for the Dying Person

"Dying . . . can be awful," says Dr. Derek Doyle, medical director of St. Columbus hospice in England, "but the death itself . . . in 99.9% of patients—is peaceful, so tranquil—I'm tempted to say, so beautiful—that one can hardly believe it . . . The tension in the face disappears, labored breathing becomes easy, the tautness of somebody who's suffered a lot and had to be uncannily brave seems to ease away. A lot of the suffering just seems to vanish, yet life is still going on. And for that last few hours or day . . . you have somebody who honestly looks happy and relaxed.[52]

While this may be the case for most patients near death, nonetheless, at some stage of dying certain patients do become tense or agitated. Perhaps this is what Dr. Doyle is referring to when he says dying can be awful. (See the case of Leah in the "Death" section.)

Breathing Exercises to Calm the Mind

The moment our body-mind is not actively engaged—that is, completely involved—we fall prey to a whirl of thoughts or fantasies. A valuable exercise for calming the body-mind and inducing a feeling of deep relaxation, and even bliss, is concentration on the breath by counting the inhalations and exhalations, or simply the exhalations. Since ancient times, breath counting has been considered by spiritual masters the foundation of body-mind discipline. Breath is thus the force unifying body and mind and providing a link between the conscious and the subconscious, the volitional and the nonvolitional functions. In fact, breath can be said to be the most perfect expression of the nature of all life. Asked, "What is the length of a person's life?" Buddha replied, "The interval between an inhalation and an exhalation." Each exhalation, it can be said, is a dying; each inhalation a rebirth.

The exercise is performed as follows: Lie on your back with knees slightly raised, the feet and back flat, and a pillow under your bent knees. Lightly clasp your hands, or place them one over the other, on top of the abdomen. If this is not comfortable, your hands can be placed at your sides. Take a deep breath, hold it momentarily, then slowly exhale. Do this once or twice, then breathe naturally.

When you inhale quietly, count "One," and when you exhale, count "Two," and so on until you come to ten. Then return to one and repeat. If you lose the count or go beyond ten, as soon as you become aware of this, return again to one and continue again to ten, counting slowly. If you are by yourself, you may count audibly; if you are with others, count silently.

Another way to perform breath counting is to count only on the exhalation. As you exhale, feel your agitated mind state and negative thoughts evaporating.

Visualization Exercises

Another useful exercise—and this can be done sitting up as well as lying down—is to imagine an elixir slowly descending through the throat, the lungs, the heart, and other vital parts of the body. As it slides through each organ, feel that organ being relaxed, cleansed, and rejuvenated. Simultaneously visualize yourself pleasantly warm and well.

As a further aid in calming your mind, try visualizing the serene countenance of Christ or a saint or the Virgin Mary (if you are a Christian); Buddha or a bodhisattva such as Kwan-yin (if you are a Buddhist); Krishna (if you are a Hindu). Those who follow a religion that does not sanction visualization, or those who have no formal religious affiliation, might find that a certain object, picture, or piece of music instills calmness. Or perhaps a certain prayer. Should feelings of anger or hatred toward any persons arise, mentally embrace that person and radiate thoughts of loving-kindness toward him or her. This may be easier said than done, but if you work at it conscientiously, what seems at first intolerable will gradually become easy.

These exercises are not just for the dying. Don't wait until you have a fatal illness to undertake them. Performed each day for about half an hour, they will do more than simply relax your body or calm your mind; they will transform your whole personality, making it easier for you to live with yourself and others. (See also Appendix E: "Meditation.")

Embracing Your Death

Reflect on these words of a Zen master:

> Your Mind-essence is not subject to birth or death. It is neither being nor nothingness, neither emptiness nor form and color. Nor is it something that feels pain or joy.

> However much you try to know [with your rational mind] that which is now sick, you cannot. Yet if you think of nothing, wish for nothing, want to understand nothing, cling to nothing, and only ask yourself, "What is the true substance of the mind of this one who is now suffering?" ending your days like clouds fading in the sky, you will eventually be freed of your painful bondage to endless change.[53]

Imagine yourself, then, fading away, slowly, very slowly, until you remember less and less. Now allow a peaceful, relaxed feeling to take over—not in a hurry but slowly.

8

TO THE FAMILY AND FRIENDS OF THE DYING

Dying in the Hospital or at Home?

Whether the dying family member will end his days in a hospital or at home is a question of prime importance for him and his family. There are many considerations that should go into such a decision. For example, the family may wish to keep the dying person at home, but are they truly aware of what this entails in their particular situation? Can they stand up to the strain of continuing to work in their outside jobs while coping with, for example, an elderly, incontinent, perhaps semiconscious parent who must be moved about in the bed to prevent bedsores from forming, must be slowly and patiently fed by hand, and must be frequently cleaned up and changed?

Do not, though, refuse to keep a dying loved one at home because you're afraid you may not be up to it. Perhaps there is semiprofessional help available a few hours a day or a few days a week that would lessen the strain, ease the workload, and allow the patient to be in a familiar environment with close and sympathetic family members and friends around him. On the other hand, the dying person may find it easier in a hospital with an understanding, empathetic staff, or in a hospice program, where he could feel relieved that they were not placing the burden of his care on the family. The state of the family finances, too, will enter in, as health insurance has its limitations, particularly with regard to home care.

This and more is discussed in the book *Home Care for the Dying*, by Deborah Whiting Little,[54] and readers are urged to avail themselves of it, as the subject is too complex to be adequately covered here. In the end, the choice is a very personal one for each dying person and his family, dependent on the circumstances at the time the decision is made—and if the circumstances change, so might the decision.

The Last Hours of the Dying

Especially in the dying person's last hours, give him your warm support, for they have a karmic bond with each and every member of the family. Be fluent listeners. Pay attention to whatever they may say, neither arguing with nor contradicting them. If they rail against God or the doctor or anyone else, let them do so. Do not force them to discuss such practical matters as the making of a will, if their mind does not move in that direction. For any member of the family to impose his or her own wishes in these last hours, when the dying person needs complete peace to concentrate their dwindling energy for the passage through death, would be karmically harmful to all involved.

The ancients knew what we modern people seem to have forgotten, that dying requires a composed, tranquil mind state to enable the transition from one plane of existence to another—an occurrence which the ancients never doubted.

Remaining with the Dying Person

Be aware that those approaching death may reach a point where they lose interest in their surroundings and withdraw from those around them into a trancelike state, often seeing or hearing things which others are not experiencing. The family should not interpret this as evidence of the deterioration of their mind or memory and assume that they can now be safely ignored. The fact is, their hearing and understanding may be even more acute. Many ancient traditions say that individuals often develop extrasensory perception during severe or terminal illness. Any *excessive* weeping or hysteria on your part, therefore, will almost certainly disturb these sensitive processes going on within the dying; therefore keep these demonstrations as far from the deathbed as possible. Providing a tranquil environment is more difficult in a hospital, where, even though a patient's family may remain calm and centered during the last hours, there can be other patients nearby who are noisy or uncontrolled, along with the ubiquitous television sets going at high volume. All this will make your job harder but not impossible.

Do not, though, interpret the dying person's withdrawal to mean you should withdraw from them. On the contrary, take every opportunity to show your empathy and love by holding the hand of the dying, embracing them, kissing them, or otherwise touching them and identifying with their needs. Even sitting quietly with them, radiating love and affection, will help dispel the clouds of loneliness and fear that often arise at this time. Even though you observe little body response to your gestures, you can be certain that your caring presence is reassuring to the dying. Abandonment is one of the greatest fears of the terminally ill.

Guiding the Mind of the Dying

When it is clear that death is imminent, it is well to ask either a close, trusted friend of the dying person or a member of the family to act as primary caregiver. His or her main function will be to read aloud from the sacred writings until the dying one takes their last breath.

You who are to guide the mind of the dying both before and after the death transition—yours is a vital role. Remember, the liberation of Essential-mind from the confines of the body through the death process offers a unique opportunity for awakening.

Both the dying person and the family should concur with your role in the dying process. You must fully respect any indication that the dying person wishes to be alone. However, when you do speak to them or begin to read, always address them by name so as to draw their attention.

Create a serene atmosphere for the last hours of the dying, whether in a hospital, a nursing home, or their own home. Obviously, there are more things you can do if the dying person is at home than if they are in the hospital. But this does not mean that you have to surrender your role if the dying person is confined to the hospital. Even if there is more than one person in the hospital room, it is still possible to carry out many of these suggestions.

Arrange the room of the dying one so that there is a feeling of comfortable familiarity. If the patient has a favorite painting, or a photograph of a family member they are close to and who cannot be present, place it where it can easily be seen. It is of prime importance that the channels of communication between you and the dying one be unobstructed by any talk irrelevant to their needs and state of mind.

Breathing with the Dying Person

For you to be composed and concentrated will help the dying person continue with equanimity on their journey into the after-death state. It can be both calming and otherwise helpful to the dying patient for you to share with them the counting of their breath for periods of about twenty minutes, perhaps several times a day, as they near the threshold of death.

You might begin by holding the dying person's hand as the two of you join in counting. First, however, quietly suggest that they concentrate on relaxing one part of their body at a time, such as each arm, each foot, the neck, and so on, until their whole body has been relaxed. Then begin quietly counting aloud to them as they breathe in and out. Count "One" on the inhalation, "Two" on the exhalation, "Three" on the inhalation, and so on, synchronizing your counting with their breathing. Breathe yourself in unison with the counting and their breathing. After counting up to ten, begin with one again.

When you observe that the dying person is no longer in a position to do anything for themselves, you may begin reciting one of the sacred texts (see "The Heart of Perfect Wisdom" and "Verses on the Faith Mind") or their favorite prayer. This will prevent their mind from drifting aimlessly. Put your lips close to their ear and utter each word distinctly. Keep in mind that the sense of hearing is the last to go. Moreover, since even medical experts are in disagreement over when death actually occurs, do not discontinue the chanting the moment the person is declared dead, but persist for a longer or shorter while, depending on the surrounding circumstances.

9

CREMATION OR BURIAL?

Six Options for Taking Care of the Body

LONG BEFORE the dying person breathes his last, he and his family have to decide how his body is to be disposed of upon death. A number of options for body disposition are available. These are succinctly set forth by Ernest Morgan in his excellent *Manual of Death Education and Simple Burial*:

1. Immediate removal to a medical school, followed by a memorial service. Generally this avoids all expense and performs a valuable service. There can be a brief gathering of the immediate family before removal if circumstances permit, but this must be done quickly.
2. Immediate cremation, followed by a memorial service. There may also be a commitment service at the crematory chapel if desired.
3. Immediate earth burial, followed by a memorial service. There may also be a graveside commitment service if desired.
4. A funeral service in the presence of the body, followed by removal to a medical school.
5. A funeral service in the presence of the body, followed by cremation.
6. A funeral service in the presence of the body, followed by earth burial.

The preceding alternatives, which are listed according to cost, with the least expensive first, assume the services of a funeral director, except possibly in cases of immediate removal to a medical school or for cremation.[55]

Prepaying Your Funeral

More and more people these days are opting to prepay their funeral. The death of a loved one is a traumatic and difficult time, filled with emotion. Decisions as to burial or cremation, style and expense of casket, whether or not to embalm, and all the other details in regard to body disposal must be made during the most painful part of the period following death—unless they have been arranged for prior to the death. The next of kin may not really know whether you would prefer burial or cremation, a pricey casket or a plain pine box. Moreover, knowing you've taken care of these details and not left them for your survivors can be a source of peace.

There are some things to keep in mind if you are considering prepaying your funeral. The American Association of Retired Persons (AARP) recommends that you plan your funeral and the disposition of your body in advance, but that you be cautious about paying in advance, for three reasons: you may change your mind about what you want, you may move away from the area, or the company providing the services may go out of business before you die.

There are generally several options available for prepayment of costs, including various prepaid plans, a bank account listing a beneficiary (sometimes called a revocable living trust or a totten trust), or a life insurance policy whose beneficiary has been instructed to use the funds for your funeral and related expenses. Prepaid plans can be categorized as follows: (1) guaranteed price, revocable (you can change your mind and receive full or partial refund); (2) nonguaranteed price, revocable (you can change your mind and get full or partial refund, but the amount you prepay may not cover the full costs when death finally arrives); (3) guaranteed price, irrevocable (price is guaranteed but you get no refund if you change plans); and (4) nonguaranteed price, irrevocable (not advised). Whatever you decide, it is wise to put your wishes in writing and make the document readily accessible to those who will be taking care of your body following your death. Do not put the information in your will or in your safe-deposit box as it may not be read until after your funeral. For further information, you may wish to obtain the AARP booklet *Prepaying Your Funeral: Some Questions to Ask* from the Special Projects Section, Program Department, AARP, 1909 K Street NW, Washington, DC 20049.

Are Funeral Directors Necessary?

It is possible to take care of all the details of body disposal without using a funeral director or a funeral home, and some people may wish to do so.

Lisa Carlson has written a comprehensive book[56] giving a state-by-state listing of laws and regulations covering disposal of bodies, and telling how she dealt with the unexpected death of her husband. She also relates how others have been able to handle burial or cremation of loved ones with few or none of the services of a funeral director. Or, instead of getting information as well as inspiration from this book, one might join one of the memorial societies set up in cities throughout the United States by people banding together in search of a send-off that would not leave their heirs ragged in the streets. Such societies usually offer inexpensive cremations or burials to members. To find the memorial society nearest you, write to the Continental Association of Funeral and Memorial Societies, Suite 530, 2001 S Street NW, Washington, DC 20009.

Wakes and Vigils

There are, of course, different ways of saying farewell to a loved family member or close friend. Not uncommon are wakes in which family members and friends stay up most of the night eating, drinking, and reminiscing about the deceased in the presence of his body. The coffin may or may not be open. There is also the rosary wake, in which family and friends stay up all night reciting the rosary.

Then there is the solitary vigil. A sensitive woman friend told me that when her father, whom she hadn't seen for some time because she lived a continent away from him, died suddenly, she had an overwhelming desire to be with him to express her heretofore unstated love for him. So she hastened to the mortuary parlor where his body lay (having first instructed the funeral director not to embalm or cut the body in any way) and then, with an understanding woman friend, she stayed with her father all night. This is what she reported: "My father had died the day before. Throughout the night my friend and I both felt his strong presence. We recited prayers together, chanted, and meditated. I had always thought of my father as a vexed man, but now he looked so peaceful and happy. For me it was truly a spiritual event. Never have I felt closer to my father than that night."

Another woman friend described what it was like to keep an all-night vigil over the body of a close relative, accompanied by his twelve-year-old son:

> Charles had committed suicide. But this night as I looked at him lying contentedly in his coffin, the frustration, the hurt, the bitterness of his life had vanished and he looked positively beatific. Even his son remarked on how serene he looked. "I have never seen Daddy looking so happy," he said. "I know he is more peaceful now than he ever was alive. I'm glad I came with you and I'm not the least bit afraid or sad."

The Body's Presence at the Funeral

A Unitarian minister who has conducted open-coffin funerals takes a decidedly dim view of their value:

> As far as I am concerned, a commercial funeral for anyone is out; I will never do another. But a *memorial* service is essential. A memorial service is for the people

> who are left alive, and the best service is one where there is no coffin at all. The immortal things which people leave on earth are their friends, their children, their relationships. These are things that have nothing to do with a . . . lifeless carcass. As far as I am concerned, the custom of the open coffin is not only an economic atrocity which adds hundreds of dollars to every funeral bill, but it gives terrible pain to the survivors. I can't count the times I have had to coax sobbing widows or parents or children away from an open coffin, and for *what*?[57]

Although the sobbing of widows or parents or children before an open coffin may strike some as proof of the unbearable pain such viewing entails for the family, ventilating their grief in this manner can be highly therapeutic. This is confirmed by a psychologist and a psychiatrist.

Ann Kliman, a psychologist in Westchester County, New York, who has been involved in crisis-situation counseling for many years, strongly believes in the therapeutic value of a funeral with an open coffin. She maintains that viewing is a crucial factor in beginning the process of mourning, especially when death is sudden or unexpected. According to her, viewing provides the opportunity to accept the fact of death and to say the last goodbyes to the deceased.[58]

The late Dr. Erich Lindemann, professor of psychiatry at Harvard Medical School, also felt that an open-coffin funeral has great value:

> When asked, "What do you consider to be the most useful part of the whole funeral process?" [Dr. Lindemann] responded, "The moment of truth that comes when living persons confront the fact of death by looking at the body." When questioned further why he thought this was true, he said, "People tend to deny painful reality. They tend to marshal their mental and emotional resources to deny the fact that death has occurred. But when they experience that moment of truth that comes when they stand before the dead body, their denials col-

> lapse. They are facing reality and that is the first important step toward managing their grief. When it is done with other people, the reality is confirmed and at the same time they are encouraged to face the feelings that are basic to the grief response. Grief is a feeling. If you deny it you have difficulty coping with it, but if you face it you start the process of healthful mourning."[59]

One's first-ever viewing of a body in an open casket can be unforgettable. I still remember my vivid impressions of seeing, as a boy of twelve, a body in an open coffin for the first time. In those days it was common practice for mourners to file past the open coffin one by one for a last view of the deceased. You weren't obliged to look at the body, but most did. I was both fascinated and repelled by the reality of death which this type of service represented. The brief ceremonies at the gravesite, the lowering of the body into the earth, the crying and wailing—all this awed and moved me. Such ceremonies, wittingly or unwittingly, provide a way to face one's own grief and a means to ventilate it. The only other experience that has had a greater impact in leading me to ponder the matter of life and death was observing the burning of bodies, many years later, in the ghats of the Ganges River in Benares (Varanasi), India.

Waiting Until the Life Force Leaves the Body

In some religious traditions, to wait a period of time before the body is buried or cremated, to allow the life force to leave the body, is considered vital. For until the life force departs, which ancient texts of Buddhists and Hindus, for example, say takes three days, the body is still considered to be alive. These ancient texts warn against tampering with the body before the life force has left it, since the person who has just died still maintains a close connection with—actually an attachment to—his body. A Tibetan master of old goes so far as to describe the cutting or burning of the body before three days have elapsed as murder.[60]

Of course, this raises the question of where the life force goes after death. When asked, "Where does the soul go when the body dies?" Jakob Boehme, the Christian mystic, answered, "There is no necessity for it to go anywhere."

When a Zen master was asked, "All these mountains and rivers and the great earth—where do they come from?" he replied:

"Where does this question of yours come from?"

When Zen master Hakuin was asked, "What happens to a person at death?" he replied, "Why ask me?" "Because you're a Zen master!" "Yes," replied Hakuin, "but not a dead one!"

Let us recall how the masters whom I quoted earlier have responded more or less to this same question. Asked to write a death verse, Zen master Ikkyū wrote:

> I shan't die,
> I shan't go anywhere,
> I'll be here.
> But don't ask me anything,
> I shan't answer.

When the Indian sage Sri Ramana Maharshi was asked where he would go upon his death, he replied:

> They say that I am dying,
> but I'm not going away.
> Where could I go?
> I am here . . .

Lastly, consider the response of Hui-neng, an outstanding Chinese Zen master of the T'ang era. When he announced to his followers that he was going to leave the world on a certain date, many of them began weeping. Astonished, he asked, "For whom are you crying? Are you worrying about me because you think I don't know where I am going? If I didn't know, I wouldn't be able to leave you this way . . . If you actually knew, you couldn't possibly cry, because True-nature is without birth or death, *without going or coming* . . ." (emphasis added)

Observe that these great masters, all of whom were facing death, refrained from saying that they or their soul or life force or consciousness was going anywhere after death. By contrast, we have certain religious authorities making the dogmatic assertion that upon the death of the body, the soul ascends to heaven or else is damned to hell. In ancient times it was asserted that the soul took up abode in the tomb or coffin of the deceased or that it lingered in or near the grave. But the masters wisely do not try to name or explain. Why not? As an old song sings:

> Fools will give you reasons;
> wise men never try.

Religious Aspects of Cremation

What are the theological aspects of cremation? Catholicism, several of the mainline Protestant denominations, traditional Judaism, and Islam all favor earth burial over cremation. The Catholic church, according to the *Catholic Encyclopedia* (1975 edition), opposes cremation "because the practice was historically an act of disbelief in immortality by members of certain societies and others, and because cremation does not show reverence to the human body, the temple of the Holy Spirit."

As for Protestantism, most of the arguments advanced by Protestant churchmen are similar to those of the Roman Catholics: that cremation is a pagan custom and thus antithetical to Christian practice. Other churchmen opposed cremation because they found no biblical warrant for it. Burial is further supported by the precedent established in the burial of Jesus Christ.[61]

Orthodox Judaism bases its insistence on earth burial on the Torah: "Dust you are and to dust you shall return" (Genesis 3:19). Liberal Judaism, on the other hand, states that there is no biblical prohibition of cremation even though burial was clearly the customary practice of the ancient Hebrews. Burial is regarded as a way of respecting the human body and protecting it from desecration or indignity.[62]

Increasingly in modern times, however, these religions are yielding to the wishes of their followers to dispose of their bodies through cremation. The reasons advanced, besides lower cost, are aesthetics and hygiene. Especially if the body has been deformed, wasted by disease, or disfigured, many apparently feel that it is more fitting to burn the body.

Among the Eastern religions, Buddhism and Hinduism both sanction cremation. The Buddha himself was cremated. On the whole, it has been the custom in Buddhist countries to cremate the dead, although burial has also been practiced. Traditionally, Chinese Buddhists have buried their dead; they may or may not still do so.

With regard to Hinduism, cremation began in India as early as the second millennium B.C. In the religion and philosophy of India it is believed that fire resolves the body into its basic elements of fire, water, earth, and air, while at the same time purifying the spirit for its reincarnation.[63]

10

CREATING THE FUNERAL SERVICE

I've a great fancy to see my own funeral afore I die.

MARIA EDGEWORTH

IN ANCIENT CULTURES the funeral was considered a rite of passage of the utmost significance to the *departed.* Unfortunately, this is not generally recognized nowadays. It is astonishing to read books on death and dying by authors who profess to believe in the continuity of life, who have much to say on how to allay grief, yet who can offer no guidance whatever to the departed in the crucial after-death state. The funeral ceremonies can, of course, do much to aid the survivors in their new relationships to one another and to the deceased growing out of his or her death; the needs to mourn and to be comforted are essential. But the primary purpose of funeral rites is, or should be, to help ease the deceased's transition to the after-death state. (See "Rebirth" section for a description of the after-death state.)

Sadly, many in our culture shy away from ceremonies larded with rituals. They react badly to what they sense is the hollowness of so much religious ritual; most ritual, they complain, becomes an end in itself. They feel, with Ambrose Bierce, that rites are "ceremonies . . . with the essential oil of sincerity carefully squeezed out of them."[64] But rites that have substance behind them—feeling and understanding—are enriching in that they provide a vivid, not easily forgotten medium for transmitting ancient truths and wisdom.

"Religion originated in celebration and concern," writes Huston Smith,

> and when people feel like celebrating [ritualistically] or are deeply concerned, they get together and act together . . . The impulse to lose and then find oneself in a fluid architecture of form and motion of which one is a significant part runs deeper in life than man: birds fly in formation; and monkeys in high spirits will fall into rhythmic line, draping themselves with rope and banana peels, simian anticipations of the elaborate, needled vestments that will appear at the human level.[65]

If the members of a family didn't at some level of their being believe that the consciousness-energy of their deceased endures somehow, why would they have a funeral service, and then later, perhaps, memorial rites? Or why would any mourners have rites of passage for their dead? At a subconscious level, funeral rites undoubtedly reflect a belief in, or else a "blessed hope" of, another existence, the nature of which is fashioned by karma. If one accepts this, the rite of passage is seen as a means of aiding the deceased in what we sense must be a difficult transition from this side of life to the other.

The funeral ceremony brings home the stark fact of death and is also a means of preserving and extending the link between the departed, the family, and the community. Otherwise, why the chanting, the singing, the benediction, the supplications, the prayers, and the sermon for the repose of the soul by the minister, priest, rabbi, or other officiant? Don't the service and the presence of all the mourners imply that they too believe that the Essential-nature of the departed does not die but somehow continues in one form or another? Isn't the funeral service really a send-off and not a write-off? I repeat: why would a family go through this elaborate ceremony if they believed the deceased was ineluctably a corpse, a lifeless bag of bones?

Lyall Watson confirms the deep significance of funeral rites:

> Implicit in every funeral practice is the assumption that death is not the end, that it marks some kind of transition. In his investigation of the Malayan death system, Robert Hertz shows how death is not regarded as an immediate or final event, but as only one phase of a gradual development. The Malays and many others recognize a death process that begins early in life, and this belief is reflected in the minds and actions of their communities. The moment that we call death is for them no more than an intermediary stage, a sign that the body should be dealt with in some provisional way . . .
>
> In our society the generally accepted opinion is that death is instantaneous. The only reason for the delay of two or three days between death and disposal is to allow preparations to be made and to give time for friends and relatives to gather. The fact that we are almost alone in this view, and that few other cultures regard death in such a precise way, cannot be accidental . . .[66]

In certain religions—notably Buddhism—the *primary* purpose of the funeral is not to pay one's respects to the deceased or console the family—although these have their place—but to awaken the intermediate being to the true nature of life and death. (See "Rebirth" section.) Solemn funeral services have another vital purpose: they make us think soberly about our own demise.

The Service

Although families with a religious affiliation may wish to have a member of the clergy hold funeral services in a church or temple or synagogue, an effective spiritual funeral or memorial service can take place anywhere, with or without benefit of clergy. The funerals described later in this chapter, which were actually conducted and can serve as models, do not depend on formal adherence to a religious sect, and yet they can truly be called religious. At the same time, they can serve as well for those who consider themselves agnostics or even atheists. The chanting or reciting of *The Heart of Perfect Wisdom*, the funeral prayer, and "The Flowers Poem," are chiefly for the benefit of the departed. The tributes to the memory of the deceased are mainly to allay the grief of family and friends. To the eulogies may be added music, poetry, additional prayers and psalms, or even dances, depending on the age and personality of the departed, her outlook on life, and perhaps other circumstances.

It has been said that a funeral is a rite of passage in which the body of the deceased is present, and that a memorial service is one in which there is no body. In the Buddhist tradition, the funeral proper and the memorial services that follow for the next forty-nine days represent continuing attempts to awaken the mind of the departed to the true nature of existence. In this view, memorial services are condensed versions of the funeral, embodying the essential rites. The reciting of the sacred texts is thought to be every bit as valid during the forty-nine day period as during the funeral proper. These rites are to be repeated every day for the first week and on the death day for the following six weeks.[67] Performed in harmony with the seven-day birth-and-death cycle in the intermediate state, they have as their purpose the awakening of the mind of the deceased before he or she enters the next realm of existence.

These forty-nine-day postmortem rites are not to be dispensed with even when death comes through sudden accident, allowing no time for the preparation of the mind of the victim, or when death overtakes him in a remote or inaccessible location, so that his body or cremains[68] are not present at the funeral. A photograph of the deceased is of special significance in helping those at the service to focus their energies toward the one who died. This focusing, in turn, aids the deceased by making available to him or her increased psychic energy.

The family would do well to participate both in the death rites and in the postfuneral ceremonies which take place in the forty-nine-day interval. In thus reaffirming their karmic link with the deceased they will ease their loneliness and constructively channel their grief. The Mind of the dead and the Mind of the living are intrinsically One. This One can in no way be diminished. Not even the dead can disappear. Where, after all, would they go?

The Funeral of Marie—A Six-year-old[69]

This service was for a child of six who died of smoke inhalation. Although neither of her parents had any formal affiliation with a temple or church, they did identify to some extent with the doctrines of Hinduism, Buddhism, and Christianity. On the morning after the death of Marie, I was asked by the parents to help organize and lead a funeral service for their daughter. With the assistance of several mourners I hastily put together a simple altar, and on this we placed a large photograph of Marie, as well as handpicked flowers, candles, and some of her favorite foods. In front of the altar Marie lay enclosed in a homemade casket.

The service began with my telling everyone that the main purpose of the funeral ceremony was to aid Marie, and that we could accomplish this by directing our love toward her through our chanting and heartfelt recitations, thereby invoking the wisdom of ancient sages in the difficult transition from this side of life to the other. I also said that while, from an ordinary viewpoint, the death of a young child is considered tragic, we had no reason to feel grief-stricken; Marie was born when she needed to be and she died when she had to die, her karma for this life having exhausted itself, young though she was.

Next we all chanted *The Heart of Perfect Wisdom* (see "The Funeral of Lillian—An Eighty-four-year-old Writer" for the significance of this inspired text) while one person beat a drum and another periodically struck a small, bowl-shaped gong.

Following the chanting we all offered up a prayer, recited with feeling three times in unison, to help invoke bodhisattvic forces for the benefit of Marie. First I recited a line and then everyone repeated it:

O Compassionate Ones,
abiding in all directions,
endowed with great compassion,

endowed with love, affording protection to
sentient beings,
consent through the power of your great
compassion to come forth;
consent to accept these offerings concretely
laid out and mentally created.
O Compassionate Ones,
you who possess the wisdom of understanding,
the love of compassion,
the power of doing divine deeds and of
protecting in incomprehensible measure:
Marie is passing from this world to the next.
She is taking a great leap.
The light of this world has faded for her.
She has entered solitude with her
karmic forces.
She has gone into a vast Silence.
She is borne away by the Great Ocean [of birth
and death].
O Compassionate Ones,
protect Marie, who is defenseless.
Be to her like a mother and a father.
O Compassionate Ones,
let not the force of your compassion be weak,
but aid her.
Forget not your ancient vows . . .

Following this supplication, the following verses were directed to Marie:

The Flowers Poem

The world is a flower.
Gods are flowers.
Enlightened ones are flowers.
All phenomena are flowers.
Red flowers, white flowers, green flowers,
yellow flowers, black flowers,

all the different kinds of the colors of
flowers, all the different kinds
of love shining forth.
Life unfolds from life and returns to life.
Such an immense universe! Oh many lives!
Flowers of gratitude, flowers of sorrow,
flowers of suffering, flowers of joy,
laughter's flowers, anger's flowers,
heaven's flowers, hell's flowers.
Each connected to the others
and each making the others grow.

When our real mind's eye
opens this world of flowers,
all beings shine,
music echoes through mountains and oceans.
One's world becomes the world of millions.
The individual becomes the human race.
All lives become the individual—
billions of mirrors
all reflecting each other.
Marie, there is death and there is life,
there is no death and no life.
There is changing life, there is unchanging
life.
Flowers change color, moment by moment.

Such a vivid world! Such a bright you! . . .
Marie, you were born out of these flowers,
you gave birth to these flowers.
You have no beginning and no ending,
you are bottomless and limitless,
even as you are infinitesimal dust . . .

Marie, you are the flower.
You are love.
All beings shine out of their uniqueness,

all melt into the oneness of colors.
You are one, you are many,
only one moment, only one unique place,
only the unique you.
Beside you there is nothing:
you dance, appearing in all.

From nowhere you came, to nowhere you go.
You stay nowhere. You are nowhere attached.
You occupy everything, you occupy nothing.
You are the becoming of indescribable change.
You are love. You are the flower.[70]

Upon the conclusion of this verse, all present went singly to the altar and made an offering of a pinch of powdered incense. This over, the 150 or so mourners began walking toward a church a mile away. En route some individuals blew conch shells, while others softly chanted the sacred word "Om," the sounds intermingling. Other marchers quietly chanted verses from the various spiritual traditions.

At the church the small casket was placed on the altar, surrounded by flowers and candles. The proceedings in the church were entirely spontaneous. Different individuals stood up and began singing a folk tune or reciting sacred words. Friends and relatives reminisced about Marie. The haunting sounds of a harmonica were heard in the elegiac "Going Home."

With the conclusion of these informal rituals, we moved to the churchyard, where Marie's grave was dug by close friends. During the digging, participants formed a large circle, joined hands, and began chanting "Om." All the while, conch shells were sounded, providing a rich and meaningful counterpoint—meaningful because in many spiritual traditions the blowing of a conch shell symbolizes the breath of a new life.

Marie's casket was now slowly lowered into the grave as the mourners crowded around. Marie's mother and others who brought flowers began tossing them on the casket, which was slowly being covered with the upturned earth.

When the grave was filled, Marie's mother carefully tamped the earth over it as though tucking her daughter in for a long sleep. As a final gesture, she set in place a wooden cross made by her husband. Once again the large gathering formed a circle, holding hands, and they slowly circumambulated the grave, all the while chanting "Om."

From a financial standpoint, the cost of this funeral was minimal. Apart from the price of the wood to make the small coffin, and what I presume was a donation to the priest for the use of the church and the privilege of burying Marie in the churchyard, the parents had no other expenses connected with the funeral. More important, this kind of funeral, of caring for one's own dead without a funeral director, helped Marie's parents and friends say goodbye in a healing way.

The Funeral of Lillian—An Eighty-four-year-old Writer

Unlike the first model service, which was unrehearsed and held out of doors, this one was formal and in the sanctuary of The Zen Center of Rochester, of which Lillian was a long-standing member. This type of service can be done for anyone regardless of his or her religious affiliation, or lack of it.

Lillian was a writer in her eighties and a well-known person in the community in which she lived. In her will she had stipulated that at her funeral we play the slow movement (the so-called Funeral March) from Beethoven's Third Symphony, the Eroica. Stately and somber, yet not without a sense of struggle and hope, the music concludes on a note of serene acceptance—qualities that mirror Lillian's own strivings for Self-fulfillment.

As family members and friends entered the sanctuary, they were greeted by the strains of this profound music, which set the tone for what followed.

An altar stood at one end of the sanctuary. On this we had placed a large photograph of Lillian, flowers, and her cremains, which had been wrapped in a damask cloth. Since red was her favorite color (she had once said it stood for life), the flowers and the cloth were of this hue. Also on the altar were lighted candles and evergreens—the flames symbolic of infinite light, the pine needles of everlasting life. The photograph enabled those present to focus and direct their energies toward Lillian.

When we started, the music was faded to a soft, background level, and it continued that way throughout the service. I explained that the main purpose of the funeral rites was to help Lillian awaken to the true nature of birth and death and not simply to extol her virtues or lament her passing.

Following this we all chanted *The Heart of Perfect Wisdom*, which encapsulates the accumulated wisdom of Buddhism's spiritual masters on the nature of ultimate reality. *The Heart of Perfect Wisdom* is considered a most potent formulation for piercing the delusive mind. It is the kernel, or core, of the message of the wisdom scriptures given by the Buddha. Also referred to as *The Heart Sutra,* it is to be grasped not through the intellect but with the heart—that is, through one's own deepest intuition. Thus "perfect wisdom" here means transcendental wisdom, as well as the path leading to the attainment of this wisdom, and the text of the teaching conducive to its realization.

The significance of chanting this sacred text is that the deceased, shorn of the limitations of a body and a mind as we ordinarily understand these terms, is now better able to absorb and be guided by its deeper meaning.

The Heart of Perfect Wisdom[71]

Form here[72] is only emptiness,
emptiness only form.
Form is no other than emptiness,
emptiness no other than form.

Feeling, thought and choice
consciousness itself,
are the same as this.

Dharmas[73] here are empty,
all are the primal void.

None are born or die,
nor are they stained or pure,
nor do they wax or wane.

So in emptiness no form,
no feeling, thought, or choice,
nor is there consciousness.

No eye, ear, nose,
tongue, body, mind;
no color, sound, smell,
taste, touch, or what the mind
takes hold of,
nor even act of sensing.

No ignorance or end of it,
nor all that comes of ignorance;
no withering, no death,
no end of them.

Nor is there pain or cause of pain
or cease in pain or noble path
to lead from pain,
not even wisdom to attain,
attainment too is emptiness.[74]

One of Lillian's close friends now read a poem written on nature and the cosmic rhythm. Upon the conclusion of the poem, Lillian's housekeeper and another friend described joyful moments with Lillian and reminisced about their many years of friendship. The funeral prayer and "The Flowers Poem" were then read, this latter being specifically directed toward her.

As the final ritual, each person present went up to the altar, looked intently at the photograph of Lillian, took a pinch of powdered incense from the box on the altar, and offered it on a burning piece of charcoal in the incense pot, making a bow of farewell with hands palm to palm.

This concluded the formal service. Everyone now retired to another room of the Center for light refreshments, where they continued their reminiscences of Lillian.

The Value of Chanting

Chanting can have a vital place in a funeral service. When it is done with sincerity and zest, the sounds and rhythms of chanting provide a way to circumvent the discriminating intellect and to drive home directly to the subconscious mind of the deceased the essential truths of existence.

It is best to have a drum of one kind or another to set and maintain the tempo of the chanting. It unifies the energy of the service—raising it up or bringing it down, or drawing it together when it becomes scattered. The drummer need not be a professional, nor the drum any special kind, though the drummer should be able to maintain a steady, pulsating beat for the duration of the chanting.

The drummer begins slowly and works very quickly up to the tempo that, once established, must be maintained until the end of the chant. Should the drummer and the chanters not synchronize, the chanting becomes disjointed and the vital energy flow toward the deceased becomes disrupted.

Equally important is the spirit in which the chanting is done, whether with sincerity and vigor or otherwise. Just as lackadaisical drumming can diminish the force of the service, so halfhearted chanting can lessen the impact of the funeral or memorial rites. When the chanting is directed to the deceased, with everyone focusing on the photograph of the deceased, the chanting is especially effective.

Zen master Hakuun Yasutani points out in his book *Eight Bases of Belief in Buddhism*[75] that a person in the after-death state does have consciousness but not what we ordinarily think of as consciousness in the "alive" state. And he or she also has sensory awareness of a kind not available to us so-called "alive" human beings. This means that the entity can "hear" *The Heart of Perfect Wisdom* and the other elements of the funeral service, but in a way that cannot be equated with ordinary hearing.

Physicists (such as David Bohm) have demonstrated that two

subatomic particles, once they have interacted, can respond to each other thousands of years later, and that particles *and people* alike may influence each other, since everything in the universe is connected. If you apply to chanting what these scientists are saying about the responsive communion between matter and people, you can begin to understand why it is that when you empty your mind of random thoughts and focus all your attention and energy on the chanting and on the person who has died, that consciousness cannot but be influenced.

Some physicians feel that sick people who are prayed for often recover more quickly than those who are not the object of prayers. In an article on religion and medicine in *The Christian Science Monitor* a practicing surgeon comments:

> The use of prayer in medicine is not a groundswell, but there is a willingness to recognize nonscientific interventions. Physicians are no longer bothered about using things whose mechanisms aren't understood . . . In my years in medical practice there are many concrete examples where I would have to give prayer the credit for the outcome, rather than my own intervention as a physician.[76]

And since the dead are not really dead, who can say that chanting and prayer at funeral and memorial services cannot help them as well?

There's another aspect to all this. Who are the people who come to a funeral? The family and close friends of the departed, right? Through a lifetime of contact and interaction between them, strong karmic bonds have been forged. These bonds are not severed at death.

In the deepest sense there is no one, nothing anywhere with whom we do not have a karmic connection. When the contact was recent (for example, this lifetime) and the bond strong (a relative or close friend), the chanting and the words are greatly intensified. I say "words," but it is really what lies *behind* the words that has the power to rouse and transform. Words that have strong spirit propelling them are like a well-aimed arrow which, once released, will not stop short of its mark.

People sometimes ask whether the subtle message of, say, *The Heart of Perfect Wisdom* can be understood by a child. In the case of six-year-old Marie, once she has died, is she still six? The knowledge in her subconscious mind—the collective unconscious, if you like—is still functional. So are the karmic impulses that propelled her into the life she just left and that will propel her into her next life. Energy cannot be destroyed; nor can the accumulated knowledge and understanding of countless lifetimes. Forgotten, yes, but not lost.

So what of this young entity? When she dies she is no longer young in the sense of her karmic heritage or physical years—she is ageless. Age is relative, and she is now no longer bound by that restriction. The age of the dead person, then, makes no difference; neither does her sex, her nationality, or even her religion. The only thing that matters is the way in which you chant, that is, whether your chanting has conviction behind it and is focused toward what we are calling the entity or not. We can go even further: it doesn't even matter whether the being who died was human. Animals, too, can be affected by a strong funeral service. All life, having its basis in this universal Mind, is irrevocably connected. In the purest and most fundamental sense there is no difference between a buddha, a six-year-old girl, an elephant, a flea, a redwood tree, and a blade of grass.

Funerals for Newborn Babies

When newborn babies die, or when a woman has a premature birth and they can't save the baby, or when the baby dies in the womb, a lot of families don't know whether there should be a funeral or not. From the Buddhist point of view a child comes to its parents because of the karmic affinity between them. Whether death takes place before birth, in infancy, in childhood, or in old age, the funeral service serves the same purpose. Because of the parents' affinity with the infant, their ability to influence her future life in the after-death state is great. Thus the funeral service represents, as in the case with older people, a once-in-a-lifetime chance to awaken her to the indivisibility of life and death, to the truth that form is only emptiness, emptiness only form—the essential message of *The Heart of Perfect Wisdom.*

Besides aiding the deceased, as we have said, and providing an outlet for the parents' grief, the funeral service is also a means of allaying possible guilt feelings of family members. And for those who participate in the service wholeheartedly, it can answer questions about the role of karma and the mystery of life and death—questions that inevitably arise following the death of an infant. The darkness surrounding death is thus to some extent dispelled. A meaningful funeral or memorial service awakens our deepest intuitions about life and death. Not only this, but the funeral service gives parents, family, and friends the assurance that they have done everything they can to help the child in the after-death state. This in itself can do much to allay the grief of parents.

Part Three

KARMA

Shallow men believe in luck,
believe in circumstance.
Strong men believe in cause and effect.

Ralph Waldo Emerson

Chance is a word void of sense;
nothing can exist without a cause.

Voltaire

11

UNDERSTANDING KARMA

Life's Seeming Injustice

EVER SINCE THE FIRST prehistoric hunters battled a mastodon and one of them lost an arm or leg in the fray, human beings have asked themselves, "Why me and not him?" In all societies and civilizations men and women have struggled to find answers to life's seeming injustice and randomness. Why is one person born deaf or blind, and another free of all physical handicaps? Why is one born with a brilliant mind and another with virtually no mind? Why are some born in the midst of plenty, while others live in poverty and misery? Where is the justice in all this?

For many the answer has been simply "It is the will of God. His ways are mysterious, and we with our limited understanding are incapable of grasping His divine purpose. Therefore 'Ours not to reason why, ours but to suffer and sigh'; we must have faith that in the end God's plan will be revealed." But for countless others these answers satisfy neither reason nor a sense of justice. On the contrary, they often create feelings of powerlessness and resentment which fester and sometimes lead to deep psychological disturbances.

Yet there is an explanation, accepted by millions of people, that opens a window on the why and how of events. This is the doctrine of karma. Though seemingly random and mysterious, karma is a law that functions consistently in dispensing justice. The endless entanglements and contradictions of human existence are clarified by this simple principle, which holds that for every effect there must be an antecedent cause, whose effect in turn becomes another cause, *ad infinitum.* In other words, the doctrine of karma teaches that what we reap accords with what we have sowed.

At the same time, the workings of karma are profound and intricate and their implications not easily grasped. With good reason the ancient symbol for karma is an endless knot.

This sign graphically depicts the infinite network of interrelationships among all forms of existence. It also symbolizes the beginningless and endless causes that condition existence.

The Wheel of Life and Death

The process of becoming is also called the chain of causation, the chain of dependent origination, or, more commonly, the wheel of life and death. As the wheel turns (or each link of the chain is activated), the residue of energy from the turn (or link) before gives rise to the succeeding turn, thus keeping the wheel in motion.[1] The wheel of life and death is a representation of the mind of the unenlightened. Buddha taught, "Everything *is:* this is one extreme view. Everything *is not:* this is the second extreme view. Avoiding both these extremes, the Tathagata [that is, Buddha; see Glossary] teaches the Norm of the Mean." Elaborating on this, Coomaraswamy writes, "This [doctrine of the] Mean asserts that everything is a Becoming, a flux without beginning [first cause] or end; there exists no static moment when this Becoming attains to Being—no sooner can we conceive it by the attributes of name and form, than it has changed to something else. In place of an individual there exists a succession of instants of consciousness."[2]

All creatures are tied to the wheel—the ceaseless round of birth and death—to the law of causation, according to which existence is determined by antecedent actions. This wheel is set in motion by actions stemming from our basic ignorance of the true nature of existence and by karmic propensities from an incalculable past. The wheel is kept revolving by our craving for and clinging to the pleasures of the senses. At the hub are greed, anger, and deluded thinking. The residue of action from each cycle carries forward to the next cycle, perpetually turning the wheel through life and death until we free ourselves from this endless circuit.

Why Believe in Karma?

Belief in the law of causation generates the conviction that just as our past actions shaped the present, so will the life we lead today determine the nature of our future. We *are* the architects of our lives. We *can* change. As the journalist John Walters writes:

> Acceptance of the theory of karma and rebirth will settle many problems regarding life which previously seemed insoluble. It brings a reasonable explanation to circumstances and events, to the tragedies and comedies of life that otherwise would make the world seem one vast madhouse or the plaything of a crazed deity. Belief in karma and rebirth results in a lasting sense of calm and understanding. Life ceases to anger and surprise us, death loses its terrors. No longer do we despairingly utter those useless words, "Why does God let such things happen?" When misfortunes strike us, we realize that payment is being made for wrong actions in a previous life. The debts are being wiped out."[3]

Karma and Causation

"Karma" encompasses greater meaning than simply "causation." Looked at superficially, this latter term appears to be simple. Let us say my elbow strikes a glass jar on a table and the jar falls to the floor and breaks. The jar fell because my elbow hit it, and the broken glass is the effect. If I am riding my bike and a tire hits a piece of glass and blows out, the cause of the blowout is the glass and the effect is the blown tire. All this is obvious. Somewhat less obviously, a parent, instead of reacting firmly but sympathetically to his unruly child, shouts at him harshly. The child, out of hurt and anguish, attacks his younger sister, continuing the cycle of bad feeling. The parent now has a doubly painful situation—one directly of his own making—to try to resolve. Causation, then, pervades all aspects of our life. In a wider sense, cause and effect is an infinite flux, permeating time and space and linking all beings and all phenomena.

Karma is a more inclusive concept than simple cause and effect because it includes moral—or intangible—causes and effects as well as physical—or tangible—causes and effects. Derived from the Sanskrit root *kri*, meaning to do or to make, "karma" refers to action—often to acts of volition—and deeds. For the *consequences* flowing from such acts, there is the more precise term *karma-vipaka,* although in common practice these days the word "karma" loosely covers both meanings. "Karma" is an evocative word that provides entrance to the subtle and intricate relationships of cause and effect, and to an understanding of the way the patterns of deeds and events fit together and interact.

Karma and Intention

Every deed performed with an intention behind it—whether it be physical or mental, good or bad—weaves a timeless pattern, leaves an ineffable mark that sooner or later will produce an effect or consequence in our own life and in the lives of others. "This mark will never be erased save by sheer exhaustion of the karma or by the interruption of an overwhelming counter-karma."[4]

However, "intention" must be understood broadly to encompass a wide range of mental activity. Thus acts performed "instinctively or habitually—such as striking out angrily without premeditation—and acts conditioned by unconscious mentation or emotion, even if we do not understand the motive impulses behind these acts, have karmic consequences. (We know from psychology that even apparently unintentional acts may have subconscious roots.)

Not all experienced effects are products of willed action, or karma. Let us say a heavy branch of a tree falls and seriously injures me as I'm walking along on a windy day. I did nothing to cause the branch to drop, although I experienced the effect of its fall. Nonetheless, I did freely put myself in the place where the branch came down, and to that extent I bear responsibility for what happened to me (perhaps the result of "bad" karma, perhaps not). The cause of the branch falling was the wind and a weakness in the branch; the cause of my injury was being under the branch when it fell. The unexpectedness of the event and my reactions to the severity of the trauma may have a long-lasting effect on me, but this is an effect of a certain cause—my reactions to the incident.

All conditioned phenomena are the result of complex interactions of causes and effects. Such phenomena arise when causes and conditions governing them mature. When conditions become altered, phenomena change accordingly.

Volitional acts "are a form of energy which radiates outward from the doer and affects both himself and others. The murderer may never be apprehended and punished by civil authorities, but the dead survive in the present, and sometime, somewhere, the energy of the past act will have an effect on both the murderer and others. The energy is never lost."[5] The late Dr. Sarvepalli Radhakrishnan, one of India's foremost scholars, called karma "the law of the conservation of moral energy." Professor Garma C. C. Chang describes it this way:

> Karma is essentially a doctrine of the intricate reciprocation between forces and actions that push forward the turning wheel of *samsara.* When expressed on a cosmological scale this force-action complex is a stupendous power that propels the universe and life; when expressed in the ethical sense, it is an unfailing, impersonal law that effectuates the moral order, "dispensing" natural rewards and retributions. Metaphysically, karma is a creative energy brought forth by the collective actions of certain groups; it sustains the order and function of a particular universe in which those groups reside . . .[6]

Karma Is Not Fate

The Buddha said, "If it be true that a man *must* reap according to his deeds, in that case there is no religious life, nor is any opportunity afforded for the complete extinction of suffering. But if the reward a man reaps *accords* with his deeds, in that case there is a religious life and opportunity is afforded for the complete extinction of suffering . . ."[7]

This passage refutes the erroneous view that all physical circumstances and mental attitudes spring solely from past causes. Furthermore:

> If the present life is totally or wholly controlled by our past actions, then karma amounts to fatalism or predestination. If this were true, free will would be an absurdity. Life would be purely mechanical, not much different from a machine. Whether we are created by Almighty God, who controls our destinies and foreordains our future, or are produced by irresistible past karma that completely determines our fate and controls our life force independent of any free actions on our part, is essentially the same. Such a fatalistic doctrine is not the Buddhist law of karma.[8]

The doctrine of karma, then, repudiates any notion of fate or fixed destiny, since circumstances and our response to them are constantly changing. Karma can be made to sound like fatalism only if one believes that the relation between cause and effect is rigid. Cause and effect, however, are dynamic, the effect always changing according to the circumstances, which are themselves both effects of past causes of current and future effects. Past karma has to be expiated, but through our present actions we have the possibility of changing the future direction of our lives. (Even to speak of past and future may be an oversimplification, but it is a necessary concession to our ordinary way of thinking and perceiving.) Fatalism, with the implication that we struggle in vain against a preordained destiny set by higher authority, is a misconception of the law of causation. If my life is already predetermined, why should I make an effort to live decently? The truth is, nothing is unchangeable, the point being that our capability for the exercise of free will is always present. Clearly, then, everyone has the potential at each moment to alter the course of his future karma. If we did not have that freedom, what would be the point of spiritual training?

Primary and Secondary Causes

Karma involves a combination of primary and secondary causes. In the case of a plant, for example, the seed is a primary cause, and fertilizer, rain, wind, sunlight, and attention of the farmer are secondary causes. Take two farmers who plant seeds of grain at the same time. One cultivates his field, fertilizing it with rich manure; the other does nothing but watch the weeds. Obviously there will be a great difference in their respective crops. (Secondary causes may thus be of essential importance.) The principle of primary and secondary causes is always functioning—whether the effect is of minor significance, such as a sneeze, or major, such as death. Similarly, when we pass from this life to the intermediate state at death, though impelled by our desire to be reborn as a human being (the primary cause), we cannot do so without parents, who are a necessary secondary cause of rebirth.

12

CHANGING YOUR KARMA

CAN "BAD" KARMA BE PREVENTED?

ALTHOUGH EFFECTS result from causes, we still have the power to influence the ultimate outcome, because running through the chain of causation is our free will. A bad effect, for example, may be turned to a good end depending upon our attitude. Suppose one is sentenced to prison. This is the effect of a previous action. How the individual chooses to deal with the situation, however, is to a large extent up to him. He may have a change of heart and become law-abiding or, as an old offender, tell himself to be more careful and not get caught the next time. He may make prison his spiritual training center by practicing meditation and reading good books. Obviously his attitude toward his confinement will greatly alter its effect upon him.

The life of Robert Stroud, the "Birdman of Alcatraz," exemplifies this principle. After spending fifty-four years in prison, he died at the age of seventy-three. Despite his third-grade education, he was able to teach himself such diverse subjects as astronomy, painting, languages, mathematics, and law. He also planned prison reforms and studied birds, becoming a world authority on bird diseases. Gradually he underwent a change in personality, becoming a loving and compassionate person.

Some of you may also be familiar with the story of the Tibetan master Milarepa. In his youth Milarepa was involved in black magic which directly led to the deaths of many people. Eventually he decided to change his life and began to train under a teacher. During his training he underwent awesome austerities, subsisting only on nettles and living without clothing in caves high in the mountains. His teacher more than once instructed him to construct a house out of heavy stones and, once it was built, ordered him to pull it down and rebuild it in another location. In the course of these hardships Milarepa came to expiate the karma of having caused the deaths of so many people, and he eventually became a great sage and teacher himself.

Simultaneous and Progressive Cause and Effect

Two other aspects of karma are what might be loosely called simultaneous cause and effect and progressive cause and effect. Suppose I cut my arm badly and cry out in pain. The wound, the bleeding, and the pain occur more or less simultaneously. Later the wound may become infected and the arm may swell, necessitating the attention of a doctor. This is progressive cause and effect.

Then there is the law of small cause and large effect. In this case time is a crucial element: the longer the lapse of time between the cause and the effect, the greater the effect. For example, if you save money, the longer you keep it in the bank, the greater the amount of interest you will receive. Conversely, if you have a debt and do not repay it for a long time, it will become bigger by reason of the interest added to it. Zen master Yasutani has said, "Think of your good deeds as savings and your bad deeds as debts."

Variable and "Constant" Karma

Within the period of a single lifetime every being has, in addition to its variable karma, a particular "constant" karma into which it is born, which includes species, race, sex, and certain other congenital conditions—a missing limb, for example. Our "constant" karma is the result of previous actions crystallized at the time of birth and unchangeable until death. For example, to be born white or black or Asian, or as a man or a woman, is unalterable karma. Though set for life, these conditions are then recast at the next rebirth, again in accordance with the individual's ever ripening past actions.

Variable karma is karma which can be modified by one's own effort. Consider the matter of health. A person may be born sickly, but by watching his health, he can make himself strong. Or he may sustain a serious injury which disables him, but by dint of hard work on himself, he overcomes that negative karma. The following story is dramatic proof of this:

A young lifeguard by the name of Doug Heir dove into a swimming pool to save someone crying for help. The force of the dive brought him to the floor of the pool, where he struck his head, breaking his neck and becoming paralyzed. This was a young man proud of his strength and abilities in sports, and now he lay unable to move, permanently disabled. His family worked with him, and he worked hard himself, on his recovery. In time the broken neck healed, and with intensive physical therapy he was able to gradually recover some use of his upper body. Thus inspired, he began weight training and then shotput and javelin throwing, though from a wheelchair. He went on to win a gold medal with a world-record-setting throw in the Paralympics in England, to attend college and then law school, and to live an independent life in his own apartment and drive his own car. In these ways he changed his karma from that of a bedridden, wholly dependent quadriplegic to an active sportsman and professional able to live on his own without help.[9]

Constant and variable karma can be seen in the matter of longevity: constant because longevity is limited by one's genetic inheritance; variable because it is also affected by one's environment and habits. A kind and honest person, one whose conduct is pure, will benefit from the state of mind which his behavior produces. He will be comfortable with himself and secure in his actions. The more humane he is, the more inclined he will be to perform compassionate deeds, and such actions will become instinctive in him. On the other hand, an irascible, cruel, and dishonest man will make both his life and those of others miserable by creating anger and tension. His corrupt acts will become habitual, and he will perform them with increasing frequency. Moreover, the greater the concentration of thought and will in accomplishing the action, the more lasting the action's effects in the results that follow. Conduct, then, influences states of mind just as states of mind determine behavior.

All actions—whether they do harm or good, whether they are intentional, unconscious, or apparently accidental—affect the doer sooner or later. Every thought, utterance, and deed is a seed that ripens until, under suitable conditions, it comes to fruition as an event or circumstance. The effect can ripen instantly, later in one's present lifetime, or in a future lifetime. Moreover, between each cause and its effect can come succeeding causes which can influence and modify the effect of the original cause. We never know when a particular karmic seed will come to fruition. It is a continuous process, for the way in which one responds to circumstances determines the quality of one's present life as well as that of future lives.

Our moral, intellectual, and temperamental differences are chiefly due to our own actions both present and past; thus karma can be seen as the force giving rise to differences between individuals—differences in abilities, dispositions, and bents as well as in size, color, and shape, and even in one's views of life. Regardless of the time, the place, or the persons involved, the ups and downs of human life are affected and influenced by this law.

Transcending Karma

Karma defines and restricts. Simply to have a certain body-mind is already a karmic restriction. We have only to point to the physical capacities of certain animals to see how limited we are in these respects. No human has the speed or stamina of a horse or a cheetah. The arboreal feats of a simian can't be equaled by a human being. A dog's sense of smell is said to be a hundred times more acute than a human's. Every creature is what it is by reason of its karma.

What we all seek, consciously or unconsciously, is release from the limitations and restrictions of the chain of causation pressing upon us. How can this freedom be gained? A deceptively simple koan tells how.

> A disciple asked a master, "When cold and heat come, how can we avoid them?"
>
> MASTER: "Why don't you go where there is no cold or heat?"
>
> DISCIPLE: "Where's the place where there is no cold or heat?"
>
> MASTER: "In winter, let the cold kill you. In summer, let the heat kill you."

The master uses heat and cold here, of course, as metaphors for birth, sickness, old age, death—karmic milestones in the life of all of us. These milestones are everywhere. To emphasize that point, the master asks, "Why don't you go where there is no cold or heat?" He is pointing a way out, but the student, not understanding, grasps at straws. "Where is that place?" he asks, and the master tells him: "In winter, let the cold kill you. In summer, let the heat kill you."

In other words, when it is cold, don't wish you were on a beach in the middle of the summer, sunning yourself—give yourself up to the cold. When it is hot, don't spend your time daydreaming of cooling breezes—accept the heat so completely that you transcend it. Pain, disease, old age, death can be overcome, the master is implying, if we don't run away from them but face them with strong spirit. Too often we tend to teeter on the edge of life, hesitant to jump in. It is like contemplating a cold shower in winter. If you *think*, "This is going to be cold!" and mentally brace yourself against it, "Brrr!" you'll start to shiver before the cold water even hits you. But don't *think* of coldness, or anything else—just jump under the shower, drenching yourself. Who then remains outside to say, "I'm cold"? No circumstance, whether bitter cold or stifling heat, whether a difficult family situation or a trying personal relationship, the master is saying, need be unnerving or lasting if we meet it head-on.

So long as one is merely on the surface of things, they are always imperfect, unsatisfactory, incomplete. Penetrate into the substance and everything is perfect, complete, whole.

How, then, do we get to the point where everything is seen as full, whole, perfect? A Zen master tells how:

> Every moment, every existence is causation itself. Outside [them] . . . there is neither I nor the world. This being the case, the man of real freedom would be the one who lives in peace in whatever circumstances cause and effect bring about. Whether the situation be favorable or adverse, he lives it as the absolute situation with his whole being—that is, he is causation itself. He never dualistically discriminates different aspects of the situation; his heart is never disturbed by any outside elements. When he lives like this, he is the master of cause and effect and everything is blessed as it is. The eternal peace is established here.[10]

The way out, then, is the way in.

Collective Karma

Joy or suffering can also follow from collective karma, in which each member of a group reaps according to what the group as a whole has sown. Even as each of us has an independent existence, at the same time we relate deeply to one another. "Given this, there is that." Everything is connected and interrelated; all things are mutually dependent for their existence. "Buddhism holds that nothing was created singly or individually. All things in the universe . . . depend upon one another, the influence of each mutually permeating and thereby making a universal symphony of harmonious totality. If one item were lacking, the universe would not be complete; without the rest, one item cannot be."[11]

We can see this principle operating on a social level. To be a parent requires children. Children need parents for their existence and nurturing. Citizens depend on the police for protection; the police depend on us for economic support. Similarly with the fire department. The city depends on the state for certain services. The state depends on cooperation with other states and on the federal government to protect its inhabitants in a variety of ways. The federal government, for its part, cannot function without the work and support of its citizens, who depend on the nation as a whole for their cultural identity and well-being. Nations, too, depend on one another in numerous ways. In the deepest sense, then, we are all in the same boat—more than that, we are extensions of one another. Karmically speaking, a common lifeline of mutual responsibility binds us all.

It is not always easy to distinguish between collective and individual karma. Suppose I neglect my health and become sick. This is individual karma and no one can substitute for me in this illness; I have to take the bitter medicine alone. However, collective karma would begin to operate if I became seriously ill, perhaps needing an operation, so that my family and friends became involved financially and emotionally. To be a passenger in a plane or car that crashes—this is also collective karma. But the fact that one passenger dies, another is only injured, and still another escapes unharmed—this is individual karma.[12]

Collective karma affects us in individual ways as well as collectively; that is, collective karma also becomes individual karma, and in this sense we often cannot speak of karma as being definitively *either* individual *or* collective. They affect and interact with each other. Think of Hitler—it was his individual karma to be a megalomaniacal mass murderer, but it was also his country's collective karma to decide to make him führer. Another example is the *Titanic* disaster. It was the captain's individual karma to choose to ignore numerous warnings about icebergs and continue on course; but it was also the collective karma of everyone on board to be on that boat with him as captain.

We cannot make predictions about collective karma any more than we can about individual karma. We can, however, look at trends. A person, country, or group holding on to destructive, degrading, self-centered practices, policies, or habits is bound to fall into painful situations. We form a unity. Our collective society, the groups with which we associate, are as much a part of us as we are of them. We can choose to spread peace or hatred.

Collective karma is always in operation, but it functions on a much grander scale than individual karma. This has two implications. One is that we are often not aware of collective karma; it is like a huge painting whose full impact is not evident until one observes it from a distance. The other is that when collective karmic events occur, they can be cataclysmic or of devastating proportions because they involve numerous people.

A distinction can also be made between collective karmic *events* and collective karma. The first is a specific occurrence, such as the sinking of the *Titanic,* the war in Vietnam, or a car accident. The second is the fundamental principle of the workings of cause and effect as it affects a body of people united by situation, location, race, creed, or ethnic group.

The Karma of Parent and Child

At the most profound level, collective karma involves the parent-child relationship, which is much deeper than that between siblings. The acceptance of their mutual karma by parents and children has far-reaching implications. No child who had been reared to believe in the validity of the law of causation, and who had accepted it, could one day fling into the face of his parents the taunt "Don't blame me! I didn't ask to be born!" for he would know that we all ask to be born and are born through parents whom we *seek* because of a karmic affinity going back before conception. He or she would be aware that the primary cause of our being propelled again and again into "re-becoming" is a clinging to the notion of a separate, individual existence and the desire to be reborn. The conjunction of a mother and a father is only a secondary, or contributing, cause of one's rebirth.[13] Nor could parents with similar awareness and acceptance of the law of causation ever exclaim in exasperation, "We just don't understand how any child of *ours* could do such a thing!" since they would realize that their sons and daughters have karmas—habit forces or tendencies of long standing—which are independent of inherited mental and physical characteristics.

Although adolescence is a time when boys and girls struggle to emancipate themselves from the influence of their parents, and parents at the same time try to maintain their tenuous control over their children, a child who understood the depth of the parent-child karmic relationship would not permanently alienate herself from her parents except possibly in cases where she had been physically or emotionally abused. That awareness would do much to blunt the sharp edges of the inevitable parent-child conflict that surfaces at this particular time. Parents would recognize that they cannot blame their children for the pains of parenthood, while children would realize that the domineering attitudes of their parents are the product of causes and conditions which they (the children) once set in motion. Both would know that mutual respect and love in the parent-child relationship, as in every other, grows from pain as well as from joy.

Although we often speak of "good" and "bad" (painful) karma, the term "karma" is generally used in reference to the latter—as when selfish actions, for instance, are called "karma-producing." In recent years, as the word "karma" has become widely used in the West, several new usages have arisen. Among these is the term "heavy karma," meaning an unusually large debt that must be expiated as a result of pain-producing thoughts and actions in this life and previous lives. The word "karma" may also imply an evil bent of mind growing out of long-standing ego-dominated behavior. We may also speak of "having a karma" with someone, implying a mutual attraction or repulsion that exists as a result of a strong relationship from a previous life. One will also hear the expression, "Karma willing, I'll see you next month," meaning that if my karma decrees that I live at least to next month and make it to our reunion, we'll meet again then.

Inevitably, in certain circles these days, "karma" has become a buzzword, the glib explanation for any out-of-the-ordinary happening. Even in Japan—a nominally Buddhist country—the word is casually tossed about, as witness this story: A high school student showed his report card to his father. Examining the report carefully, the father was dismayed to find a string of low marks. "Why are your grades so bad?" he sternly demanded. The boy offhandedly replied, "Guess it's just my karma, Dad." Whereupon Dad gave the boy a hard slap. "Why did you hit me?" his son protested. "Because that's *my* karma," answered the father.

"Karma" is sometimes used in reference to a relationship that has played itself out, such as a job or love affair that one is no longer interested in. Not infrequently, though, announcing that one's karma with someone has ended is often a lame attempt to extricate oneself from an unpleasant situation. Correctly, karma cannot be used as justification *for doing or not doing anything*. It can only be pointed to as an explanation of something that has already occurred.

Lightening the Karmic Burden

The workings of karma are complex and often inscrutable. A child is instantly killed by a car, and in their anguish and despair the parents protest, "Why did this have to happen to *our* child? She was such a generous, loving person, with no malice in her. Why did *she* have to die so young and so violently when others whose lives are selfish and cruel die in their own bed at an advanced age? Where is the justice of it?" And if previously they had faith in the goodness of God, they now feel disillusionment and bitterness toward Him. "Why would a loving and just God permit this?" they demand.

Even a person who accepted karma might initially ask such questions when tragedy struck. But on deeper reflection, one would realize that the question was not "Why?" but "How?"—"How can I expiate the karma which brought this about and not create more of it in the future?" The best way to do this is to accept the situation and use it as an opportunity to repay a karmic debt. This does not mean passively accepting whatever misfortune comes your way when you *can* change the situation. By "rolling with the punch," however, one lightens one's pain and lessens one's karmic burden.

Furthermore, there is no residue of resentment or bitterness. In families where a child dies, parents who reflect gratefully on the joy and love she brought into their lives eventually find such thoughts a tremendous aid in allaying the terrible hurt. Here, too, our attitude affects our karma.

One who truly understood that the painful events of his life represent the flowering of seeds once planted by him would inevitably say, "I don't know why this has happened, but since it has, I must have helped cause it." This is not the same as saying, "Such and such an experience is happening to me because I need to develop such and such a characteristic"—for example, more compassion.

In the context of an awareness of karma, suffering would be seen as the inevitable consequence of a series of causes and effects that we ourselves initiated. Eventually one develops the faith to accept that whatever happens to us is primarily the result of our own actions. We might make what we perceive to be mistakes, but in an ultimate sense there are no mistakes; we simply live in accord with our past and current karma. To deeply perceive this is to be taught by life rather than overcome by it. By thus accepting and acquiescing in the effects of our actions, we begin to lessen the karmic burden and eventually the pain-producing causes.

Once, a mother whose son had been imprisoned for selling drugs said to me, "What have I done to deserve this? Why *me?*" A physician friend who was present at a talk on karma in which I had related the foregoing incident commented, "Whenever something painful happens to me and I ask, 'What have I done to deserve this?' invariably the answer comes as 'Plenty!' " This has got to be the response of all of us if we are honest with ourselves, for none of us is free from the guilt implied in the question. Yet the sense of guilt may be turned to a positive end by reflecting, "What causes, what incidents brought about the painful result? In what way did my own behavior contribute to it?" Such questioning can be revealing and thus therapeutic. Life does not exist in a vacuum. The more we understand the interconnectedness of all life, the better we understand the motivations behind our actions and the consequences of our behavior. In the end, others as well as we are the beneficiaries.

When Others Are Wrong I Am Wrong

It would be hard, I think, to find a higher ethical principle than that enunciated by the sixth patriarch of Zen, who said, "When others are wrong I am in the wrong. When I have transgressed I alone am to blame." Such a deep sense of personal responsibility could come only from one who truly understood the law of causation at a profound level. Such a person would know that the network of interrelationships between all forms of life is so vast and complex that we cannot, in a cosmic sense, disavow responsibility for whatever happens anywhere—least of all for the repercussions on our own and others' lives of our thoughts, speech, and actions.

Someone once came to me for help in resolving the angry feelings he had for a former girlfriend. I asked him what he had been doing to this end and he replied that he had been directing loving thoughts toward her. I suggested he start reciting a repentance verse and begin directing feelings of contrition toward her. He was taken aback. "Why should I apologize to *her?*" he insisted. "*She* was the one who hurt *me.*" "But," I told him, "the fact that you felt pain means you did something to earn it; no doubt you caused her pain as well. You equally share responsibility for this situation."

How do we explain the unwillingness of so many to reflect on their past wrongs which have caused hurt to others, and their failure to see how the tangled web of these actions continues to cloud their lives and those of others? To what can we attribute our reluctance to make a searching and fearless moral inventory of ourselves? Author J. Glenn Gray believes this attitude is traceable to the rise of modern psychology and the predominance of naturalistic philosophers, "who have tended to view guilt feelings as a hindrance to the full development of personality and the achievement of a life-affirming outlook."[14] Worse, people have tended to use such notions to justify antisocial behavior. And so we blame the parents for being too strict or too lenient, but the offender is blameless. Or else we find society at fault and not the criminal. The individual is thus released from responsibility for past deeds and from the hard duty to improve his character. Overlooked is the fact that at every step of the way a person has the choice to follow the honest and moral road or to deviate from it.

13

THE INTERCONNECTEDNESS OF ALL LIFE

We Are Our Brothers

To fully understand karma it is essential that we recognize the interdependence of all life—that we are not alone but move in an intimate dance with all creation. If I move, you move; if you do wrong, I do wrong; if I do good, you too do good. The joys and triumphs of all humanity are also mine as long as I am able to take joy in the good fortune of others without being envious. Similarly, when I am able to cry with the pain of those who suffer, my compassion is working and I do what I can to help those in need. But, as Dolores Leckey observes, "Every time one of us truly rests, the world rests a little, so intimately connected are we with one another." Yet equally true, we come into this world alone and we will leave it alone, sustained by our wholesome karmas and hindered by our unwholesome ones.

> In between [birth and death, writes an anonymous author] we must find whatever meaning we can in our lives. We must reach out to others and celebrate with them those special times in which we honor the past and look with hope towards the future. For it is only in these moments that we transcend our human limitations, break

free from the bonds of our solitary existence, and taste the sweetness of life.

To feel that when others are in the wrong I too am wrong, and that when I have transgressed I alone am to blame, doesn't mean that for every wrong committed I must accept blame at a literal level and take the corresponding punishment. Let us suppose you did everything you could to help end the Vietnam War. In that event you might well say, "Why should I feel responsible for the bombings and other horrors that were committed there?" Of course, few people could really say they did *everything* within their power to stop the war. But many did try hard. So where does the responsibility lie? It lies in the need to rid ourselves of greed, anger, and other destructive elements of our personality. It also lies in developing our full potential as compassionate human beings and in actually expressing that compassion throughout our lives. We are our brother's keepers—no, in the deepest sense we *are* our brothers, for we are not apart from them.

Karma and Suicide

Any intentional act that is egoistically motivated has negative karmic consequences. The willful taking of one's life is such an act. Human life is preeminently precious because it is only from that state that we can come to enlightenment and attain true liberation.

The Buddhist injunction not to kill is part of a total effort to prevent destruction of human consciousness and community. No society can be indifferent to the taking of human life.[15] Suicide implies a rupture of human equilibrium in the society of which one is a part; it does violence to our fundamental instinct for life. The Talmud says, "Whosoever saves a single life, it is as if he had saved the whole world." It is true that from the absolute standpoint of Essential-nature, suicide, like any other phenomenon, is void of any fundamental reality. However, the fact is that we exist simultaneously on two levels: the phenomenal (or relative) and the unconditioned (or absolute). Actually, these are not two, though in our speaking about them in the language of our dualistically oriented mind, they seem to be separate. But in moments of utter clarity we may recognize that the phenomenal is the Void and that the formless is the phenomenal. Thus, while in an absolute sense suicide affects no one, since there is no one and nothing to be affected on that level, at the same time, we also exist in the relative dimension of time and space, of human relationships. On this level, the loss is enormously painful to many people—family, friends, and acquaintances. Because my ego-based action—killing myself—was the source of this pain, I am guilty of producing an immense amount of negative karma, the effects of which will adversely influence not only me but many others as well. It is in the world of form that karma is created, manifested, and expiated. To make statements relating only to life on the plane of the absolute, or undifferentiated, is a fatal mistake; it is as blind as seeing only the relative side of life. The formless aspect can never be considered without the differentiated; the two are inseparable.

Speaking of the individual's relation to the community, William James affirms that these two are mutually conditioning: "The community stagnates without the impulse of the individual. The impulse dies away without the sympathy of the community." When the poet John Donne says, "Every man's death diminishes me," he is affirming the spiritual and scientific truth that all life is interrelated, and that what happens in one place can have its repercussions millions of miles away. The individuals who make up a particular society are like the threads of a fine brocade. Remove even one thread and you have marred the entire pattern of the fabric to some extent. It is violent death through murder, suicide, and war that is particularly disruptive.

Now, some people may feel that one should be able to do what one pleases with one's own body. But, is it really "ours"? If it were, we ought to be able to control aging and death itself. Obviously we are not able to do that. Similarly, if our minds were really our own, we should be able to totally control our thoughts, and we can't do that either. Our body has its own laws, which it obeys regardless of our wishes. So whose body, whose mind is it? Our body-mind is the crystallization of the way we have thought, felt, and acted; it's the gift of our karma, which enables us to be reborn as a human being, with all the joy, pain, and potential attendant upon having a physical existence. Nonetheless, clinging to body and mind as *my* body, *my* mind is the first fatal step on the road to self-imprisonment. As W. H. Auden states in his "Canzone":

> Our claim to own our bodies and our world
> Is our catastrophe.

As human beings, we represent the culmination of the struggle to evolve from the most primitive life forms into this present body, with its highly intricate brain and marvelously complex physical structure. Through the grace of good karma most of us have achieved "a faultless body and a blameless mind." Ours therefore is a sacred obligation to protect them for ourselves and others.

> O man's most wonderful work—
> Just to walk upon the earth!

Karma and Abortion

In the case of abortion, in the most profound sense, neither the doctor's instruments nor anything else can destroy the real life of the fetus, for its ever-abiding True-nature is indestructible. Looking at abortion from a relative view, however, one can see that all the participants in an abortion—that is, the parents and the doctor (or other person) who performs it—share in the effects of that action.

No matter what we do, for whatever reason, we are planting seeds with every single action and will have to deal with their fruit when the time comes. What kind of karma we are creating for ourselves and for others depends on the degree of selfishness, or lack of it, which motivates our action. If a pregnant woman sincerely feels that she is emotionally incapable of lovingly caring for her child, she may create less painful karma by aborting the embryo than by crippling her growing child later on. If she has an abortion because she resents any interference with the gratification of her selfish desires, she inevitably creates painful karma. If giving birth to a baby seriously endangers the life of the mother, then saving the mother's life—she being the more developed one—may take precedence over saving that of the embryo. Clear awareness and affirmation of the law of cause and effect, and complete willingness to assume responsibility for what needs to be done, will help clear the mind of guilt, anxiety, and remorse, which are also seeds for new obstructions.

Karma and Euthanasia

None of us wants to see someone dear to us suffer, of course. But the karma of the one who takes her own life and that of those who aid and abet life-taking are not the same. Deliberately to take your own life carries with it a heavy karmic penalty, for all the reasons you have heard. To respond to another's entreaties to end his life because of great pain and suffering incurs karmically less serious results. (This latter does *not* include counseling another to take his own life—an action that may have more severe karmic consequences.) It may strike some of you as selfish to be thinking of your own karma when someone dear to you in great pain pleads with you to end his or her life. But that is really secondary to a consideration of that person's karma. Might it not be kinder, karmically speaking, not to accede to that person's request for the person's *own* sake? There are no easy answers to these questions, for each situation is a unique set of circumstances, and each person must make his or her decision based on those circumstances—with the full knowledge that, whatever is decided, cause brings effect.

Karma and Retribution

Karma is not a matter of an eye for an eye and a tooth for a tooth in the narrow sense. There isn't necessarily a one-to-one correspondence between the evil or good a person does in one lifetime and the results that will be experienced in another. The fact that in a previous life one may have cut off a person's hand doesn't necessarily mean that in this lifetime he will lose his own hand. The ever changing events continuously interweave with one another. The currents of karma, both good and bad, intermingle, flowing from past lives to the present life and from this life to future lives. Our karma is thus determined by the sum total of our actions, good and bad, and by the larger karmic flux of which we are a part. These actions in turn create a pattern, a predisposition, as a result of which we respond to events in a certain way. That is, our karma creates a pathway, or perhaps a rut, which we tend habitually to follow.

Karma Realized Now and in the Future

Just as our actions can produce positive, negative, or neutral karma, so the results of karma can occur during three periods in time. Some karma bears its fruit in the present life, or as soon as the act is performed. The effects of the act, though, may not occur until the next lifetime. And in some instances many lifetimes may elapse before an effect is felt. In some cases the karmic force may be so weak that it produces no reaction at all. So retribution experienced in this life is the matured result of karmic seeds sown either in a past life or in the present one; and the accumulated effects of actions in this life, good or bad, are experienced in this life or in subsequent ones.

Instead of the terms "positive" and "negative," it might actually be more precise to speak of wholesome and unwholesome volitions. An unwholesome volition is one rooted in greed, hate (anger), or delusion (erroneous thinking)—in a word, in self-centeredness. A wholesome volition is rooted in the opposite of those passions, namely, generosity, love, contentment, clarity of mind.

In the light of what we've said about karma realized now and in the future, it may be easier to understand how it happens that one who has led a decent life will suddenly go off the deep end and commit a terrible wrong—to the dismay and consternation of his family and friends, who have always looked upon him as a pillar of virtue. What happened? He has been hit with past karma brought into play by certain causes and conditions.

When we look at human existence from the perspective of only one lifetime, it sometimes seems that the wicked prosper and the good suffer, that the decent person has unhappiness as his lot while the evildoer lives happily. But this is only the outcome of past good and evil karma. If it were possible to track lifetimes, we would see that eventually the evildoers get their just desserts.

Karma and the Intention to Learn

I've heard some people say that the cause of our suffering in this world might be due not to something wrong we did in the past, but to a need on our part to learn something—for example, awareness or humility. Some people even go so far as to say we *choose* to undergo painful experiences in order to learn from them. But these notions are a distortion of the Buddhist teaching of karma. Consider this situation: I start across a busy intersection while the light is still green, and because I am inattentive, I get hit by a car and am badly hurt. My injury did not result from my need to learn the value of mindfulness. Whether I become more attentive in the future as a result of the accident is up to me, but the accident did not happen in order to teach me to be attentive.

Or take another case. Let us say your husband is mistreating you. Through what you did in the past—perhaps within recent memory, perhaps not—you have "earned" the abuse being heaped on you now. But there is a vital difference between accepting responsibility for the abuse being inflicted on you and lying belly up to invite further punishments—taking it without trying to change your circumstances. If you continue to allow your husband to beat you, not only are you perpetuating your pain and grief; you are also helping him perpetuate the bad karma he is creating for himself. Remember, we have the power to change our karma. You could choose to leave the relationship, perhaps moving to a distant area to live, or you could undergo psychological counseling to understand and change your own behavior patterns that may have contributed to the situation, or you can simply sit back and tell yourself, "It's my karma."

I understand many people these days believe that we cause our own illness and so we also have the power to completely cure ourselves either by willing the disease away or by employing alternative therapies alone. Although it is true that our minds and bodies are shaped by our karma—which includes our choice of parents and therefore possible genetic predisposition to certain diseases—we can't overlook the fact of environmental and other influences.

We are a very complex interaction of mind, body, emotion, and will. These four are inseparably connected, although for convenience, we divide them into individual components. And so sickness of the body-mind is no simple thing. Take the common cold: it's known that it is caused by a virus, but that physical exhaustion, depression, and stress can also determine whether a person exposed to the virus actually gets the cold. Or take cancer, perhaps the most complex and mysterious of illnesses: it has no simple origin and no simple cure. While a person's cheerful, optimistic attitude and will to overcome the disease have been known to make a difference in certain cases, they don't at all in others. "Doctors are men," says Voltaire, "who prescribe medicine of which they know little to cure diseases of which they know less in human beings of which they know nothing."

It flies in the face of what we do know about the etiology of sickness to assume that we alone cause our illness and therefore that we can cure ourselves of it. True, an intemperate lifestyle—bad diet, lack of exercise, alcohol and drug abuse, mental confusion, depression, inability to cope with stress, and other factors—can precipitate an illness; it is dangerous to assume, however, that you need only apply some willpower or positive imaging—or even surgery, radiation, and chemotherapy—to effect a cure. For the person who is ill, it can be a traumatic experience to believe he can cure himself—or he's not living right—and then to fail. And it is irresponsible and insensitive to say to him, "You've made yourself sick; just make yourself well! If you can't, something's rotten about you."

This smacks of the religious belief popular in certain times in history, that those who suffer illness and misery do so because they have fallen from God's grace and so are begetting His wrath. If it were true that disease and pain are the outcome of a life of impurity, how do we explain that such an imposing spiritual figure as Sri Ramana Maharshi died of cancer? (See "Sri Ramana Maharshi.")

Karma and Compassion

Compassion and wisdom are two of the cornerstones of Buddhism, of which karma is a fundamental teaching. Some people misinterpret the doctrine of karma, believing that by alleviating the suffering of another they are interfering with their karma. But this contradicts the well-known pronouncement of the Buddha: "One thing I teach, and one thing only—suffering—its causes *and the way to overcome them.*" (Emphasis added.) And the Buddha was most emphatically not referring only to the suffering of the individual listeners, but to that of all beings. One who truly understands and accepts the law of karma spontaneously offers sympathy, understanding, and help to another in pain, simply because he would know that he himself at one time or another had had to bear the painful consequences of his own past wrongdoing.

But what is compassion? Is it merely sympathizing with those in pain, or actively helping to relieve their suffering, like the Good Samaritan who doesn't walk past the injured or the ailing but stops to help? Is it aiding the poor and the homeless? Enlightened compassion involves much more than engaging in such temporary measures. Even if you feed a hungry man, he's going to get hungry again, so unless you teach him how to grow his own food, or teach him a skill so he can earn enough money to buy his own food, your compassion is not of the deepest kind. The same principle applies to the homeless. While they are entitled to help in finding and holding their places in the society of which they're a part and to whose development they have contributed (in perhaps invisible ways), our compassion is not yet truly enlightened unless we can get them to see that their own karma has been a vital element in bringing them to their present condition—that even if society has pushed them to the ground they still have the power to get up and change their karma.

I was once asked, "If you accept that all misery is self-created, and that in this life you need to atone for past misdeeds, how are you going to empathize with the sufferings of another person?" The law of cause and effect does not imply that all misery is self-created. What happens to one of us affects all of us, though the effect isn't always obvious. Nor is it accurate to say we are here merely to atone for past wrongdoings. We are here to work out past karma, both positive and negative—a statement which has a much broader implication than that of paying off past karmic debts. You can think of our present life as a huge school or arena where we seek to develop ourselves physically, mentally, morally, and spiritually—in other words, to raise the level of our own consciousness and the consciousness of others. That is why we are strongly attracted to certain parents and to certain other people, including a spouse, whose actions often pain us and whom we in turn pain. The development of our full potential necessitates undergoing pain and struggle. We may resent that pain, and we may hate the person or persons we blame for it, yet our karma propels us toward such persons precisely because at this stage of our life the pain is essential for our growth and spiritual advancement. If we gratefully accept the pain and see it as an opportunity to grow, to purge ourselves of past unwholesome karma, we have already taken a giant step upward.

It's all too easy to throw around the arcane word "karma" with an air of omniscience. The fact is, all ego-motivated acts create karmic consequences, but that doesn't mean those acts have no other implications. Let us say a man and his child are brutally murdered in a terrorist hijacking of a plane. Was this their karma? Yes, because they chose to be on the plane and so become the victims of the collective karma of all those on board. To say this, however, is not to excuse the horrors and evils of terrorism or make light of the tragedy of such killings. If we see somebody suffering, we need to help her if at all possible. That person's karma *might* be pain and poverty; nevertheless, we must act. This is *our* karma. We cannot ignore individual suffering, for only by responding to it do we express our compassion and demonstrate our humanity. Would a compassionate, undeluded individual, when confronted with human misery, turn away from it with the thought "It is self-created; it's no business of mine"? The answer is a flat no. Why not?

Because enlightened compassion is not the outcome of conscious choice; it is the upwelling of a deep instinct in all of us, which if not obstructed by deluded thinking operates freely. Besides, to be helped may be a person's karma as much as his suffering is.

To say, "It's my 'bad' karma" after an unhappy event in one's own life is a positive thing, especially if it leads one to reflect on the significance of the shifting circumstances of his life. But to say "Too bad, but that's your karma" gratuitously to someone in misery is not only insensitive but, in many cases, only partially true. Besides, common decency—respect for another's feelings—is a social imperative in any civilized society. An individual may have brought on his sufferings by past misguided actions, or his sufferings may be due to collective karma. Nonetheless, a truly sympathetic human being would act immediately and directly to do everything he could to alleviate another's pain and suffering. Helping another would be helping himself. No man's karma is exclusively his own, and no one's suffering is exclusively her own. A web of relationships sustains and nourishes each of us.

Karma and Change

The truth is we can never know precisely what our karma is because its origin may be obscure. It is constantly shifting, adjusting, moving, being expiated, and being newly formed. This old Chinese story about a farmer whose horse ran away illustrates the dynamic quality of karma. When his neighbors came over to console him, sighing, "Too bad, too bad," the farmer said, "Maybe." The next day the horse returned, bringing with him seven wild horses. "Oh, how lucky you are!" exclaimed the neighbors. "Maybe," replied the farmer. On the following day when the farmer's son tried to ride one of the new horses, he was thrown and broke his leg. "Oh, how awful!" cried the neighbors. "Maybe," answered the farmer. The next day soldiers came to conscript the young men of the village, but the farmer's son wasn't taken because his leg was broken. "How wonderful for you!" said the neighbors. "Maybe," said the farmer.

Obviously, then, trying to extrapolate future karma from a certain event would be as foolhardy as looking at pictures of babies you've never seen before, singling one out, and attempting to describe what her future will bring.

Creating Good Karma

Insofar as we free ourselves of greed and anger, cultivate compassion and wisdom (seeing things as they really are) and immerse ourselves in *all* the circumstances of our life, we accumulate wholesome—or at least not unwholesome—karma. The Buddha's precepts provide excellent guidelines:

1. not to kill but to cherish all life;
2. not to take what is not given but to respect the things of others;
3. not to misuse sexuality but to be caring and responsible;
4. not to lie but to speak the truth;
5. not to cause others to use substances that confuse the mind, nor to do so oneself, but to keep the mind clear;
6. not to speak of the shortcomings of others but to be understanding and sympathetic;
7. not to praise oneself and condemn others but to overcome one's own shortcomings;
8. not to withhold spiritual or material aid but to give it freely where needed;
9. not to indulge in anger but to exercise forebearance.

There are others, but these are the most important.

Although observance of this or any other moral code is the first indispensable step on the road to a genuine spiritual life, only an awakening to the true nature of life and death can provide unshakable contentment—in this or any other life.

To sum up: Our life situation is not ordered by either gods or devils but is the consequence of our own actions, arising from our thoughts, speech, and emotions, whether we are aware of the meaning of good and bad or not. These actions echo within us and influence our personality. When our attitudes change, our circumstances likewise change.

Our horizons would expand and our lives would take on fresh meaning if we began training ourselves to see that even the minutest event in our lives has karmic significance. We would gain a new awareness of our own power and dignity even as we became more humble, for we would realize that we are not isolated fragments thrown into the universe by a capricious fate, but part of one vast ocean in which all currents intermingle. Wonder and joy would replace boredom and discontent.

PART FOUR

REBIRTH

I am just as certain as you see me here
that I have existed a thousand times before
and I hope to return a thousand times more.

GOETHE

After all, it is no more surprising to
be born twice
than it is to be born once.

VOLTAIRE

All life is phoenix-like,[1] *recreating itself*
again and again from its own ashes.

AUTHOR UNKNOWN

14

THE CASE FOR REBIRTH

What Lies Beyond?

"As far back as I can remember I have unconsciously referred to the experiences of a previous state of existence . . . As the stars looked to me when I was a shepherd in Assyria, they look to me now a New Englander . . . And Hawthorne, too, I remember as one with whom I sauntered in old heroic times along the banks of the Scamander amid the ruins of chariots and heroes."[2]

Perhaps you've heard or read statements such as this before and dismissed them as no more than the fantasies of a starry-eyed New Ager or an Eastern guru. Surely no one with both feet on the ground could believe that he had lived in other bodies in times past, and that he even remembered those lives. Yet these are not the ravings of a lunatic or the pseudophilosophic musings of someone strung out on drugs. These are the words of Henry David Thoreau—a man of lively mind, to be sure, but as American as apple pie.

Belief in Afterlife

It can fairly be said that no notion has persisted for so long and in so many guises as the idea that the death of the physical body is not the end of individual existence. That all living beings, including the unseen inhabitants of other realms, have previously existed in some form or another and will continue to be reborn was almost universally accepted in the ancient world. Even in prehistoric times, people have clung to a belief in the hereafter with fierce tenacity, refusing to believe that a person's influence ended at death. The pervasiveness of these beliefs is seen in the diversity of civilizations which believed them: civilizations in Egypt, India, Ireland, Greece, and South America. Through myths and legends, through sacred texts and rituals, faith in the continuity of existence has been handed down to the present time. According to the noted anthropologist Sir James Frazer, individuals in primitive societies no more doubted their immortality than they did the reality of their conscious existence.[3]

Ancient Egyptians did not question the reality of an afterlife, and they made certain that the dead wanted for naught, furnishing them with a prodigious amount of paraphernalia for their journey and eventual encounter with Osiris. The dead were, in a sense, as alive as the living, for why else would such solemn religious rites as animal sacrifices and offerings of food and wine be made?

The Greeks were heartened by the concept that their souls, newly released from the body, would fly like freed birds to the bliss of Elysium. Early Christians, prior to the Second Council of Constantinople in A.D. 553, believed in re-becoming, a conviction that was in accord with the Gnostic belief that angels may become men or demons, and that from the latter they may rise to become men or angels.

In our own time, too, we persist in refusing to accept death as the incontrovertible end. According to a Gallup poll taken in 1980–81, nearly 70 percent of Americans believe in life after death.[4] While most people's concept of an afterlife is based on a union with God, reunion with loved ones, and/or life in a heavenly realm, a surprising 23 percent believe in reincarnation. What is surprising is not that such a great number believe in the continuity of existence, but rather that so *few* Americans embrace what is, for a large proportion of the world's population—Hindus, Buddhists, and Jains, as well as others—incontrovertible.

Many outstanding individuals of our age—Carl Jung, Ralph

Waldo Emerson, Albert Schweitzer, Henry David Thoreau, and Mohandas Gandhi, to name a few—believed in reincarnation, transmigration, or rebirth (terms which, though used interchangeably, are not really identical—see "Rebirth Distinguished from Reincarnation"). Belief in reincarnation, if not rebirth, is not inimical to contemporary Christian and Jewish beliefs. Dr. Leslie Weatherhead, minister of London's City Temple for almost three decades, felt that reincarnation offered a key to unlock many problems for Christians. He pointed out that Jesus never denied it, that it was a prevailing belief in Jesus' day, and that it was an essential part of the Essene teachings.

Passages in the Old Testament and the Kabala, sacred texts of Judaism, contain references to metempsychosis, or transmigration. It is also universally accepted by the Hasidic movement. Commenting on the origins of Jewish belief in transmigration, Rabbi Moses Gaster says, "There cannot be any doubt that these views are extremely old [in Judaism]. Simon Magus raises the claim of former existences, his soul passing through many bodies before it reaches that known as Simon . . . The [Hebrew] masters of the occult science never doubted its Jewish character . . ."[5]

The Intermediate Realm

It is the teaching of sages from Buddhist and other cultures that at the moment of death we begin our transitional existence, which is the intermediate realm between death and rebirth. (See Diagram 4.) This realm is very different from the physical plane, but in one respect it is identical. For just as our ego-based perceptions affect the way we relate to and interact with our environment and events in this world, similarly does our karma, stemming from both the last and many former existences, affect the way we relate to the experiences of an intermediate life.

There are said to be three primary stages in the transitional state. The initial stage consists predominantly of physical sensations of freedom and is relatively short in duration. At this point a tenuous connection to the physical body still remains. One may be acutely aware of the actions and words as well as the thoughts of living loved ones. This sensitivity and awareness mean that any

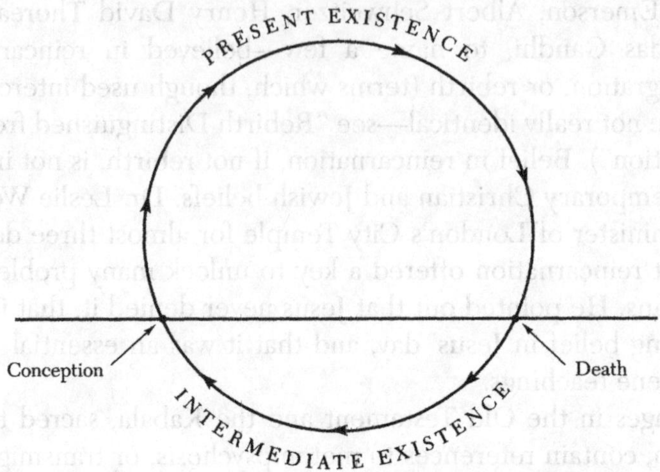

DIAGRAM 4: *The Circle of Continuing Existence*

words *directed to the deceased* at this time—as in chanting, for example—can bring about an awakening.

The second stage encompasses diverse sensory experiences and lasts longer than the first. In the final stage the entity is drawn, according to its karma, to a particular rebirth. The process from death to rebirth is said to take place in cycles of seven days or multiples thereof—usually forty-nine days. But this figure is not fixed. It can occur in a day or a week or not until many years later. Presumably the time of rebirth is determined by, among other factors, the attraction of the being to parents with whom it has a karmic affinity.

As was mentioned earlier, the seventh, eighth, and ninth levels of consciousness do survive death. (See "The Nine Levels of Consciousness.") Karma, or the force of will, continues in its cyclic propulsion through death, after-death, and rebirth. But we also possess a semblance of our other senses in the intermediate existence. At the moment of death the first six levels of consciousness become transmuted from a physical orientation to a nonphysical. Until we take on a "solid" body again, sight, hearing, smell, taste, touch, and intellect are incipient, functioning in a tenuous way. Without a body as a vehicle they cannot be fully utilized, but neither are they completely absent. Zen master Yasutani explains it this way:

> This intermediate being is constantly changing and does not have any rigid form. It is said to be much superior to present-life existence. It is like an electric current: it can pass through all obstacles and even fly hundreds of miles in a moment. It is also said to have intellect, emotion, and will of a tenuous nature as well as the five sensory organs.
>
> It is said that the intermediate being has some mysterious power to see, feel and find its parents, and that it is able to see the sexual intercourse by which it may be conceived.[6]

It is as difficult to give a precise description of the *intermediate state* as it is to give one of this world—only more so. Since, as I've said, the experience of passage is colored by our karma, it will differ from person to person. However, it is possible to give what might be called an Everyman's (or -woman's) description of this state.

Let me capitulate in some detail the masters' accounts of the stages of the journey from death to rebirth. During the first stage the most striking element is the thought of how easy it is to die. Unlike the sometimes prolonged act of dying, which may be difficult and painful, death itself is as simple, easy, and natural as a leaf's fluttering off a tree. Many people see their whole life played out rapidly before them in the instant before physical death. Soon after that, as the intermediate state of existence is entered, there may be a feeling of floating or flying, similar to sensations people often have in dreams. There is an awareness of great calmness and tranquility, a sensation of relief and utter ease. One might even wonder, "What was all the worry about?" With the last breath all worries and cares of the mundane world are cast aside. The entity may then be drawn to a tunnel of bright white light and may sense that loved ones or a wonderful experience lies in wait at the end. The feeling is like that of walking into a lover's embrace, or like the joyful anticipation of a child waiting to open presents on Christmas morning.

The events and experiences of this first stage are substantially the same whether a person has very negative, pain-producing karma or relatively good karma. However, the way a person with bad karma relates to these experiences will be considerably different from the way a person with good karma does. The former might, for example, feel cynical, suffused with apprehension and suspicion. At first such a person may feel that he "got away with it," that is, with the crimes and evil perpetrated in his life, but he will soon become uneasy. What is happening will be perceived as a loss of control, and his anxiety will grow.

The second stage of passage is deeply influenced by a person's mind state at the time of death. Also of great importance are the life experiences of the being both in its last previous lifetime and in its many former lifetimes, as well as the kind of guidance received in the immediate post-death state. Here again is where strong, meaningful chanting at the funeral can be effective. (See "The Value of Chanting.") Thus the experience of the second stage varies extensively from person to person. The experiences encountered, however, are all projections of one's own consciousness, and if this is understood and firmly imbedded in the mind, one will not be frightened by the apparitions that may appear.

Upon entering the second stage, the intermediate entity may feel confused, as if awakening from a deep, drugged sleep. Everything will seem vaguely familiar and dreamlike, as though the being were caught in a constant state of déjà vu. Many different things may happen now. The senses, which were once accustomed to the simple and mundane things of the physical world, will be assaulted by various frightening, terrible, or exquisitely beautiful sights, sounds, and smells. Loud, startling noises, sudden bangs, cracks, and rumbles will be heard. Howling wind and raging fires may appear. The entity may feel as if it is sinking into an abyss or becoming paralyzed. Words are spoken, but no sound is heard; sounds are heard, but no words are spoken. Thoughts wander randomly, as in a delirium. It is not possible to focus on objects, because they move away or become transparent. Nothing appears solid, nothing has substance. It is possible to move like a flash of lightning, at great speeds through objects. All of the senses, though of a tenuous nature, are present, but they are no longer attuned to the physical realm.

It is vital to understand that the way an individual reacts to the transitional experiences greatly depends on the kind of life he led before dying. Whether he is frightened by these experiences or unmoved by them depends on the degree to which he saw through his clinging attachments to the material world. And his reactions to events now will determine much of what is yet to come.

The masters have assured us that everything one experiences in this state is as unreal and devoid of substance, as empty of all abiding reality, as what is experienced in the dimension of waking consciousness. All lights, visions, and apparitions of every kind should therefore be regarded as mere projections and reflexes of the entity's mind states. Since the terrifying things it encounters cannot cause harm, it need not cower before them. The being should now remind itself of the need to be free from all clinging attachments to objects as well as experiences. If the entity was experienced in meditation during former existences and developed concentrative powers to a high degree, it will still have the ability to focus its mind. It is possible to accomplish this if there is single-minded concentration on the truths one has understood. Although the entity may feel as if it is in the midst of a raging storm, it can become tranquil and centered through the concentrative power of its mind.

When the second stage draws to an end, the third stage begins. As with the first two stages, here too karma plays an all-important role. This is the time when one, so to speak, looks into the mirror of her karma and finds herself committed to a particular course of action. According to the causes and conditions established, the entity will be drawn to one of a number of realms in which rebirth will take place. Those who have led destructive, pain-producing lives will be inexorably drawn to a rebirth that will entail great suffering. Those who have led more wholesome lives will also be drawn toward rebirths that are in accord with their deeds.

It should be emphasized that the impulse to be reborn is devoid of all self-conscious reflection or cognition. It is rather a blind yearning toward the mother-to-be on the part of one who will be reborn as a male, or toward the father-to-be for one who will be reborn as a female. This instinct is governed by our karma, which induces us to be attracted to a particular type of environmental and physical existence—well-to-do or humble, male or female, human or nonhuman, dark- or fair-skinned, Chinese, Mexican, African, or American. The body can thus be described as a crystallization of thought patterns conditioned by our karma—a process that began before birth and that will continue after it in an infinite expansion of life.

We can rightly say that we contain the seeds of past memories and the vestiges of recollections of former lives, not excluding the former lives of others. The scholar John Blofeld describes this well:

> What we call "life" is a single link in an infinitely long chain of "lives" and "deaths." Perhaps, if our unconscious could be raised to conscious level, we should be able to perceive the entire chain stretching back far enough to exceed the most generous estimates of the length of time human beings have populated this earth. (And why just this earth? Why should not many of our previous lives have been passed upon other earths contained within this stupendous universe?) Perhaps the recollection would include hundreds or thousands of millions of lives lived here or elsewhere, and at this or other levels of consciousness, perhaps in states of being previously unsuspected.[7]

Rebirth and the Aim of Life

The ultimate aim, to use this imprecise term, of a person with an aspiration to awakening is not rebirth—and with it the inevitable pains and sufferings attendant upon a body—but the unconditioned state of pure consciousness. What the true aspirant seeks is release from the pain and frustrations of numberless lives, from the endless wheel of rebirths, both for himself and for all beings.

As author John Blofeld has written:

> It is the outflows resulting from our varied responses to the play of phenomena which harness us to the wheel of life—"the torture wheel upon which the victim's

> bones are broken one by one and his flesh lacerated until, in his ignorance, he prays for the permanent death that is forever denied him. Bound by our own folly and stupidity to this wheel, we are dragged upwards and downwards through realms of life and death; every phenomenon produces a reaction within us, leading to some sort of outflow from our minds, which acts upon phenomena and causes them to react upon us yet again, and so on, endlessly, until wisdom is painfully achieved."[8]

As this vivid description makes clear, yet another rebirth is nothing to look forward to.

Simply stated, what propels us again and again into rebirth is the desire, the craving, the will for another body, coupled with the tightly held notion of oneself as a discrete entity. Rebirth, then, is the inevitable consequence of our not having attained full awakening and total integration in this lifetime. At the same time rebirth is another opportunity for awakening, assuming of course that one incarnates as a human being again. Remember, it is only through a human body that we can come to enlightenment—this is why human life is so precious. "Reexistence," then, is a halfway house on the way to one's true home. As Gandhi said (speaking of attaining the goal of *ahiṃsā* or nonviolence), "I cannot think of permanent enmity between man and man, and believing as I do in the theory of rebirth, I live in the hope that if not in this birth, in some other birth I shall be able to hug all humanity in friendly embrace."[9]

Rebirth Distinguished from Reincarnation

The doctrines of transmigration and reincarnation imply the existence of a soul and are simplifications of the teaching of rebirth, which is, admittedly, more difficult to grasp. The problem lies in the key term "soul." What we call our soul, or our self, is actually no more than a current of consciousness comprised of "thought-moments[10] of infinitestimal duration succeeding one another in a stream of inconceivable rapidity."[11] The speed and progress of this process, although always of lightning-fast duration, change according to the nature of the stimulation. If the catalyst is slight, the process functions without full cognition.

We can compare the process to a movie: the illusion of motion is created by numerous still frames moving in swift progression. It is also like a river: the body of water rushing before us is in reality made up of innumerable droplets of water flowing together.

The Buddhist scholar Francis Story explains "soul" more precisely:

> Much misunderstanding of the Buddhist doctrine of rebirth has been caused in the West by the use of the words "reincarnation," "transmigration" and "soul" . . . "Soul" is an ambiguous term that has never been clearly defined in Western religious thought; but it is generally taken to mean the sum total of an individual personality, an enduring ego-entity that exists more or less independently of the physical body and survives it after death. The "soul" is considered to be the personality-factor which distinguishes one individual from another, and is supposed to consist of the elements of consciousness, mind, character and all that goes to make up the psychic, immaterial side of a human being.
>
> The Buddha categorically denied the existence of a "soul" in the sense defined above. He recognized that all conditioned and compounded phenomena are impermanent, and this alone makes the existence of such a "soul" impossible.[12]

Reincarnation implies an independent, migrating soul substance that embodies itself in a new form. The teaching of rebirth, or the continuity of life, repudiates such a notion.

What Passes Over?

While there is no thread of continuity tangible to the senses, there is nonetheless a stream of continuity which can be called neither different nor identical. As the scholar T. R. V. Murti explains, "Rebirth does not mean the bodily transportation of an individual essence from one place to another. It only means that a new series of states arises, conditioned by the previous states."[13]

Many analogies have been used to describe the transmission process. Take a flame. If you light a candle with a match, is the flame in the candle the same as or different from the flame of the match? We have to say not the same and yet not different. Another analogy, one used by Ananda Coomaraswamy, is that of a billiard ball rolling against another such ball. "If another ball is rolled against the last stationary ball, the moving ball will stop dead and the foremost stationary ball will move on . . . The first moving ball does not pass over, it remains behind, it dies; but it is undeniably the *movement of that ball,* its momentum, its karma, and not any newly created movement, which is reborn in the foremost ball."[14]

If life is a sequence of moments linked in a chain of causation, the moment beyond death is the next link in the chain. As there has been a sense of continuity and yet no continuous self, there is nothing surprising in that sense of continuity's extending beyond the moment of death. Life is a series of events or happenings, and death takes its place in the series of events, giving rise to the next event. Thus there is no self that is reborn; there is an ongoing continuity of "again-becoming." In each moment of life the individual is born and dies, yet he continues. The same is true of the moment of death."[15]

So rebirth, or better, "again-becoming," does not involve the transfer of a substance but is better described as the continuation of the process which occurs at every moment of consciousness, continuing to operate to both affect and effect our rebirth.

We can't, then, say that the being that has just been reborn *is* your grandmother, nor can we say that it is *not.* The karma energy of the last thought of this life is the precipitating cause of our next life. This present life provides the basis for the quality of our death, which in turn conditions the nature of our next life.

What *is* it, then, that is reborn? To give it a name is to twist the truth to suit ourselves. An enlightened master said simply, "Not he, yet not another." Buddhaghosa, another sage, said, "It is a mere material and immaterial state, arising when it has obtained its conditions . . . it is not a lasting being, not a soul."

The Power of Will

The power of will is a tremendous force to be reckoned with. Anyone who has had a two-year-old can attest to that. This will has the power to extend through lifetimes.

Swami Vivekananda (1863–1902) wrote vividly of the will that perseveres through successive births:

> Such a gigantic will as that of a Buddha or Jesus could not be obtained in one life, for we know who their fathers were. It is not known that their fathers ever spoke a word for the good of mankind. The gigantic will which manifested Buddha and Jesus—whence came this accumulation of power? It must have been there through ages and ages, continually growing bigger and bigger until it burst on society as Buddha or Jesus, and it is rolling down even to the present day.[16]

Of all the needs we have—to create, to know, to experience life—nothing can compare with the will to develop oneself spiritually in order to free oneself and others from suffering. Yet it takes countless *lifetimes* of dedicated effort and single-minded determination in order to develop one's potential to the fullest so that this can be accomplished. It is impossible to burst full-blown into the world as a completely enlightened person without such preparation. Since the will to live again is conditioned by a need for self-development, a person will very likely be drawn to the state of existence most conducive to that activity. Remember: it is the *desire* or craving for a continuation of life, and the clinging to a notion of a separate individuality, that propel us again and again into new rounds of birth and death. V. F. Gunaratna puts it epigrammatically: "The will-to-live makes man re-live."[17]

It is important to understand that rebirth doesn't always lead upward; we devolve as well as evolve. Don't forget that a person's succeeding life isn't always a step up. If that person has set up negative causes and conditions in the past, they will ripen eventually, and that could mean a drop to a much lower rung on the ladder of existence. Given most people's limited vision, it is extremely difficult and painful to continue to do the things one needs to do to develop into a fully grown human being. What we *think* we want is often just a reflection of our superficial desires. Our deepest yearnings push and pull us on a subconscious level and drive us to what we truly need—even if it's not what we *think* we need or want. Oscar Wilde expressed this perfectly when he said that there are two kinds of unhappiness in the world: not getting what you want, and getting what you want.

A person who has truly seen into his True-nature—and this is possible for each one of us—has the advantage of knowing what he or she has to do. This is often accompanied with the strength—developed through steady and regular practice of meditation—to transcend the pain and difficulties that may accompany self-development.

There is another element also at work here. We could call it the principle of "like attracts like." The subconscious mind exerts a tremendous power to draw to itself others of similar inclination. People feel most comfortable with those who share similar interests and values: artists enjoy hobnobbing with other artists, musicians enjoy the company of musically inclined people, and the spiritually minded will commune with those who share their interests. On the other hand, thieves associate with underworld characters, drinkers with alcoholics, drug addicts with pushers; neurotics seek the company of other neurotics, and the mentally disturbed gravitate toward people who are unbalanced. On both a conscious and subconscious level we create our environment even as we participate in it.

It is impossible to live a life full of fear, anger, and pain-producing actions and then, at the moment of death, escape from karmic retribution by having a "good" thought. The last thought of a dying person has an initial impact on the rebirth, but the cumulative effect of the events of his or her life exerts a tremendous additional influence. Although a person might be afraid of rebirth and try to suppress the desire for another body, it is not possible to do so, because the habit forces of many lifetimes are still operating at the moment of death. Their next rebirth would be conditioned by their fear of retribution in that life. Accordingly, they might be reborn agoraphobic or severely repressed, or as a withdrawn, timid individual afraid of their own shadow. But in any case, they certainly would be reborn. Fear is a clinging to that which we fear; perversely, it is this clinging that brings us the very thing we fear or would most like to avoid.

Can Fear Be Carried from Life to Life?

There are many cases of people who have severe, unexplained fears that have been present from their earliest childhood. Children sometimes have aversions that border on the hysterical. I remember one mother telling me about her child. She said that he had been petrified of large bodies of water from the time he was an infant. He would be fine in the bathtub, but if they went on an outing to the beach, he screamed in such terror that they had to leave. He is a teenager now and he still does not enjoy being around lakes or oceans, although he is no longer as visibly frightened.

How would you explain such a phenomenon? If you look at the problem from the point of view of rebirth, it is entirely possible that the young man died at sea in a previous lifetime and took with him into his current life a terror connected with the experience. Naturally, there can be other interpretations for such fears, but this one is seldom, if ever, considered by traditional psychoanalysts.

Remembering Past Lives

Some people argue that if rebirth were true, we would all have some recollections from previous lives. But this doesn't really make sense. Do you remember all you did and learned in high school, or even in college? Yet you know that you were there. How many people remember all the incidents of their childhood, much less their birth itself? No one. Yet they never doubt that they were born. Many people cannot even recall their dreams of the night before. Since people's memories vary greatly in their capacity for both vividness and recall, memory is but shallow and inadequate proof of happenings of the past. Commenting on this phenomenon, Lama Govinda writes:

> They forget that active memory is only a small part of our normal consciousness, and that our subconscious memory registers and preserves every past impression and experience which our waking mind fails to recall.
>
> There are those who in virtue of concentration and other yogic practices are able to bring the subconscious into the realm of discriminate consciousness and thereby to draw upon the unrestricted treasury of subconscious memory wherein are stored records not only of our own past lives but the records of the past of our race, the past of humanity, and of all pre-human forms of life, if not of the very consciousness that makes life possible in this universe.[18]

Anyone who has had a loved one suddenly die knows that it is often very difficult to remember the events that took place immediately following the death. At such a time, everything may become suspended, vague, blurred; one may be in a state of shock. How much more difficult, then, must it be to remember the events of one's own death and subsequent rebirth. Also keep in mind that after death the consciousness-energy goes into an intermediate state, in which sensory impressions are not registered as clearly as they were during the physical existence. (See "The Intermediate Realm".)

Nevertheless, there are numerous case histories of people who have remembered one or more of their previous lives. One of the most convincing, thorough, and meticulously researched books on this subject is Ian Stevenson's *Twenty Cases Suggestive of Reincarnation.*[19] Dr. Stevenson has been Carlson Professor of Psychiatry at the University of Virginia Medical School and has served as chairman of the department of neurology and psychiatry. He currently heads the division of personality studies. While Stevenson's research does not provide proof in the conventional scientific sense, it offers persuasive testimony in a uniquely unbiased way, testimony that is devoid of the bizarre or supernatural trappings with which so many of these stories are presented elsewhere. Much of Stevenson's research was done in the Near and Far East, but he has also pursued cases in Africa, Europe, and this country. The focus of his studies is primarily children between the ages of three and five who spontaneously began talking about a previous lifetime.

It is very unlikely that these stories were just made up by the children or that they were deliberate fabrications put into the children's mouths by their parents. For one thing, the family, including the child, had nothing to gain from setting up such a ruse. There are no financial rewards given to people who report these memories, nor is there much in the way of publicity. Remember, in many cultures of the East memories of previous lives are not looked on as anything unusual. Since rebirth is accepted as a fact, it is a common assumption that some people will remember who they were in another life.

In a number of cases, moreover, the parents of these children were downright angry with them for persistently babbling on about their other family, the one they used to live with. Some parents punished their child for continuing to insist she had lived another life in another city. Stevenson affirms this when he says, "Even in cultures where reincarnation is accepted, parents sometimes think such memories are harmful. They are often upset by what the child remembers. Parents would not be particularly pleased to have a murdered child, not to mention a murderer, reincarnate in their family."[20]

In most of the cases reported by Stevenson, however, it was the child's determination to see the family of her past, and her unwavering stance about the facts of that existence, that finally forced the parents to ascertain whether or not what she said was true.

Another point is that there were usually a great many witnesses to the truth of the statements these children made. Stevenson and his coworkers cross-examined several children over a long period of time, and their stories proved amazingly accurate when verified.

Any discrepancies in their accounts are recorded, and often these involve such minor things as mispronounced names or the statement that a house was green instead of blue.

Finally, much of the information related by these remarkable children was of such a nature that no one in their family could possibly have had access to it. Just think: A child of four announces that his real name is not Edward but John. He gives his address in another town; neither he nor his parents have ever been there. He gives the names of his former parents, their occupations, and the stores where they commonly shopped. Then he relates various incidents that took place during that life—usually family events of a mundane nature, but occasionally peculiar occurrences. His parents eventually track down the address where the child used to live and take him there. Along the way he is able to recognize various landmarks and point out the house where he used to live—despite its having been painted in the intervening years. In some cases the child has picked out relatives from a large crowd of people. In other instances, he has pointed out changes in the house or surrounding area that only someone familiar with the vicinity could have recognized. In still more unusual cases, the child has spoken idiomatic phrases, or even carried on long conversations, in the language of his former existence, a language with which neither he nor his parents were even marginally familiar.[21]

It is less common for adults than for children, but there are some who do have this ability. Edgar Cayce, arguably the most noted and gifted psychic of our time, is an example of someone who was able to see into not only his past lives but those of others as well. His "readings," which illuminated in detail the workings of the law of causation and rebirth, are world famous. Cayce was born in 1877 on a Kentucky farm and raised by strict fundamentalist Christian parents. Although uneducated beyond the ninth grade, at age twenty-one he learned to induce extraordinary medical clairvoyance through self-hypnosis. After twenty-two years of healing others—frequently strangers living thousands of miles away—he discovered that his powers could be enlarged to see into their past lives. At first these "life readings," as they came to be called, caused the humble and self-doubting Cayce considerable anguish, for the doctrine of rebirth seemed to him in conflict with his literal interpretation of the Bible. But once he reconciled them, he devoted the rest of his life to helping many thousands of people trace their afflictions and limitations in the present to specific conduct in the past.

Scores of such cases, with the details confirmed, are presented in *Many Mansions* by the psychologist Gina Cerminara. Also included in the book is the case of a man anemic since birth who had, five lifetimes previously, seized political control of a country, shedding much blood. Another man's chronic digestive weakness was traced by Cayce to two previous lifetimes of gluttony. And in another case, a woman's poverty and misfortunes were seen as caused by her misuse of authority and wealth in a previous life in which she was part of French royalty.

In my years of teaching I have had several students who, I was convinced, had the ability to recall previous lifetimes. In Zen, however, there is no encouragement or emphasis given to this type of endeavor, since the purpose of spiritual training is not the development of psychic abilities but rather Self-realization, or enlightenment. It is very easy to get sidetracked from the path of spiritual discipline when one has strong psychic perceptions. It was for this reason that the thirteenth-century Zen master Dōgen said:

> There are those who have the supernatural power to know their past lives, whether as humans, animals, or some other form of sentient life. However, this supernatural power is not acquired by becoming enlightened . . . but is rather the result of bad karma in past lives . . . Even if you can understand the events of five hundred lifetimes a little, it is not really much of an ability.[22]

One of my students, who had many such memories, told me she was happy when the memories began to fade in intensity, enabling her to concentrate on what needed to be done in *this* life.

Nevertheless, these recollections can sometimes be helpful. One student told me the following story. For years she and a young man with whom she worked closely—he was one of her supervisors—

had an extremely antagonistic relationship. Try as she might, it was impossible for her to overcome her negative feelings for him. One day while she was meditating she suddenly saw herself dressed in unusual garb. She knew she was somewhere in middle Europe in the thirteenth century. (She told me the exact location and date.) Next she saw herself leaning over a cradle and looking at her baby boy; with anguish she realized he was deaf, blind, and mute. She then saw herself strangling the baby and feeling the baby's anger, which was directed toward her. When she remembered this, she was filled with horror and self-loathing. An instant later she saw herself in her next lifetime just as she was being condemned to burn at the stake by the very same being she had murdered in her previous life. She looked at the man with abhorrence and was shocked to see that it was the man whom, in this lifetime, she found so hard to tolerate.

Soon after she had this recollection, painful as it was—she told me she cried in despair for hours remembering the horrendous thing she had done—she decided to tell her antagonist about the memory. She told me:

> I was very apprehensive about telling John these things. I wondered if he would think I was a weirdo and our relationship would become worse than ever. But I felt it was our only chance to change the terrible karma we had been building together. When I told him the memory, he began to cry. I was crying too. Afterward he said to me, jokingly, "Well, Mom, I guess we've got a lot to work out. But knowing now that what we did to each other in the past is what is affecting our relationship today—this will make it easier to bury the hatchet." From that time on we became close friends.

Another case involved a husband and wife who were going through a painful divorce. The wife in particular was filled with bitterness toward her husband, who had been not only unfaithful to her but also, she felt, mentally abusive. One day the woman came to me and said that she remembered being with her husband in another lifetime, this time not as his wife but as a woman who wished to marry him. When he told her that he would not accept her, she became enraged and tried to poison him. After remembering this, she told me, she felt that she had a karmic debt to pay her husband, and that this was why she was suffering so much in their current relationship. She also said that she felt it imperative that they come to some accord in this lifetime, or else the negative karmic pattern that they had built up would be perpetuated. She and her ex-husband, it might be mentioned, now have a cordial relationship.

Stevenson mentions one case where a woman's memories of having committed suicide in her previous life deterred her from killing herself again. The knowledge that nothing would be over or solved and that she would have to face her problems in her next life was enough to make her reconsider and change her life.

For many people it is a kindness that they *don't* remember what they did in the past. Let me tell you about an incident that took place about fifteen years ago. A young man came to our center who was not very stable psychologically, but who felt a need for spiritual practice and tried hard to meditate. One day he was persuaded by a friend to see a psychic. That was the last we saw of him until he reappeared several years later—disheveled, destitute, and seriously disturbed. He had been told by the psychic that in his last life he had been a Nazi responsible for the deaths of many people. That information, along with some other events, was so traumatic that it precipitated a severe psychological collapse—one from which he has never recovered. This is an extreme example, but it probably is not unique.

Many people would be horrified to learn of the terrible things they had done in previous existences, and unless they had some means of understanding and atoning for their actions in past lives, they would become ill or very depressed. Emerson warned about dragging around "the corpse of memory." And Gandhi, in speaking of this same subject, said, "It is nature's kindness that we do not remember past births. Where is the good . . . of knowing in detail the numberless births we have gone through? Life would be a burden if we carried such a tremendous load of memories. A wise man deliberately forgets many things . . ."[23] Owen Rutter expressed the same sentiment when he wrote, "The obscuring of memory is surely merciful. The remembrance of all the wrongs we have done and all the wrongs which have been done to us, throughout our chain of lives, would be an intolerable burden. Most of us have enough to contend with in this life without burdening ourselves with the recollection of the dangers, the fears and the hates of other lives."[24]

It is worth noting that even those who are psychic and able to recall their own previous lives, make the mistake of believing that the only other lifetimes they lived were the ones they remember. They become very attached to those lives and say with pride, "In my last lifetime I was such and such a person." Unfortunately, all too often people who claim to have genuine memories of previous existences exhibit a singular predilection for lifetimes in which they were famous personages. Just think of all the people who have claimed to be Napoleon in a previous life! And he, ironically, often said, "Do you know who I am? I am Charlemagne." But in the greater scheme of things, what difference does it make? *Everyone* has had *innumerable* previous lifetimes—"as many as the sands in the river Ganges," as the ancient texts say. All life is life after death. It is folly to speak of the remembered lifetime as the only one! Nor should one identify with a remembered life of fame or power more than with one of humble circumstance.

Another important element is this: it is very difficult, if not impossible, to accurately interpret the data from former existences unless one is of a psychic bent himself. Even then mistakes can be made. Karmic connections and motivations are often vague, as I said earlier when we were discussing karma, and rarely can you easily relate a cause in one lifetime with an effect in another.

15

FURTHER IMPLICATIONS OF REBIRTH

The Moral Effects

There are obvious moral implications inherent in the law of rebirth and its other half, karma. To remember the pain-producing actions of one's previous lives, and to see their consequences in subsequent lives, lead one to the inescapable conclusion that in a basic sense we are the masters of our destiny. We ourselves are responsible for our life situation, be it good or bad. The salubrious effect of this belief has not been lost on the millions of Buddhists and other believers who look to themselves as the cause of their tribulations. One who is certain that sooner or later—if not in this life then in some other—what is reaped will be in accord with what has been sown will think twice before committing some evil.

The noted Orientalist Max Müller, speaking of rebirth, wrote:

> Whatever we may think of the premises on which this theory rests, its influence on human character has been marvelous. If a man feels that what, without any fault of his own, he suffers in this life can only be the result of some of his former acts, he will bear his sufferings with more resignation, like a debtor who is paying off an old debt. And if he knows besides that in this life he may

actually lay by moral capital for the future, he has a motive for goodness . . . Nothing can be lost.[25]

There is more evidence of the moral effect this belief exerted on people in times past. A British census of approximately one hundred years ago gave these figures on crimes committed in India: "Among Europeans, 1 conviction for every 274 people; among native Christians, 1 in every 799 people; among Buddhists, 1 for every 3,787 people."[26]

Two indispensable elements produce the deep awareness essential to establishing moral behavior. They are a concern for the karmic consequences of our actions in subsequent existences, and an uncertainty about the fruits those actions will bear. To be unable to establish the specific incident from a previous lifetime which produced our suffering in this life, and yet to affirm, "My own acts are the ultimate cause," is indicative of a deeply spiritual orientation.

Heredity, Environment, or Karma?

Physical characteristics are not intrinsic to the life force or thought force that passes over from death to rebirth. What is inherited from our previous lives is manifested through genetic constitution, external circumstances, and certain tendencies. Fears, affinities, and various other emotional inclinations may also pass over. The interplay of external conditions with karmic forces molds and influences the new being, who also has the power to alter his circumstances. While it is axiomatic that a baby born to black parents will be black, or one born to Caucasians will be white, there is nevertheless a wide range of characteristics over which the individual's attitude has its pull. Francis Story describes it this way:

> Here the principle of attraction comes into play; the thought force gravitates naturally towards what is most in affinity with it, and so to some extent creates, and certainly modifies, its circumstances. These also act upon

> the awakening consciousness, so that heredity and environment both have a share in molding the new personality. If the past karma was bad, these external conditions will reflect that "badness," so that it is only by a new effort of will that the mind can rise above their influence and fashion for itself a better destiny.[27]

Of course, some people might look similar, if not the same, from lifetime to lifetime—provided, of course, they are born as humans each time. There are many intriguing cases of people with unusual physical characteristics who claim to have had those identical marks in a previous life. Birthmarks, too, may well be an inherited physical karmic tendency, since no one knows why certain people have them and others do not. Stevenson has been doing some fascinating research on birthmarks for over a decade. Comparing the past-life memories of children who have unusual birthmarks and birth defects with postmortem reports of injuries in their alleged previous life, he has found a correlation between the injuries in the previous life and the birthmarks in the present. He feels that these records will "provide the strongest evidence we have so far in favor of reincarnation."[28]

If our physical and emotional characteristics did come solely from heredity and environment, how would one explain the unusual circumstances surrounding identical twins separated at birth? Studies have shown the astonishing similarities of these twins' behavior, including such things as the names of people they married, dates of marriage, names and ages of their children, and predilections in clothing, food, hobbies, and occupations. Even if it were true that all these coincidences were purely a result of their shared genetic background, there is still room for consideration of karma and rebirth's having exercised an influence on their lives. Why is this so? Because everyone *chooses* his or her future parents. Thus, from a Buddhist point of view, we also choose the appropriate genetic influences, as well as the immediate pre- and postnatal environment, that will affect our future behavior.

It can be said that heredity and environment are, on the physical plane, the manifestations of the spiritual laws of rebirth and karma.

Since it is virtually impossible to isolate which of the factors—karma, genetics, or environment—is exerting the most influence on a person's life, all one can do is to say the data supports both explanations, and to bear in mind that karma is transmitted in part through heredity and environment. As we know, the genes an individual receives from his ancestors through his parents are only one contribution to the personality.[29]

Without some belief in karma and rebirth, how would one explain, for example, such occurrences as early childhood phobias, the spontaneous development of extraordinary abilities in children, incidents of transsexuality, idiot savants, childhood autism, child prodigies born to ordinary parents, and even exceptionally strong preferences dating from infancy? Those who believe in rebirth have no trouble accepting that these phenomena are related to or stem from incidents that took place in past lives. "It is only if rebirth is taken to mean the transmigration of a 'soul,' " writes Francis Story, "that there is any conflict between [rebirth] and the known facts of genetics."[30] One geneticist with whom I spoke told me, "No geneticist who is not a Nazi would try to make a strong case for the immutable determination of behavior by the genes. There is hard evidence that our genetic makeup may predispose us to certain *patterns* of behavior. Nevertheless, other factors also play important determining roles."[31] Clearly, then, biological and sociological explanations still leave many questions unanswered.

Parents, Children, and Rebirth

The karmic bond between parent and child is very strong. Since parents are the vehicles for our births, we owe them a tremendous debt of gratitude. We are attracted to and born through parents (one or both) with whom we have a karmic affinity. That affinity also forges the bond between them and us. In healthy family relationships it is the unconditional love children feel from their parents that supports them throughout their lives. Human children have an exceptionally long period of total dependence, and without the love and help of parents or another adult, they cannot survive.

It has actually been shown that infants who are deprived of love will fail to thrive and may even die. They become depressed and withdrawn, showing signs of both physical and psychic distress.

Think of all the times you've seen movies or heard stories of a young man on the threshold of death calling out to his mother or father. For better or worse, our parents' influence—their presence or absence, their care or lack of it, their morals or debaucheries, their ideals or hypocrisy—pervades our lives, even as we simultaneously affect our parents.

Now, one question that arises is, if beings are so strongly attracted to their parents, how do you explain miscarriages and stillbirths? Or, even more puzzling why would a mother abort her child? Actually, the great anguish these events cause for the parents, especially the mother, is evidence of the strong attraction that exists between the parents and the unborn child. Only the rare mother-to-be is indifferent to the fact of her pregnancy and the child she carries. It is not uncommon for women to be more careful of their bodies during this time: they stop drinking alcohol and caffeine, stop smoking, start exercising, and begin eating more balanced meals—all for the sake of their babies. Unfortunately, there are also cases of mutually negative attachment, such as when the being-to-be is drawn to a drug addict who makes no attempt to cure her addiction for the sake of the baby.

Negative mutual attachment is also evident in cases of abortions undergone without coercion. Although the unborn being is attracted to a particular set of parents, the mother, because of karmic circumstances at the time of conception, is unable to acquiesce in the being's choice of her as a mother. Talking with women who were contemplating an abortion, I have seen the confusion, anxiety, and pain which they faced. Their decision to abort was made in anything but a casual or indifferent manner and was arrived at after much deep searching. There was an undeniable bond between the mothers and these unknown beings within them—a bond that was severed with great pain. It is important to recognize that more than one set of causes must be present for someone to be reborn, the will to live being only one cause. Also indispensable are parents who are physically able to reproduce, and the mother's willingness to carry the baby throughout the pregnancy. This is not to say that the mother is responsible for miscarriages and stillbirths. There can be, however, contributing factors of both a physical and a karmic nature that make the pregnancy impossible to continue. Remember that the being-to-be is only one half the picture. While it has its karmic impulse to be born, the mother also has her karma, one which might not include having a child at that time.

Another possibility is that the karma of the unborn child was not strong enough to carry him throughout the pregnancy. Perhaps his karmic bond with the mother was tenuous; or perhaps, due to effects stemming from causes in previous lifetimes, he was only able to sustain a short existence in this life. We really don't know.

In the case of early miscarriages, it may be that the life force never joined with the ovum and sperm to produce a viable embryo. But this, too, is conjecture. Orthodox Buddhist psychology believes that from the moment of conception the being-to-be has a mind that is aware at a "bare state of subconsciousness identical with the . . . adult consciousness during dreamless sleep."[32]

You can see, then, that the sad occurrences of miscarriages, stillbirths, and abortions do not mean that the craving for life and attraction to the parent are absent; rather, these events mean that there are additional karmic factors at work.

Rebirth and Special Affinities and Aptitudes

A person who is immersed in a certain endeavor throughout his life—for example, mathematics—can become so obsessed with the subject that it becomes the focal point of his existence. The same can be said of music, dance, art, sports—the list could go on and on. Such a passion would decidedly affect a person's karma and subsequent rebirth.

As we know, there are many children who seem to inherit the aptitudes of one or both of their parents for such things. If a father is an artist and his daughter is similarly inclined, someone is bound to say, "She gets her talent from her father." And if neither the father nor the mother has a skill that their child displays, you will probably hear, "It must have come from Grandpa," or Great

Auntie, or someone else in the family tree. But occasionally a child develops a talent that cannot be so easily explained—no one in the family has ever had this ability to anyone's knowledge. Might it be possible that the child possessed his or her talent even *before* being born into this life?

Consider the uncanny abilities of child prodigies. From ancient times to the present there have been numerous instances of remarkable children who have displayed extraordinary precocity in such fields as music, art, language, science, or mathematics. It is common knowledge that Mozart, who was born into a musical family, was composing by the age of four, but we must also consider Handel, whose interest in music was roundly discouraged by his parents. There are many other cases of children who developed outstanding talents at an early age, such as Giannella de Marco, who in 1953 at the age of eight conducted the London Philharmonic Orchestra; Dimitris Sgouros, who at the age of seven gave his first solo piano recital, and at the age of twelve graduated from the Athens Conservatory of Music with the first prize and the title of professor of piano; Marcel Lavallard, who was an accomplished artist by the age of twelve; and Tom Wiggins, the blind child of a slave, who was a concert pianist by the age of four, despite the fact that his intelligence was so low he could barely speak. Yet never has science adequately explained why such phenomena occur. Is it not more plausible to believe that these remarkable cases stem simply from accomplishments in a former life? Dr. Leslie Weatherhead suggests that rebirth is the answer:

> Is it an accidental group of genes that makes a little girl of eight a musician far in advance of grown men and women, who have slaved for many years in that field? Is it a piece of luck that a boy of fourteen can write perfect Persian? If so, life seems unjust as well as chancy. Or is it that they have been here before? Plato believed wholeheartedly in reincarnation, and his famous "Theory of Reminiscence" asserted that "knowledge easily acquired is that which the enduring self had in an earlier life, so that it flows back easily." In the dialogue *Meno*, Socrates

shows that an untutored slave boy knew mathematical facts which in this life had never been taught him. "He had forgotten that he knew them . . . To Socrates it was self-evident that the boy's capacity was the result of an experience he had had in a previous lifetime."

One wonders why men have so readily accepted the idea of a life *after* death and so largely, in the West, discarded the idea of a life *before* birth.[33]

Near-Death Experiences

It was primarily the research and writing of Dr. Elisabeth Kübler-Ross in the mid-1970s that brought the phenomena of near-death experiences to light. She stirred up a great deal of controversy when she claimed that the extraordinary similarities in hundreds of stories from people who had had near-death experiences proved that there was life after death. At first she found that many people were reluctant to discuss their experiences for fear of being labeled insane. But when they did talk about what had happened to them, she was struck by the harmony and beauty of what others assumed was an ordeal.

In the last twenty-five years, so many people have reported these episodes that there are now even clubs where people can compare what happened to them. A Gallup poll reported that "35 percent of those who had suffered a brush with death had felt the near-death phenomenon. Using those figures, Gallup estimated eight million Americans have undergone such experiences."[34]

Kübler-Ross claimed that many of the people who underwent these experiences "resented our desperate attempts to bring them back to life. Death is the feeling of peace and hope. Not one of them has ever been afraid to die again."[35] Other studies have shown that people who have undergone a near-death episode become more sensitive, more religious, and less materialistic than they were before. Experiencers often find themselves consumed with a desire to be of service to others. Dr. Bruce Greyson, a psychiatrist at the University of Connecticut Health Center, says that "The most common aftereffect is that they no longer are afraid of dying. They are freed up to live their lives."[36]

A couple of years ago I talked at some length with one of my students who had had a near-death episode. He was in the hospital when he stopped breathing. He said that he felt himself gently float out of his body and that he watched the frantic efforts to resuscitate him. He told me he was able to read a small sign on the other side of the room. He could also see his doctor's distraught face, even though the doctor's back was to him, and he was able to read the doctor's thoughts. Later, when my student was past the crisis, he spoke with his doctor, who verified what he (the doctor) had been thinking at the time. My student said he felt great peace and wondered what all the fuss was about. In the end, the thought of leaving his wife and children made him decide to return to his body, albeit reluctantly.

The experience had a dramatic effect on this man. Soon after he regained his health, he sold his business and went into a different line of work—one that he had always wanted to be in but that had before seemed impossible. He also made several other major changes in his lifestyle—all for the better. And he told me that the experience totally erased all fear of death. "Death," he said, "has completely lost its mystery for me. I am absolutely not afraid to die."

What is going on here? Some physicians dismiss these reports as no more than hallucinations caused by chemical reactions in the brain—reactions induced either by lack of oxygen or by drugs in the system. Others admit that they really haven't the foggiest notion as to what's going on, but that obviously *something* is happening.

From a spiritual point of view, something indeed is going on. What these people are experiencing is the initial phase of the journey to rebirth, the *first* stage of death. The near-death experience is analogous to taking an airplane trip to a foreign country very different from our own and barely getting out of the airplane at the airport. Many experiences await you, as they do for everyone else on board, but until you actually leave the airport and begin your sojourn, your experience and those of the other passengers are roughly equal. Many people who have had a near-death experience, and researchers too, mistake these experiences as *the* afterlife, not realizing that there are stages of death leading to inevitable rebirth in another existence.

We see in the laws of karma and rebirth the very keynotes to the evolution of humankind. Swami Paramananda superbly summarizes the beauty of these laws:

> Reincarnation is not, as is supposed by many hasty thinkers, a pagan doctrine; it has its roots in the very foundation of the spiritual world. It explains the incongruity of life in the light of reason. It offers us consolation in the deepest sense. It makes clear that our disadvantages and our sufferings are not imposed upon us by an arbitrary hand, but are the fulfillment of just laws. Also it teaches us that our lost opportunities are not taken away from us forever. We are given new chances that we may learn, that we may evolve . . . Nothing of real value is ever lost, nor our misdeeds, our cruel and treacherous acts, forgotten until we have atoned for them. It is not that some being is keeping account of our thoughts and deeds, but we ourselves keep a complete record . . . and we reap the sum total of these thoughts and deeds in our every embodiment.[37]

The most profound mysteries of life and death are within our grasp. If we understand that life holds the secret of death, just as death embodies the secret of life, we can live with greater peace in our hearts and greater love for all living beings.

APPENDIXES

APPENDIX A

LIVING WILLS

WE LIVE IN A WORLD of ever-expanding medical treatment options, where more decisions are the responsibility of patients than ever before.[1] Some of the most important medical decisions we will ever make arise as we near the end of our lives. By preparing adequately for death we not only reduce the decision-making burden on our families, we also engender greater clarity in ourselves. The best way to plan for death is to:

1. create advance medical directives, setting forth in writing our wishes as best we can;
2. appoint a health care agent to deal with the unexpected circumstances that are sure to arise; and
3. find out what kinds of end-of-life assistance are available from our physician.

LIVING WITH TECHNOLOGY

In the developed world, life has become inextricably integrated with technology. We are born, live and die in an engineered realm. Eighty percent of us die in hospital beds.[2] It is said that "Nature never failed the heart that loved her," but for most of us, that love is one-sided. We are but half-hearted naturalists. We welcome the joy of natural good health, but we fight against the equally natural ills to which we are also susceptible.

This supplement was written by Casey Frank, a senior disciple of Roshi Philip Kapleau and an attorney working in the area of bioethics.

Through medicine we reduce pain and disability and improve the quality and length of life. We explicitly choose when to *do* much that in the past would simply have happened *to* us. We control reproduction, extend life, and have an increasing number of options around how we die. End-of-life choices evoke profound concerns and anxieties, both because they are unfamiliar to us and because they are of ultimate consequence. However, they are the ineluctable extension of a world where autonomy has become paramount.

The Rise of Patient Autonomy

Historically, physician beneficence toward patients was the controlling principle of medical practice. More recently, patient autonomy has become the ascendent ethic.[3] Autonomy is usually seen as the right to refuse treatment. This right became rooted in law following a landmark case where it was ruled that: "Every human being of adult years and sound mind has a right to determine what shall be done with his own body."[4] Patient autonomy has also expanded to encompass the right of surrogates to refuse treatment on behalf of patients[5] and a patient's limited right to die.[6] A difficulty arises when we cannot make or communicate our wish to receive treatment—or to be left alone.

This determination of when we are actually unable to make and communicate our own medical treatment decisions is usually made by the treating physician, who tests whether we lack the capacity to give informed consent. Informed consent requires that we understand the risks and benefits of any medical decision. It is limited to that issue alone.

Our treatment decisions must be voluntary and informed—that is, based on adequate information supplied to us by our physician. Properly, physicians look to see that we:

1. express treatment choices;
2. understand and retain sufficient medical information over time;

3. are able to articulate relevant issues; and
4. can do a simple risk-benefit analysis.

Next, we must be able to communicate our choices clearly. If we are unconscious, delirious, or paralyzed, this is obviously impossible and makes informed consent unrealizable. It is, in effect, the same as mental incapacity. Thus, it is vital that we plan ahead while we have the time and faculties. The best way to do this is by creating written advance directives. Everyone who is not a minor should do this. Some of the most famous and contentious situations regarding patient autonomy have involved people who were in their twenties and in good health before they became incapacitated, like Karen Quinlan and Nancy Cruzan.

Advance Directives

Advance directives allow a patient not only to refuse unwanted treatment but also to request it as desired. The purpose of advance directives is to predict our future treatment decisions and provide guidance to caregivers and family members. These directives usually come into play only when a patient is unable to give informed consent directly, as discussed above. If a patient doesn't provide guidance for future decisions, then families and physicians must make these decisions in an atmosphere of urgency and uncertainty. Directives give voice to a patient's views when they cannot be voiced directly. They do not deprive a person of personal autonomy but preserve and extend it into the future.

These advance directives have become more popular since they were used by President Nixon and Jackie Kennedy. President Bill Clinton and Hillary Clinton have also announced their intention to provide advance directives for their own care and treatment.[7] All federally funded hospitals must provide written guidance for creating directives upon the admission of a patient (although they cannot require their creation).[8]

What if you become incapacitated before creating an advance directive? If you have no close relative, a guardian may need to be appointed. The power of a guardian is based on a court order issued after a formal hearing. A guardian must act in the best interests of the incapacitated person.[9] A court-appointed guardian is less subject to challenge than a health care agent. The procedure of appointing a guardian is more expensive and time-consuming than that of creating advance directives and thus is utilized only as a last resort. As a practical matter, as long as there are written directives or, alternately, if there is someone to speak for the patient and there is no conflict among family members, a guardian should not be necessary.[10]

Health Care Agents

The most important advance directive appoints a health care agent, also known as a surrogate, or proxy, who can make decisions on behalf of a patient. The majority of health care decisions that need to be made involve day-to-day care and treatment or placement options—not just "pulling-the-plug." Because there is no way to address every medical possibility in advance, it is essential to have an agent who can respond to the unforeseeable.

An in-depth discussion of your options with your physician is essential to clarify your own wishes. You must then communicate your decisions and your sensibilities to your agent. Though the directive appointing the agent should be in writing, nothing can replace face-to-face communication in helping an agent understand your views. You should also discuss these issues with your family, to avoid surprises and reduce the possibility of dissension later on.

The legality of withholding food and water is a special case in many states. Often food and water cannot be withdrawn unless all treatment has also been withheld. Further, the presumption that a patient wants them is stronger than for less "essential" treatments. Thus, you should express your wishes explicitly in writing if you wish to have food and water withheld, and you should clarify under what circumstances this measure should be implemented.

Living Wills

The best known advance directives are living wills, written to prohibit the excessive prolonging of the dying process. Living wills are valid only if a patient is in a terminal medical condition from which there is no reasonable expectation of recovery. Living wills are limited to *refusal* of treatment. Because they are limited in what they cover, they are no substitute for the appointment of an agent. Another limitation of living wills with no agent is that they may be ignored by your physician unless you have an agent to interpret and facilitate them.[11] However, if your state legally allows it, a combined directive, which both appoints an agent and gives specific instructions though a living will, is ideal. Further, if you have no one to act as your agent, a living will can afford the best opportunity for expressing your wishes.

Remember, advance directives on the whole are not limited to mere refusal of treatment. They are also your opportunity to communicate the level of treatment you desire. For example, your advance directive can specify the desired level of pain relievers you wish to receive and in what circumstances food and water should be withheld. Advance directives give us the opportunity to share our personal decisions about these issues.

Some Troublesome Issues

One makes a directive while still somewhat distant from the events that it addresses. Usually people who have chosen to forego life-sustaining treatments do not later change their minds.[12] The very process of creating an advance directive helps you to think through and stabilize your treatment choices. But there have been cases where people have recovered from an unconscious condition thought to be irreversible[13] and this, understandably, raises a disturbing question about the wisdom of withholding life-sustaining treatments. However, these are rare exceptions. Very few persons rendered unconscious by trauma for months ever return to functional lives.[14]

Another emerging risk of advance directives is the possibility that they may leave a patient at the mercy of a financially frugal HMO or an unscrupulous nursing home administrator, who might want to save money by withholding treatment prematurely, inadvertently hastening a patient's death. This problem can be mitigated by having a health care agent.

Resources

Forms to guide the creation of advance directives are available from Choice in Dying, 200 Varick Street, New York, NY 10014, Tel: (800) 989-9455; website: www.choices.org; email: cid@choices.org. In Europe, contact the *World Federation of Right-to-Die Societies,* 61 Minterne Avenue, Norwood Green, Southall, Middlesex, England UB2 4HP; Tel: (44)181-574-3775.

You may wish to have your lawyer draw up your advance directives. It is advisable to use the form accepted in your state, although you can customize it to suit your choices. Using your state's accepted form ensures that it will be legally enforceable and familiar to your health care provider. Have your directives witnessed by two adults and notarized. And it is essential to give copies to your doctor, your lawyer, close family members, and anyone else who might be in a position to make—or contest—a decision about your medical treatment. Keep a copy of the directives in a very convenient place readily available in an emergency.

Physician Assistance for the Dying

So-called physician-assisted suicide has polarized public opinion in the United States. Adamant opponents liken it to Nazi eugenics; adamant supporters cast it as a simple question of personal freedom. "Physician assistance for the dying" is really a better way to describe this process, as a patient's quest for a dignified death and a physician's assistance at the end of life involve much more than the solitary issue of assisted suicide. Pain relief, other palliative or comfort care, mutual communication, respect for the autonomy of the patient, and respect for the judgment of the physician are all important. We need to explore these issues with our physicians while we are lucid, so we can understand what kind of help might be provided to us.

Many see a physician's role to be that of a collaborator with his patients—one that continues until death itself. This goes beyond the mere prolongation of life and could even include helping someone to die.[15] Certainly most physicians strive to help their patients heal without wanting to consider the final option. However, some incurably ill patients suffer mightily in spite of the best efforts of their physicians.[16] Although physician assistance in dying invokes legitimate concerns, it would be overly partisan to reject it out of hand.[17] Following is a discussion of several key issues in this debate.

Untreated Mental Illness

Physician assistance in dying should only follow the patient's competent, settled decision to die. Mental states where we cannot grasp the consequences of our decision, treatable clinical depression, or temporary feelings of despair may make death seem desirable.[18] In these circumstances, physician-assisted suicide cannot be justified. The consequences of an intentional death are so great that they must be reflected upon with deliberate seriousness, as discussed earlier in the section "Suicide and Euthanasia."

Untreated Physical Symptoms

The wish to die is often related to unrelieved or under-treated physical pain. For this reason, all options to relieve a patient's physical pain should be thoroughly explored before physician-assisted suicide is considered. A much-needed emphasis on palliative care, including pain-relief, is gaining support in many states. Hospice physicians and oncologists are among the most skilled in adequate pain relief.[19]

Vulnerability of the Disenfranchised

Members of minorities, the disabled, the elderly, and the poor are especially vulnerable to the inherent biases that characterize society. Consequentially, these groups fear that, since they are disenfranchised, they may be more likely to be encouraged to die. Surveys appear to show that this is why a clear majority of the poor, the elderly and blacks oppose legalization of physician-assisted suicide, even though an overall majority of Americans support it.[20]

Physicians' Objections

Even if we accept that patient autonomy has become paramount, physicians should not be required to sacrifice their own moral integrity to meet the patient's wishes.[21] Many physicians make a clear distinction between their duty to "first do no harm" and assisting a patient to intentionally end his or her life. They are concerned that such assistance will dilute the mission of the profession. Physicians with good-faith conscientious objections could simply excuse themselves from participation. The recently proposed laws that would legalize physician assistance in dying would also protect physicians' right to do so.[22]

The Law

In 1991, Dr. Timothy Quill published an explicit account of his efforts to assist a severely ill patient to die.[23] Although the actions described were widely practiced and ages-old, they had usually been performed *sub-rosa.*[24] Indeed, one of Dr. Quill's aims was to stimulate an open discussion of these practices and to end their secretive application.[25]

Two legal cases, including one in which Dr. Quill was the defendant, were combined and decided by the U.S. Supreme Court. The Court ruled that the right to die can be limited by states to the patient's refusal of treatment. Thus, no patient currently has a right to affirmative assistance in dying under the U.S. Constitution.[26] In some states such assisted suicide still constitutes manslaughter.[27] Until states give physicians license to act freely in concert with their patients at the end of life, patients are limited to explicitly refusing treatment and to receiving treatments that are classified as having a "double effect." For example, the administering of opiates to reduce pain can have the added effect of suppressing respiration and shortening life. The intended effect is pain relief; the unintended but unavoidable—and thus permitted—effect can be death.

Conclusion

According to a recent study, 53 percent of physicians treating AIDS victims have assisted a patient in dying.[28] Is it better to accept this reality or hold fast to an older view of a doctor's role? The American Medical Association opposes physician-assisted suicide and submits that better care will eliminate the need.[29] Others have suggested criteria for the direct regulation of physician assistance in dying.[30] Clinical criteria, guidelines, and the necessary forms are available from some physician groups, in spite of the fact that the process is currently illegal.[31] Resolution of this momentous issue is nowhere near consensus, so it must be resolved by each of us as best we can.

APPENDIX B

HOSPICE CARE

THE HOSPICE MOVEMENT, which has so revitalized the care of the terminally ill in England and America, was begun by health care professionals who were dissatisfied with the quality of care available to those whose diseases could not be cured and who were nearing death. Typically, before hospice, these patients found themselves in the intensive care unit of a hospital, treated more like an object or a diseased entity than a dying human being, despite the very best of intentions. Instead of being lent support and comfort in their last hours, they were stripped, willy-nilly, of their dignity and composure by the very institutions and machines designed to help them. Alternatively, those who were nearing death would have been at home, isolated from loved ones by mutual exhaustion, by feelings of uncertainty and guilt, by the disease and its pain, or by the sedation prescribed to blunt that pain.

The family of the dying patient is often beset with stresses—physical, emotional, spiritual, and financial—that very often lead to disease, both physical and mental, in the bereaved. Meanwhile, for the dying patient these stresses are not uncommonly exacerbated by medical protocols and an institutional environment designed for those who will recover, not for those who are dying.

The search for a better context in which to care for the dying led to a rediscovery of the medieval concept of hospice. The word *hospice* comes from the Latin word for hospitality; and the medieval hospice, or place of hospitality, opened its doors to those who most needed help: the pilgrim, the traveler far from home, the sick, and those with incurable diseases. Some hospices were large, well appointed, and famous—such as the hospice of the Knights Hospitaller at Rhodes—while others must have been the simplest of cottages; but all had in common the ideal of service. Whether run by monks or nuns, members of lay orders, or simply those who felt a vocation of caring, hospices, at their best, embodied a spiritual attitude that has all but vanished in the evolution of the modern hospital.

Of course, much of the problem has to do with attitudes about death that we have in the West. Arnold Toynbee put it, "Death is un-American." Death threatens our cherished myths—of technical omnipotence, of the forever fresh and conquerable frontier, of the permanence of our productions. Our denial of death amounts to a denial of life, and in this milieu the modern hospice has arisen as a compassionate affirmation of life, with power to heal the living as well as the dying. Hospices, both ancient and modern, are built on the quiet confidence that death, like life, is a kind of pilgrimage, though a beginningless and endless one.

In a hospice setting the patient is seen not as a person with an incurable and terminal disease, but as a person with symptoms (for example, pain) that can be treated and usually controlled to a great extent. This palliative care is not aimed primarily at extending life but at increasing the quality of that life. Symptoms are treated as synergistic, that is, they are not regarded as being in isolation from each other. As one British hospice director says to his staff: "Don't just treat the pain, treat the situation." All this results in a positive attitude among hospice workers, the patient, and the family. The foremost goal of hospice care is an alert, pain-free existence for patients in order to help them live as fully as possible until they die.

Most hospices encourage people to remain at home, where this is appropriate, since inpatient care is limited by space to those who need it most. More important, when the family can provide a substantial portion of the care, there is a greater chance for personal growth, for resolution of long-standing family problems, and, after the patient's death, there is less chance of guilt and self-doubt. Volunteers are often crucial in assisting the family to keep a person home through difficult experiences. Hospice staff is on call twenty-four hours per day, seven days per week.

All hospices offer some type of inpatient care. Inpatient care can be in a stand-alone hospice building or in a designated unit on a hospital floor where the staff has been trained in hospice work. But what is universal in these settings is that the patient will be allowed to rest, their pain will be skillfully addressed, and their family will have unlimited access.

An important part of a well-run hospice program is the volunteers who assist it. Volunteers often seem able to meet a patient on the patient's own ground. Because no one is paying them to work, they are uniquely able to help a patient keep his or her sense of self-worth. Volunteers are an important part of the spiritual atmosphere of a hospice, and they frequently become closer friends of the dying than professionals are able to. By providing respite for the family, sitting vigil at the time of death, or by just providing a caring presence for the dying, they bring the spirit of hospice to life.

Hospice is now widely available. There are over twenty-five-hundred hospices across the United States. Hospice care is fully covered by Medicare and Medicaid as well as by most insurers. If you have a family member you wish to refer to hospice, you may call the hospice directly or you may wish instead to call your physician to ask him or her to do this for you. The reason it is helpful to have the doctor involved in the referral is that the doctor will be asked by the hospice to state that to the best of his knowledge the person's prognosis is less than six months. The patient need not be aware of the prognosis; he or she only needs to know that no more aggressive treatment will be sought.

Those who are interested in hospice care should investigate as much as possible the quality of care provided and the degree to which hospice principles are followed in a given hospice, using the same care they would exercise in choosing a doctor.

Hospice Care

The following organizations supply information on hospice care:

National Hospice Organization
1901 N. Fort Meyer Drive, Suite 307
Arlington, VA 22209
(703) 243-5900
The web site is: www.NHO.org

Children's Hospice International
1101 King Street, Suite 131
Alexandria, VA 22314
(703) 684-0330

APPENDIX C

WHAT TO DO UPON SOMEONE'S DEATH: A CHECKLIST

THE FOLLOWING is a list of things that need to be done immediately following a death. It was compiled, in part, from Ernest Morgan's *A Manual of Death Education and Simple Burial*[32] and Deborah Whiting Little's *Home Care for the Dying.*[33] If organs are to be donated—and organs can only be accepted under certain circumstances of death and condition of the body—the family should let the hospital know before death. The hospital will contact the appropriate transplant coordinator, who may get in touch with the family. The organs of a person who dies at home are not suitable for donation.

1. Call the person's physician within an hour after the death. If the medical examiner or coroner must be notified, ask the doctor to do so.

   If the death occurs in a hospital, advise the nurse that you believe the person has died. The nurse will call the doctor to have the person declared dead. Generally, unless organs are to be donated, the family will have plenty of time to say their final farewells before the body is removed from the room, especially if the mortician is not notified until the family has finished.

2. If the body is being donated to a medical school, call the school, inform them that the donor has died, and arrange for transportation.
3. If funeral arrangements have already been made, notify the mortician as to when you want the body to be transported.
4. If pallbearers are to be used, select and notify them.
5. Notify anyone else who is to have a role in the services.
6. Arrange for family members or friends to take turns answering the telephone and the door at the home of the deceased. Keep a careful record of all calls.
7. List immediate family, close friends, and employer or business associates of the deceased, and inform them by telephone of the death.
8. Coordinate the supplying of food for the next few days and take care of other things that need to be done, such as cleaning. When coordinating the food supply, keep in mind the presence of possible out-of-town relatives and friends.
9. If child care is required, arrange for it.
10. Arrange accommodations for visiting relatives and friends.
11. Decide where memorial gifts can be sent if flowers are to be omitted. If flowers are to be accepted, decide what is to happen to them after the funeral.
12. Write an obituary for the newspapers. This commonly includes the age, place of birth, cause of death, occupation, college degrees, military service, organization memberships, any outstanding accomplishments, names of survivors in the immediate family, and names of any memorials set up in lieu of flowers. It is unwise to list publicly the date and time of services, as this gives a clear indication to thieves of when the house of the deceased will be empty.

    Deliver the obituary to the appropriate newspaper offices; there may be a charge to print it.

13. If the deceased was living alone, notify the utilities and the landlord of the death; notify the post office and indicate where to forward mail.
14. Notify the lawyer and the executor of the estate. Get original copies of the death certificate, as these will be required by several institutions.
15. Notify by mail any distant friends and relatives.
16. Investigate possible insurance and death benefits (Social Security, credit union, trade union, fraternal, military, and so forth) and any income for survivors from these.
17. Review all debts and installment payments. There can be delays in the transfer of assets and in other financial settlements at the time of death; if such delays will occur, make arrangements with creditors to delay any payments that do not carry insurance clauses that would cancel further payments outright.
18. To those who telephoned or sent flowers or other memorials, as well as those who helped with food, child care, or other matters, send appropriate acknowledgments and thanks. Include any nurses or other health care professionals who helped care for the person prior to death.
19. If the person died at home, arrange for return of any rented equipment.

APPENDIX D

CONSOLING THE BEREAVED: DO'S AND DON'TS[34]

1. DO let your genuine concern and caring show.
2. DO say you are sorry about what happened to their loved one and about their pain.
3. DO allow them to express as much grief as they are feeling and are willing to share.
4. DO be available to listen, run errands, help with children, or whatever else seems needed at the time.
5. DO allow them to talk about their loved one as much and as often as they want.
6. DO talk about the special memories and endearing qualities of the one who has died.
7. DO reassure them that they did everything they could, that the medical care their loved one received was the best, or with whatever else you know to be *true and positive* about the care given to the one who died.
8. DO, in asking how they are, be specific. "The last time I talked to you, I remember . . ." "I've been thinking about you a lot, and wondering how things are going for you since . . ."
9. DO thank them for sharing their pain.
10. DO send them a personal note.
11. DON'T say, "It was God's will," "I know how you feel," "Time will heal."

12. DON'T say, "God is teaching you to trust Him and increase your faith."
13. DON'T say, "Be strong; others need you."
14. DON'T say, "It could have been worse; at least your wife lived," "At least one child made it," "The baby was a girl and you wanted a boy," "The baby would have been retarded."
15. DON'T say, "These things don't just happen; there has got to be a good reason."
16. DON'T simply say, "How are things going?"
17. DON'T let your own sense of helplessness keep you from reaching out to a bereaved person.
18. DON'T avoid the grieving because you feel uncomfortable.
19. DON'T avoid mentioning the deceased person's name out of fear of reminding the bereaved of their pain.

APPENDIX E

MEDITATION

What Is Meditation?

Although there are many kinds, meditation at its highest is a form of mental and spiritual training that aims at stilling and focusing the normally scattered mind, establishing a measure of physical and mental repose, and then becoming an instrument for Self-discovery. Meditation can also be a method of cleansing the mind of impurities and disturbances, such as lustful desires, hatred, ill will, indolence, restlessness, worry, and cynical doubt. When the dusts of these hindrances are wiped from the mind mirror through disciplined meditation, we come to see things as they are in their True-nature, undistorted by our mental or emotional colorations. A lesser fruit of meditation is the strengthening and calming of the nervous system, and the tapping of physical, mental, and psychic energies. This last is analogous to a generator-battery; a special kind of energy (called samadi power) is generated and stored in the meditator's lower belly, enabling him or her to respond instantly to urgent situations without strain or wasted effort. Gradually the winds of anger, greed, and folly subside and the meditator is returned to the stillness of the world of no-thing-ness, the luminous Void, our true home. In correctly practiced meditation, the practitioner develops greater vitality, equanimity, mindfulness, and a responsiveness to the circumstances of his life. Meditation, then, is a healing practice in which the heart is calmed and the spirit strengthened.

APPENDIX E

Meditation at Rest and in Motion

Broadly speaking, meditation embraces much more than formal sitting (the more common designation for this type of meditation) in a stable, motionless posture and trying to concentrate the mind. To enter fully into every act with total attention and clear awareness is no less meditation. "Meditation is to be aware of what is going on—in our bodies, in our feelings, in our minds, and in the world."[35]

The two, formal meditation and meditation in motion, are mutually supportive. If you "sit" every day for a certain period, a special kind of energy develops; this energy enables you to perform your daily tasks with singlemindedness and clear awareness. Conversely, if you perform your daily tasks mindfully—whether working on a computer, attending meetings, laying bricks, cooking dinner, playing with your children or whatever—it is easier to empty and concentrate your mind when you sit in meditation.

Meditation can be done by anybody; it requires no special talents. Being free of any philosophic or religious content, it is for anybody and everybody. If you are already meditating, you can easily adapt your spiritual practice to the meditations that follow. (Meditations on death and specific meditations for the dying person at the point of death and during the intermediate state between decease and rebirth are described in the "Death" and "Dying" sections, respectively.)

Don't wait until you become seriously ill before beginning to meditate; start while you are in good health. Faithfully pursued, meditation will add depth and clarity to your life.

When you are ready to meditate, choose a secluded area—the privacy of your own room, a basement, an empty attic, a corner of the backyard, or any similarly isolated place. Since the most intrusive sounds are those of the human voice, whether heard directly or on TV or radio, such sounds should be avoided if possible. Natural sounds, on the other hand—such as a bird's singing, a cricket's chirping, a cat's meowing, or a dog's barking—are ordinarily not a disturbance to the meditator. Especially felicitous is the pitter-patter of rain or the steady gushing of a water fountain or waterfall;

both these sounds can have a calming effect on the mind of the meditator.

In your meditation, face a wall, curtain, or divider that is unpatterned. A plain beige, tan, or cream color is most restful for the eyes, which are best kept half open. (See "Eyes and Hands.") A distance of two to three feet from the wall to your knees is best. If you sit too close, you may strain your eyes.

Posture

For a normal, healthy person, a stable sitting posture either on a mat on the floor or in a chair is best. With your body in a stable, unmoving position, you will not have to contend with as many random thoughts as you would if you were constantly fidgeting, for such thoughts are stirred into activity through movement. If you have chosen to sit on a mat, begin by taking a comfortable posture sitting on a firm cushion, preferably in one of several cross-legged sitting positions.[36] Wear loose, comfortable clothing so that your circulation is not restricted. To stabilize your body, both knees should touch the mat or carpet. If your knees are off the mat, your body is under strain; to relieve the resulting discomfort, you will constantly move. To avoid a proliferation of random thoughts—the greatest obstacle to concentration—your back needs to be erect and your head straight, not tipped forward.

Sitting in a straight-back chair can also be an effective way to meditate. A small cushion can be inserted under your buttocks to aid in keeping your back erect and your feet firmly planted on the floor. A Scandinavian-designed kneeling chair may also be used to good effect.

Even if you are bedridden, you can derive benefits from meditation while lying in bed following these guidelines:

Breathing

Breathing is best done naturally from your lower belly rather than your chest, with your attention directed toward a point the width of four fingers below your navel. The advantage of this is that it tends to center your body-mind in that area, thereby preventing tension from developing in your head and shoulders, reducing the number of wandering thoughts and soothing the nervous system. The breath should not be "pushed down" or manipulated in any way except at the beginning of a round of sitting, when it is advisable to take one or two deep breaths, slowly exhaling after each one, to harmonize breath and mind. While doing this, imagine you are exhaling all tension and negative thoughts. After that, let your breath take its own natural rhythm.

Eyes and Hands

Keep your eyes half open and unfocused. ("Unfocused" means you are not trying to perceive what is in front of you.) Closing them entirely encourages sleepiness or the incidence of visions of one sort or another. The most effective position for your hands is in your lap, palms up, close to your abdomen, with your left hand in the palm of your right, thumbs lightly touching, and your elbows close to your body but relaxed. The advantage of this posture is that it establishes the maximum repose.

How Long to Sit

How long should you meditate at one sitting? This, of course, depends on the time available to you as well as on the maturity of your practice. It is advisable to start with a shorter period—say ten or fifteen minutes each day—and gradually increase the time as your body-mind accustoms itself to the routine of motionless meditation. It is better to meditate for shorter periods regularly than for a longer period sporadically.

When to Sit

Is there a best time for sitting? Although early morning is recommended—at that time of day it is quiet, there are few cars on the street, the telephone normally doesn't ring, you are rested, and you haven't eaten yet—you can meditate at any time.

Concentrating the Mind

Although there are many methods of concentrating the mind, the most common and simplest is counting the inhalations and exhalations of the breath. When you inhale, think to yourself "One," and when you exhale, "Two," and so on until ten. After that, return to one and go to ten again. Whenever you lose count or go beyond ten, return to one and resume the counting. The numbers need not be visualized; you need only concentrate fully on each number. Avoid simply counting mechanically.

Another method is to be aware of the rhythms of your breath—that is, becoming completely one with your inhalations and exhalations.

The value of these exercises lies in the fact that all reasoning is excluded and the discriminative mind put at rest. Thus the waves of thought are stilled and a gradual one-pointedness of mind achieved. Be aware that fleeting thoughts which dart in and out of the mind are not an impediment. Do not try to expel them; simply concentrate on the counting or the rhythms of the breath.

NOTES

INTRODUCTION

1. Marcus Borg, "Death as the Teacher of Wisdom," *Christian Century*, February 26, 1986.
2. Carl Jung, *Modern Man in Search of a Soul*, Harcourt, Brace, New York, 1955.
3. W. Y. Evans-Wentz, *The Tibetan Book of the Dead*, 3rd edition, Oxford University Press, London, 1970.
4. See Karlis Osis, "Deathbed Observations by Physicians and Nurses," *Journal of the American Society for Pyschical Research*, October 1963.
5. Philippe Ariés, *Western Attitudes Toward Death*, trans. Patricia M. Ranum, The Johns Hopkins University Press, Baltimore, 1975.
6. Review of *Healing the Wounds* in *Newsweek*, January 27, 1986.
7. See *Reincarnation: The Phoenix Fire Mystery*, ed. Joseph Head and S. L. Cranston, Julian Press/Crown Publishers, Inc., New York, 1977, for ample evidence that the doctrine of metempsychosis was once widely accepted in Western cultures and religions.
8. Quoted in Jung Young Lee, *Death and Beyond in the Eastern Perspective*, Gordon & Breach, New York, 1974.
9. Heinrich Zimmer writes, "It is easy for us to forget that our strictly linear evolutionary idea of time . . . is something peculiar to modern man. Even the Greeks of the day of Plato and Aristotle . . . did not share it. Indeed, St. Augustine seems to have been the first to conceive of this modern idea of time. His conception established itself only gradually in opposition to the notion formerly current." (From *Myths and Symbols in Indian Art and Civilization*, ed. Joseph Campbell, Princeton University Press, Princeton, N.J., 1971.)
10. Quoted in *Familiar Medical Quotations*, ed. Maurice B. Strauss, M.D., Little, Brown and Co., Boston, 1968.

One: Death

1. Lyall Watson, *The Romeo Error: A Matter of Life and Death,* Anchor Press/Doubleday, Garden City, N.Y., 1975.
2. Ibid.
3. Dogo and Sekiso are Japanese spellings of Chinese masters' names.
4. Zenkei Shibayama, *Zen Comments on the Mumonkan,* Harper & Row, New York, 1974.
5. Over the centuries it was traditional for the masters to put brush to paper shortly before death in the form of an edifying verse.
6. George Santayana (1863–1952).
7. Quoted in Philip Kapleau, *The Wheel of Death,* George Allen & Unwin, Ltd., London, 1972.
8. Quoted in *Reincarnation: The Phoenix Fire Mystery,* ed. Joseph Head and S. L. Cranston, Julian Press/Crown Publishers, Inc., New York, 1977.
9. *The Wheel of Death,* op. cit.
10. That is, solids (earth), liquids (water), heat (fire), gas (air).
11. All the foregoing accounts are taken from *The Wheel of Death,* op. cit.
12. Adapted from Zen master Hakuun Yasutani, "Commentary on the Koan Mu," in Philip Kapleau, *The Three Pillars of Zen,* Anchor Press/Doubleday, Garden City, N.Y., 1980.
13. *Chuang Tzu,* trans. Herbert A. Giles, George Allen & Unwin, Ltd., London, 1961.
14. Quoted in *Kahawai,* Vol. 6, No. 1, Winter 1984.
15. Zen is not contrary to what is natural. When one is in a fearful situation, it is natural to be afraid. But facing death is not considered a fearful situation for a spiritually developed person.
16. Quoted in Francis Dojun Cook, *How to Raise an Ox,* Center Publications, Los Angeles, 1978.
17. Engaku Monastery. Soyen Shaku was in the United States in 1905–6.
18. *Chuang Tzu,* op. cit.
19. *The Three Pillars of Zen,* op. cit.
20. Carl Jung, *Modern Man in Search of a Soul,* Harcourt, Brace, New York, 1955.
21. From an article in the *Albuquerque Journal,* August 17, 1986.
22. *The Romeo Error: A Matter of Life and Death,* op. cit.
23. Plato, *Apology,* trans. Benjamin Jowett, quoted in *The Wheel of Death,* op. cit.
24. Ignace Lepp, *Death and Its Mysteries,* trans. Bernard Murchland, Macmillan Publishing Co., New York, 1976.

25. Ibid.
26. Quoted in Harold S. Kushner, "Why I Am Not Afraid to Die," *Reader's Digest,* August 1986.
27. Moses Maimonides (1135–1204), rabbi, physician, and philosopher.
28. C. S. Lewis, *The Problem of Pain,* Collins, London, 1940.
29. Philip Kapleau, *Zen: Merging of East and West,* Anchor Press/Doubleday, Garden City, N.Y., 1989.
30. Huston Smith, *The Religions of Man,* Harper & Row, New York, 1958.
31. Zen master Bassui (1327–87), quoted in *The Three Pillars of Zen,* op. cit.
32. Abraham a Sancta Clara, an Austrian Augustinian monk and prolific author of theological writings.
33. Zen master Soen Nakagawa.
34. John C. H. Wu, *The Golden Age of Zen,* United Publishing Center, Taipei, Taiwan, 1975.
35. Quoted in Lisa Carlson, *Caring for Your Own Dead,* Upper Access Publishers, Hinesburg, Vt., 1987.
36. Quoted in Edward Conze, *Thirty Years of Buddhist Studies,* Bruno Cassirer Ltd., Oxford, 1967.
37. "The Problem of Death in East and West," *The Eastern Buddhist,* Vol. 19, No. 2, Autumn 1986.
38. Quoted in Lynne Ann DeSpelder and Albert Strickland, *The Last Dance: Encountering Death and Dying,* Mayfield Publishing Co., Palo Alto, Calif., 1983.
39. Adapted from George Bond, "Buddhist Meditations on Death," *The History of Religions,* Vol. 19, No. 3, February 1980.
40. Sigmund Freud, *Thoughts for the Times on War and Death,* (II) "Our Attitude towards Death" (1915). SE. Vol. 14, p. 289. Hogarth Press, London, 1957.
41. Quoted in Rollo May, *Love and Will,* Dell, New York, 1969.
42. Zen master Hakuin (1686–1769), quoted in Philip B. Yampolsky, *The Zen Master Hakuin: Selected Writings,* Columbia University Press, New York, 1971.
43. Quoted in Museo Universitario, Universidad Nacional Autonoma de México, *La Muerte: Expresiones Mexicanas de un Enigma* (Death: Mexican Expressions of an Enigma), Mexico City, 1975.
44. Ibid.
45. Ta Hui, *Swampland Flowers,* trans. Christopher Leary, Grove Press, New York, 1977.
46. That is, "I stand ready to sacrifice not merely my present life but my next six lifetimes on behalf of the emperor."

47. *Death and Its Mysteries,* op. cit.
48. Earth, water, fire, ether: the basic elements of the universe, according to the ancients.
49. See glossary.
50. Quoted in Arthur Osborne, *Ramana Maharshi and the Path of Self-knowledge,* Rider & Co., London, 1963.
51. Arunachala is the name of the mountain next to Sri Maharshi's ashram, and, for the master, was another name for True-nature. Shiva is one of the Hindu deities.
52. *Ramana Maharshi and the Path of Self-knowledge,* op. cit.
53. The appellation the Buddha used in referring to himself.
54. That is, present-day Bodh gaya, the city in India where the Buddha attained supreme enlightenment at the age of thirty-five.
55. Quoted in *The Wheel of Death,* op. cit.

Two: Dying

1. Fred Wistow, "Death in the Family: Healing the Loss of a Parent," in *The Family Therapy Networker,* The Family Therapy Network, Inc., 1986.
2. *Visuddhimagga.*
3. Jacques Lusseyran, *And There Was Light,* trans. Elizabeth R. Cameron, Parabola Books, New York, 1987.
4. Zen master Yasutani, quoted in Philip Kapleau, *The Three Pillars of Zen,* Anchor Press/Doubleday, Garden City, N.Y., 1980.
5. See "Concentration and Euphoria: Mind Functioning at Peak Can Produce Altered States," *The New York Times,* March 10, 1986.
6. Leonardo da Vinci (1452–1519), *The Notebooks,* Vol. 1, Ch. 1.
7. Mihajlo Mihajlov, "Mystical Experiences of the Labor Camps," in *Kontinent 2,* ed. Vladimir Maximov et al., Anchor Press/Doubleday, Garden City, N.Y., 1977.
8. *And There Was Light,* op. cit.
9. "Mystical Experiences of the Labor Camps," op. cit.
10. P. T. James, *Cover Her Face,* Warner Books, New York, 1982.
11. Quoted in Morton Hunt, "Body and Mind," *The New York Times,* March 27, 1988.
12. The Life Center is a nonprofit organization providing group and individual services for children and adults experiencing serious illness or loss, at no charge.
13. Huston Smith writes of the Buddha: "He was undoubtedly one of the greatest rationalists of all times, resembling in this respect no one as

much as Socrates . . . The remarkable fact, however, was the way this objective critical component of his character was balanced by a Franciscan tenderness so strong as to have caused his message to be subtitled 'a religion of infinite compassion.' " *The Religions of Man*, Harper & Row, New York, 1958.

14. See entry for "Skandhas" in the glossary.
15. Quoted in John Bowker, *The Problems of Suffering in Religions of the World*, Cambridge University Press, London, 1970.
16. *The Religions of Man*, op. cit.
17. The word "nothing," when written with a capital *N*, has the metaphysical sense of the viable Void out of which all forms emerge and to which they return according to causes and conditions. With a small *n* it can be taken to mean little or no worldly possessions in this context.
18. The original word is *nirvana*, which here can be understood to mean release from the chain of causation and re-becoming.
19. Quoted in *The Problems of Suffering in Religions of the World*, op. cit.
20. Ibid.
21. John Blofeld, *The Zen Teaching of Hui Hai*, Samuel Weiser, New York, 1972, Introduction.
22. *The Problems of Suffering in Religions of the World*, op. cit.
23. Ibid.
24. *The Religions of Man*, op. cit.
25. Lama Anagarika Govinda, *The Psychological Attitude of Early Buddhism*, quoted in *The Problems of Suffering in Religions of the World*, op. cit.
26. Ronald Melzack and Patrick D. Wall, *The Challenge of Pain*, Basic Books, New York, 1982.
27. Robert G. Twycross and Sylvia A. Lack, *Symptom Control in Far Advanced Cancer: Pain Relief*, Pitman, London.
28. "Pain and the Dying Patient," an audio tape made under the auspices of St. Christopher's Hospice, Sydenham, England.
29. *Random House College Dictionary*, ed. Jess Stein, revised edition, Random House, New York, 1975.
30. Edwin S. Shneidman, quoted in the pamphlet, *Suicide: The Will to Die*, National Association of Blue Shield Plans, 1973.
31. Lynn Ann DeSpelder and Albert Strickland, *The Last Dance: Encountering Death and Dying*, Mayfield Publishing Company, Palo Alto, Calif., 1983.
32. Edwin S. Shneidman, quoted in op. cit.
33. Susan J. Smith, "A Matter of Life & Death," *Times-Union*, Rochester, N.Y., October 29, 1986.

34. Quoted in *Encyclopedia of Religion and Ethics,* ed. James Hastings, Charles Scribner's Sons, 1951, Vol. 12.
35. Ibid.
36. Ibid.
37. Ananda K. Coomaraswamy, *Buddha and the Gospel of Buddhism,* G. P. Putnam's Sons, New York, 1916.
38. *Random House College Dictionary,* op. cit.
39. Susan J. Smith, "In the Era of the 'Negotiated Death,' When to Start—and End—Treatment?" *Times-Union,* Rochester, N.Y., October 27, 1986.
40. "Is It Wrong to Cut Off Feeding?" *Time* magazine, February 23, 1987.
41. "Back from the Dead," *Time* magazine, October 6, 1986.
42. The Multi-Society Task Force on PVS, "Prognosis for Recovery," *The New England Journal of Medicine,* June 2, 1994.
43. "Euthanasia and Religion," *Times-Union,* Rochester, N.Y., October 31, 1986.
44. James Rachels, *The End of Life: Euthanasia and Morality,* Oxford University Press, New York, 1986, as reviewed in Andrew H. Malcolm, "Choosing to Die," *New York Times Book Review.*
45. *Quoted in Sandol Stoddard, The Hospice Movement: A Better Way to Care for the Dying,* Vintage Books, New York, 1978.
46. Quoted in Ibid.
47. Adapted from Philip Kapleau, *The Wheel of Death,* George Allen & Unwin, Ltd., London, 1972.
48. One of the most admired of Zen writings, written by the Third Zen Patriarch, Seng Tsan. This English translation was done by members of The Zen Center, Rochester, N.Y.
49. Quoted in *High Holiday Prayer Book,* ed. Morris Silverman, Prayer Book Press, Hartford, Conn., 1939.
50. From the Book of Psalms, *The Holy Bible.*
51. Lama Anagarika Govinda, *Foundations of Tibetan Mysticism,* E. P. Dutton, New York, 1960.
52. "Dying: The Last Taboo," a British Broadcasting Company television program.
53. Zen master Bassui, quoted in *The Three Pillars of Zen,* op. cit.
54. Deborah Whiting Little, *Home Care for the Dying,* Dial Press/Doubleday, Garden City, N.Y., 1985.
55. Ernest Morgan, *A Manual of Death Education and Simple Burial,* 10th edition, revised and expanded, Celo Press, Burnsville, N.C., 1984.
56. Lisa Carlson, *Caring for Your Own Dead,* Upper Access Publishers, Hinesburg, Vt., 1987.

57. Quoted in Editors of Consumer Reports, *Funerals: Consumers' Last Rights,* W. W. Norton & Co., Inc., New York, 1977.
58. Ibid.
59. From an NFCA pamphlet, *With the Body Present,* quoted in *Funerals: Consumers' Last Rights,* Ibid.
60. Quoted in Glenn H. Mullin, *Death and Dying: The Tibetan Tradition,* Arkana, Boston, 1986.
61. Paul E. Irion, *Cremation,* Fortress Press, Philadelphia, 1968.
62. Ibid.
63. Ibid.
64. Ambrose Bierce, *The Devil's Dictionary,* Hill and Wang, New York, 1957.
65. *The Religions of Man,* op. cit.
66. Lyall Watson, *The Romeo Error: A Matter of Life and Death,* Doubleday & Company, Inc., Garden City, N.Y., 1975.
67. As rebirth within forty-nine days is not fixed, in many Buddhist countries the services are repeated at specific intervals beyond the end of the sixth week up to a period of fifty years.
68. A word derived from "cremation" and "remains," which is becoming increasingly accepted in general English usage.
69. The names of all the deceased in these sections have been changed.
70. Adapted from a Japanese poem, author unknown.
71. These verses are an abbreviated version of the full text and convey its core meaning.
72. On the level of transcendental wisdom.
73. The elements of existence.
74. Quoted in *The Wheel of Death,* op. cit.
75. Hakuun Yasutani, *Eight Bases of Beliefs in Buddhism,* trans. Eido Tai Shimano, Youval Tal Ltd., Jerusalem, 1966.
76. "The Blending of Religion and Medicine," *The Christian Science Monitor,* December 29, 1987.

Three: Karma

1. According to classical Indian philosophy rooted in Hinduism, the wheel of life contains twelve spokes: (1) ignorance (blindness to the true nature of existence) leads to (2) karma-producing actions; these actions lead to (3) consciousness; consciousness leads to (4) material form and mental functions; material form and mental functions lead to (5) the six senses (the faculties of thinking, seeing, hearing, smelling, tasting, and feeling); the six senses lead to (6) contact; contact leads to (7) sensation; sensation

leads to (8) craving; craving leads to (9) clinging; clinging leads to (10) formation of being; formation of being leads to (11) birth; birth leads to old age and (12) death—and it starts all over again. In these twelve links or cycles of causation and becoming, it is impossible to say which one is the first cause, because the twelve make a circle, a wheel. Circles, of course, have no beginning and no end.

2. Ananda K. Coomaraswamy, *Buddha and the Gospel of Buddhism*, G. P. Putnam's Sons, New York, 1916.
3. John Walters, *The Essence of Buddhism*, Thomas Y. Crowell, New York, 1964.
4. D. T. Suzuki, *Outlines of Mahayana Buddhism*, Schocken Books, New York, 1963.
5. Francis Dojun Cook, *How to Raise an Ox*, Center Publications, Los Angeles, 1978.
6. Garma C. C. Chang, *The Buddhist Teaching of Totality*, Pennsylvania State University Press, University Park, Pa., and London, 1971.
7. Quoted in Philip Kapleau, *The Wheel of Death*, George Allen & Unwin, Ltd., London, 1972.
8. Narada Thera, *The Buddha and His Teachings*, Vajrirama, Colombo, Sri Lanka, 1964.
9. Lynn Rosellini, "Learning to Live Again," *Reader's Digest*, May 1986.
10. Zenkei Shibayama, *Zen Comments on the Mumonkan*, Harper & Row, New York, 1974.
11. Junjiro Takakusu, *Essentials of Buddhist Philosophy*, ed. Wingtsit Chan and Charles A. Moore, 3rd edition, Office Appliance Co., Ltd., Honolulu, 1956.
12. Adapted from *The Wheel of Death*, op. cit.
13. The ideas are that discarnate consciousness can produce a change in the objective world through the power of karma, which is ever at work among all sentient beings—and that by the power of karma there are certain relationships created in the external world. Birth itself is conceived as really due, not to an external power which produces it, but to the inner working of the karma principle—the principle of cause and effect—which produces the state of consciousness in human beings on their being born into the world. In other words, the world of form is nothing less than the product of mind considered individually or collectively. Most of the environment of men is due to their individual karma, but there is also a collective, or social, karma at work as well; taken together, these two types of karma explain the existence of the world as we know it. See Coates and Ishizuka, *Honen's Life and Teaching*, Chionin, Kyoto, 1925.

14. J. Glenn Gray, *The Warriors,* Harper Colophon Books, New York, 1970.
15. Arthur J. Dyck, *On Human Care,* Abingdon Press, Nashville, Tenn., 1977.

Four: Rebirth

1. See "phoenix" in "A Note on the Drawings."
2. Henry David Thoreau, *The Writings of Henry David Thoreau,* Houghton Mifflin, Cambridge, Mass., 1894.
3. Sir James Frazer, *Belief in Immortality,* The Macmillan Co., New York, 1913.
4. George Gallup, Jr., with William Proctor, *Adventures in Immortality,* McGraw-Hill Book Co., New York, 1982.
5. *Encyclopaedia of Religion and Ethics,* ed. Rabbi Moses Gaster, Scribner's Sons, Hames Hasting, N.Y., 1955, Vol. 12, quoted in *Reincarnation: The Phoenix Fire Mystery,* ed. Joseph Head and S. L. Cranston, Julian Press/Crown Publishers, Inc., New York, 1977.
6. Hakuun Yasutani, *Eight Bases of Belief in Buddhism,* trans. Eido Tai Shimano, Youval Tal Ltd., Jerusalem, 1966.
7. John Blofeld, *The Wheel of Life,* Shambhala, Berkeley, Calif., 1972.
8. John Blofeld, *The Zen Teaching of Hui Hai,* Samuel Weiser, New York, 1972.
9. Quoted in *Reincarnation: The Phoenix Fire Mystery,* op. cit.
10. These thoughts or mental processes result from our conscious awareness of external or internal stimuli. Eastern psychology identifies seventeen stages in the thought process. They consist of (1) the unconscious, which can be likened to someone in a deep, dreamless sleep; (2) vibrations of the unconscious, which take place during sleep when the senses receive stimulation from an external object, or in the waking state between conscious thoughts; (3) arrest of the unconscious, which happens when the unconscious is stopped and the conscious arises, but the catalyst is not yet recognized; (4) thought-moment, which is the vague awareness of a disturbance from any stimulus; (5) fivefold consciousness, which is consciousness relating to a particular sense, that is, what appears is merely sensed; (6) reception, in which the sensed stimulus is received; (7) investigation, or the discriminating intellect, which investigates the stimulus; (8) decision, when a decision is made with regard to the stimulus; (9–15) thought impulses, full perception, introspection, and action, the stages during which conscious decisions can be made with regard to a particular course of action—these stages are the point at which we create karma;

(16–17) registration of the experience, which occurs only if the impression was very strong. Adapted from V. F. Gunaratna, *Rebirth Explained,* The Wheel Publications No. 167/169, Buddhist Publication Society, Kandy, Sri Lanka, 1971.

11. Francis Story, *The Case for Rebirth,* The Wheel Publications No. 12/13, Buddhist Publication Society, Kandy, Sri Lanka, 1959.
12. Francis Story, "Rebirth and the Western Thinker," *Light of the Dhamma,* Vol. 5, No. 2, April 1958. (*Dhamma* is the Pali rendering of the Sanskrit word *Dharma.*)
13. T. R. V. Murti, "Radhakrishnan and Buddhism," in *The Philosophy of Sarvepalli Radhakrishnan,* Tudor Publishing Co., New York, 1952.
14. Ananda K. Coomaraswamy, *Buddha and the Gospel of Buddhism,* G. P. Putnam's Sons, New York, 1916.
15. Adapted from John Bowker, *The Problems of Suffering in Religions of the World,* Cambridge University Press, London, 1970.
16. Swami Vivekananda, *The Yogas and Other Works.* Vivekananda was the most distinguished disciple of Sri Ramakrishna and founder of the Ramakrishna (Vedanta) Order in America.
17. *Rebirth Explained,* op. cit.
18. Lama Anagarika Govinda, *Foundations of Tibetan Mysticism,* E. P. Dutton, New York, 1960.
19. Ian Stevenson, M.D., *Twenty Cases Suggestive of Reincarnation,* American Society for Psychical Research, New York, 1966.
20. From an interview with Ian Stevenson in *OMNI,* January 1988.
21. This phenomenon, called *xenoglossy,* is extremely rare, but there are a number of well-documented cases of both children and adults who have displayed this ability. In some cases the language spoken was an obscure ancient tongue known only to a few linguists.
22. From Zen master Dōgen, *Shobogenzo,* trans. Francis Dojun Cook, in *How to Raise an Ox,* Center Publications, Los Angeles, 1978.
23. From a letter to Madeleine Slade, quoted in *Reincarnation: The Phoenix Fire Mystery,* op. cit.
24. Owen Rutter, *The Scales of Karma,* quoted in Christmas Humphreys, *Karma and Rebirth,* Curzon Press, London, 1983.
25. Max Müller, *Three Lectures on the Vedanta Philosophy,* Longman, Green, London, 1984, quoted in *Reincarnation: The Phoenix Fire Mystery,* op. cit.
26. Quoted in *Reincarnation: The Phoenix Fire Mystery,* op. cit.
27. "Rebirth and the Western Thinker," op. cit.
28. *Twenty Cases Suggestive of Reincarnation,* op. cit.

29. G. H. Beale, lecturer in genetics, Edinburgh University, quoted in *The Case for Rebirth*, op. cit.
30. *The Case for Rebirth*, op. cit.
31. Private communication February 1988, Barbara Handelin, Ph.D.
32. *Rebirth Explained*, op. cit.
33. Leslie D. Weatherhead, *The Case for Reincarnation*, reprint of a lecture given to the City Temple Literary Society, New York, 1957.
34. From an article by Michael Geczi in the *Wisconsin State Journal*, July 6, 1986.
35. From an article in *Newsweek*, July 12, 1976.
36. Ibid.
37. Swami Paramananda, *Reincarnation and Immortality*, The Vedanta Centre, Cohasset, Mass., 1961.

APPENDIXES

1. Elisabeth Rosenthal, "Hardest Medical Choices Shift to Patients," *New York Times*, January 27, 1994, A1.
2. Sherwin B. Nuland, *How We Die: Reflections on Life's Final Chapter*, Knopf, New York, 1994.
3. Beauchamp & Childress, *Principles of Biomedical Ethics*, Oxford University Press, New York, 1989, 67.
4. *Schloendorff v. Society of New York Hospital*, 105 N.E. 92, 129–130 (N.Y. 1914).
5. *Matter of Quinlan*, 355 A.2d 647 (N.J. 1976).
6. *Cruzan by Cruzan v. Director, Missouri Dept. of Health*, 497 U.S. 261, 271 (1990).
7. Michael Kramer, "Pulling the Plug," *Time* magazine, October 3, 1993.
8. 42 U.S.C. § 1395cc(f).
9. See, for example, C.R.S. § 15–14–311(2).
10. Intra-family conflicts are not uncommon. In the case of *In re Martin*, 517 N.W.2d 749 (1994), the spouse's interpretation of the comatose patient's wishes was flatly contradicted by his sister and mother, placing the controversy before a court.
11. Susan Gilbert, "Doctors Often Fail to Heed Wishes of the Dying Patient," *The New York Times*, November 22, 1995, A1.
12. Marion Danis, M.D., et al., "Stability of Choices about Life-Sustaining Treatments," *Annals of Internal Medicine*, April 1, 1994, 567.
13. Bill Inman was brain damaged from an auto accident, in a coma for a year, and was not expected to recover. Four years later he was living at

home, speaking, able to feed and dress himself, and was learning to walk. David McQuay, "A One in a Million Miracle," *The Denver Post*, July 21, 1985.

14. The Multi-Society Task Force on PVS, "Prognosis for Recovery," *New England Journal of Medicine*, June 2, 1994, 1572.
15. Timothy E. Quill, M.D., *Death and Dignity*, W. W. Norton, 1993, New York, 51–52.
16. Ibid., 156.
17. For a fuller discussion of objections to physician-assisted suicide, see "When Death is Sought: Assisted Suicide and Euthanasia in the Medical Context," New York State Task Force on Life and the Law, New York, 1997.
18. Jane E. Brody, "Depression May Lead Dying Patients to Seek Suicide," *New York Times*, June 18, 1997, B10.
19. *Death and Dignity*, op. cit., 79–80.
20. David E. Rosenbaum, "Americans Want a Right to Die. Or So They Think," *New York Times*, June 8, 1997, E3.
21. "The American College of Physicians Ethics Manual," *Annals of Internal Medicine* (1992), 117: 948.
22. See, for example, *The Oregon Death with Dignity Act*, Or. Rev. Stat. § 127.800 (1994).
23. "A Case of Individualized Decision Making," *New England Journal of Medicine*, March 7, 1991, 691–694.
24. D. A. Asch, "The Role of Critical Care Nurses in Euthanasia and Assisted Suicide," *New England Journal of Medicine* (1996), 334(21): 1374–1380.
25. *Death and Dignity*, op. cit., 175.
26. *Vacco v. Quill*, 117 S. Ct. 2293 (1997).
27. C.R.S. § 18-3-104(1)(b) (1987 and Supp. 1997).
28. Lee R. Slome, Ph.D., et al., "Physician-Assisted Suicide and Patients with Human Immunodeficiency Virus Disease," *New England Journal of Medicine*, February 6, 1997, 417.
29. "Doctors Design Rules on Care for the Dying," *New York Times*, June 23, 1997, A12.
30. *Death and Dignity*, op. cit., 161–165.
31. "Physician-Hastened Death: Advisory Guidelines for the San Francisco Bay Area," are available from: Steve Heilig, Bay Area Network of Ethics Committees, c/o San Francisco Medical Society, 1409 Sutter Street, San Francisco, CA 94109.
32. Ernest Morgan, *A Manual of Death Education and Simple Burial*, 10th edition, revised and expanded, Celo Press, Burnsville, N.C.

33. Deborah Whiting Little, *Home Care for the Dying*, Dial Press/Doubleday, Garden City, N.Y., 1985.
34. Compiled by the Compassionate Friends, an organization of families who have lost children.
35. Thich Nhat Hanh, Buddhist monk and peace activist.
36. For detailed descriptions and illustrations of various meditation postures and their significance, see Philip Kapleau, *The Three Pillars of Zen*, revised and expanded edition, Anchor Press/ Doubleday, Garden City, N.Y., 1980.

GLOSSARY

Abbreviations: *Skt.: Sanskrit; Ch.: Chinese; Sp.: Spanish; J.: Japanese; Tib: Tibetan*

ARS MORIENDI (The Art of Dying): a medieval text on dying, reprinted in part in the modern book *The Craft of Dying.*

BARDO (Tib.): the intermediate state between clinical death and rebirth. See also "The Intermediate Realm."

BECOMING: stands against "being"; constant change.

BIRTH AND DEATH: see **SAMSĀRA**.

BODHISATTVA (Skt.): literally, "wisdom being"; a spiritually awakened individual who, having attained enlightenment, dedicates himself or herself to helping others do the same.

BUDDHA (Skt.): a word used in two senses: (1) ultimate Truth or absolute Mind, and (2) one awakened or enlightened to the true nature of existence. *The* Buddha refers to a historical person with the given name of Siddhartha and the family name of Gautama, who was born around the year 563 B.C. He was the son of the ruler of the Shakyas, whose small kingdom lay at the foothills of present-day Nepal. Siddhartha was married at sixteen and had a son, who later became his disciple. At the age of thirty-five, after six years of hard search and struggle, Siddhartha became surpremely enlightened. Thereafter, until his death at eighty, he preached to all who would listen, always suiting his exposition to the capacity of his hearers' understanding. He is regarded by Buddhists neither as a supreme deity nor as a savior, but is venerated as a fully awakened, fully perfected human being who attained liberation of body and mind through his own human efforts.

BUDDHISM: or more precisely, the way of the Buddha. It has two main branches: the Theravada, mainly found in Southeast Asia, and the Mahayana. The latter arose in India, whence it spread to Tibet, Mongolia, China, Korea, and Japan. Zen is a sect of the Mahayana.

CALAVERAS (Sp.): "living" skeletons; in the Mexican culture *calaveras* are beings who are alive but in another dimension.

CHANTING: intoning of religious works in a blend of harmonic monotones. To be effective, chanting must be clear, wholehearted, and concentrated, with the voices of the various chanters merging harmoniously.

CREMAINS: a word entering common usage, coined from "cremation" and "remains," to denote the remains of a person whose body has been cremated.

DHARMA (Skt.): a fundamental Buddhist term having several meanings, the broadest of which is "phenomenon." All phenomena are subject to the law of causation, and this fundamental truth comprises the core of the Buddha's message.

DUKKHA (Skt.): a word frequently translated as "suffering" or "unsatisfactoriness," but implying much more: pain, grief, affliction, distress, or frustration.

EGYPTIAN BOOK OF THE DEAD: one of several ancient Egyptian texts dealing with death and the hereafter.

ENLIGHTENMENT, SELF-REALIZATION, AWAKENING: spiritual awakening to one's True-nature and to the Truth lying beyond all dualism and discrimination. This term has no connection with the eighteenth-century philosophic movement.

ESP: extrasensory (paranormal) perception.

ESSENTIAL-NATURE: see TRUE-NATURE.

EUTHANASIA: originally an easy and painless death; now refers chiefly to "the art or method of causing death painlessly so as to end suffering."

FIVE AGGREGATES, FIVE SKANDHAS: form, sensation, perception, mental formations, and consciousness. See also SKANDHAS.

FOUR NOBLE TRUTHS: (1) the Universality of Suffering, (2) The Causes of Suffering, (3) The Cessation of Suffering, and (4) The Path Leading to the Cessation of Suffering. See also "The Dilemma of Pain."

HOSPICE: originally a medieval place of shelter for travelers, pilgrims, and the sick, often run by monks or nuns; now either a residential facility or home care for the terminally ill. Hospice programs in the United States generally accept only those patients with six months or less to live. See also Appendix B, "Hospice Care."

KARMA: literally, "doing" or "acting"; our thoughts and actions and the consequences flowing from them; cause and effect. See also "Karma" section.

KOAN (J., pronounced "ko-an"; Ch. *kung-an*): in Zen, a formulation, in baffling language, pointing to ultimate Truth.

MANTRA: a sacred sound or syllable used to meditate on. See also **OM**.

MEDITATION: from the Latin *meditatio*, a "thinking over," "contemplation." There are many kinds of meditation, but essentially the term denotes one-pointed concentration on a sacred word or image that is visualized, or on a concept (such as God or love) that is thought about or reflected on, or both.

METEMPSYCHOSIS: transmigration; the passing of a soul after death into some other body, either human or animal.

MYTH: not an untrue story, but a truth so majestic, so all-encompassing that it cannot be embraced within mere fact. For Joseph Campbell, author of *The Power of Myth*, it is "a metaphor for what lies behind the visible world."

MYSTIC: according to *Webster's New World Dictionary*, "a person who professes to undergo mystical experiences by which he intuitively comprehends truths beyond human understanding." In Zen a mystic is one who has awakened to the nonduality of the world of phenomena and the world of no-form, and whose life has been transformed by this unique experience.

NIRVĀṆA (Skt.): extinction of ignorance and craving, and awakening to inner peace and freedom. *Nirvāṇa* (with a small *n*) stands against *saṃsāra*, that is, birth and death. See also "Gautama the Buddha."

NOBLE EIGHTFOLD PATH: the Buddha's formula leading to awakening. See also "The Dilemma of Pain."

NO-MINDEDLY: with the mind totally void of random or distracting thoughts.

OM (Skt.), also spelled **AUM**: a sound-symbol of the energy powering the universe—the energy of which all things are a manifestation; an object of religious meditation to harness certain energies for healing or enlightenment purposes.

ONENESS: with a small *o*, absorption to the point of self-forgetfulness. With a capital *O*, the experience of the Void, or no-thing-ness.

PALINGENESIS: from the Greek *palin*, "again," and *genesis*, "generation"; the doctrine of successive rebirths.

PARINIRVĀṆA (Skt.): literally, complete extinction of craving and ego. *Parinirvāṇa* usually refers to the state of perfect emancipation reached by Gautama the Buddha upon his passing away. See also "Gautama the Buddha."

REINCARNATION: rebirth of a soul in another body. See also "Rebirth Distinguished from Reincarnation."

REPENTANCE: in the Christian tradition, connected with sin, remorse, condemnation. In Buddhism, sin is ignorance of the true nature of existence; repentance is deep regret for one's basic ignorance and the determination to overcome it.

ROSHI (J.): a title in the Zen sect that means, literally, "venerable teacher" or "master." It implies long training and that the approval to teach has been given by one's own teacher.

SAMADHI POWER: the energy that arises through the complete absorption of the mind in itself; heightened and expanded awareness; a state of intense yet effortless concentration. See also "What Is Samadhi?"

SAṂSĀRA(Skt.): birth and death; the world of relativity, of impermanence, of constant change.

SKANDHAS (Skt.): The five skandhas or aggregates consist of form, sensations, perceptions, mental formations, and consciousness. Form comprises past elements of consciousness that have formed the body and are represented by the body. These include sense organs, sense objects, and their mutual relationship. Here we have the beginning of individuality and the division of experience into subject and object. In the second cluster are the feelings—that is, the self reacting to its surroundings. These feelings comprise pleasure and pain, joy and sorrow, disquiet and equanimity. In the third group are the perceptions of discriminating awareness, which comprise the reflective or discursive as well as the intuitive faculty of discrimination. In the fourth group are the mental formations—the forces or tendencies of the will. These represent the active principle of consciousness. That is, these mental constructs are the consequences of past karma and the progenitors of future karma. They are produced by conscious volition and are what put things together and build up the patterns of personality and karma. The last component is consciousness, which combines and coordinates all the sensory perceptions. Thus the egocentric self creates its own world instead of perceiving the world as it really is. The aim of spiritual training is to see into the ultimate unreality of the ego-I and to transform these five aggregates of the confused and unenlightened mind into enlightenment, or a selfless-I.

SOUL: "generally taken to mean the sum total of an individual personality, an enduring ego-entity that exists more or less independently of the physical body and survives it after death . . . the 'soul' is considered to be the personality-factor which distinguishes one individual from another . . ."—Francis Story.

SRI (Skt.): a Hindu title of address, equivalent to the English "Mr."; also, an honorific title applied to a religious or spiritual teacher in the Hindu tradition.

TANHA (Skt.): commonly translated as "thirst for," "craving," "desire." See also "Existential Pain: The Four Noble Truths of Suffering."

TAO (Ch.): see WAY.

TATHAGATA (Skt.): the appellation the Buddha used in referring to himself. It literally means "Thus-come," the "Thus" indicating the enlightened state.

TIBETAN BOOK OF THE DEAD: a traditional Tibetan text of instructions for the dead and dying. According to the Tibetan tradition, it is the work of the ancient sage Padmasambhava; it tells how to prepare oneself for death and the passage to rebirth.

TRANSMIGRATION: the passing of a soul into another body after death. See also "Rebirth Distinguished from Reincarnation."

TRUE-NATURE: see "True-nature Is Not Soul."

VISUDDHIMAGGA: a text written in the fifth century A.D. by Buddhaghosa, a Buddhist monk-teacher.

WAY, TĀO: the fundamental principle and reality of the universe; ultimate Truth.

ZEN (J.): an abbreviation of *Zenna,* which is a transliteration of the Chinese *Channa* (or *Chan*), which in turn is a transliteration of the Sanskrit *Dhyana.* This last has many meanings in Hinduism; in Zen Buddhism, however, the term Zen generally refers to the cultivation, chiefly through meditation, of one-pointedness, stillness, and stability of the body-mind.

ZEN BUDDHISM: a sect of Buddhism that is free of dogmas and creeds and whose teachings emphasize the fundamental, personal experience of awakening and its integration into one's life.

ZEN MASTER: a person of deep, awakened understanding and compassion who has integrated his understanding into his life and whose actions reflect this.

BIBLIOGRAPHY

Death and Dying

Articles, Pamphlets, Reports

Abe, Masao, "The Problem of Death in East and West," *The Eastern Buddhist*, Vol. 19, No. 2, Autumn 1986.

"Back from the Dead," *Time*, October 6, 1986.

"The Barbie Trial: J'Accuse," *Newsweek*, May 11, 1987.

"The Blending of Religion and Medicine," *The Christian Science Monitor*, December 29, 1987.

Blodgett, Richard, "Our Wild, Weird World of Coincidence," *Reader's Digest*, September 1987.

Bond, George, "Buddhist Meditations on Death," *The History of Religions*, Vol. 19, No. 3, February 1980.

Borg, Marcus, "Death as the Teacher of Wisdom," *Christian Century*, February 26, 1986.

"Concentration and Euphoria: Mind Functioning at Peak Can Produce Altered States," *The New York Times*, March 10, 1986.

Deciding to Forego Life-sustaining Treatment, President's Commission for the Study of Ethical Problems in Medicine and Biomedical and Behavioral Research, 1983, reprinted by Concern for Dying, New York.

Earnshaw-Smith, Elisabeth, "Emotional Pain in Dying Patients and Their Families," *Nursing Times*, November 3, 1982.

"Euthanasia and Religion," *Times-Union*, Rochester, N.Y., October 31, 1986.

Fadiman, Anne, "The Liberation of Lolly and Gronky," *Life*, December 1986.

"First Do No Harm: The Making of a Neurosurgeon," *Reader's Digest*, November 1987.

Garfield, Charles A., "Consciousness Alteration and Fear of Death," *Journal of Transpersonal Psychology*, Vol. 7, No. 2, 1975.

Bibliography

Goleman, Daniel, "The Mind over the Body," *The New York Times*, September 27, 1987.

Holden, Ted, "Patiently Speaking," *Nursing Times*, June 12, 1980.

Hunt, Morton, "Body and Mind," *The New York Times*, March 27, 1988.

Irvine, Patrick, M.D., "Sounding Board: The Attending at the Funeral," *The New England Journal of Medicine*, June 27, 1985.

"Is It Wrong to Cut Off Feeding?" *Time*, February 23, 1987.

Kahawai, Vol. 6, No. 1, Winter 1984.

"The Key Figure Is the Organ Donor," *Santa Fe Reporter*, April 9, 1986.

Khantipalo, Bhikku, *The Wheel of Birth and Death*, The Wheel Publications No. 147/148/149, Buddhist Publication Society, Kandy, Sri Lanka, 1970.

Kushner, Harold S., "Why I Am Not Afraid to Die," *Reader's Digest*, August 1986.

"The Nature and Nurture of Pain Control," *World Medicine*, February 21, 1984.

"One Against the Plague," *Newsweek*, July 21, 1986.

Osis, Karlis, "Deathbed Observations by Physicians and Nurses," *Journal of the American Society for Psychical Research*, October 1963.

Owen, David, "Rest in Pieces," *Harper's*, June 1983.

Parabola: Myth and the Quest for Meaning, Vol. 2, No. 1, Winter 1977.

Queenan, Joe, "A Send-off from This 'Vale of Tears,'" *The New York Times*, November 1, 1987.

Santmire, H. Paul, "Nothing More Beautiful than Death?" *Christian Century*, December 14, 1983.

Smith, Susan J., "In the Era of the 'Negotiated Death,' When to Start—and End—Treatment?" *Times-Union*, Rochester, N.Y., October 27, 1986.

———, "A Matter of Life & Death," *Times-Union*, Rochester, N.Y., October 29, 1986.

———, "When Prolonging a Life Prolongs Suffering," *Times-Union*, Rochester, N.Y., October 28, 1986.

Suicide: The Will to Die, National Association of Blue Shield Plans, 1973.

Twycross, Robert G., *Principles and Practice of Pain Relief in Terminal Cancer*, Sir Michael Sobell House, Churchill Hospital, Headington, Oxford, OX3 7LJ, England.

Books

Abe, Masao, *Zen and Western Thought*, ed. William R. LaFleur, University of Hawaii Press, Honolulu, 1985.

Allen, John, ed., *One Hundred Great Lives*, Greystone Press, New York, 1948.

Bibliography

Anderson, Ray S., *Theology, Death and Dying*, Basil Blackwell, Oxford and New York, 1986.

Anthony, Dick, Bruce Ecker, and Ken Wilber, eds., *Spiritual Choices*, Paragon House Publishers, New York, 1987.

Ariés, Philippe, *Western Attitudes Toward Death*, trans. Patricia M. Ranum, The Johns Hopkins University Press, Baltimore, 1974.

Bankei, *The Life and Teaching of Zen Master Bankei*, Introduction by Norman Waddell, North Point Press, Berkeley, Calif., 1984.

Bendit, Laurence J., *The Mirror of Life and Death*, 2nd edition, The Theosophical Publishing House, Wheaton, Ill., 1968.

Birnbaum, Raoul, *The Healing Buddha*, Shambhala, Boulder, Colo., 1979.

Blofeld, John, *The Zen Teaching of Hui Hai*, Samuel Weiser, New York, 1972.

Bowker, John, *The Problems of Suffering in Religions of the World*, Cambridge University Press, London, 1970.

Brown, Norman O., *Love's Body*, Random House, New York, 1966.

Budge, E. A. Wallis, trans., *The Egyptian Book of the Dead*, Dover Publications, Inc., New York, 1967.

Callanan, Maggie, and Patricia Kelley. *Final Gifts: Understanding the Special Awareness, Needs and Communications of the Dying*, Bantam, New York, 1992.

Carlson, Lisa, *Caring for Your Own Dead*, Upper Access Publishers, Hinesburg, Vt., 1987.

Carse, James P., *Death and Existence*, John Wiley & Sons, New York, 1980.

Chang, Garma C. C., *The Buddhist Teaching of Totality*, Pennsylvania State University Press, University Park, Pa., and London, 1977.

Childress, J. F., and J. Macquarrie, eds., *The Westminster Dictionary of Christian Ethics*, Westminster Press, Philadelphia, 1986.

Conze, Edward, *Thirty Years of Buddhist Studies*, Bruno Cassirer Ltd., Oxford, 1967.

———, ed., *Buddhist Texts Through the Ages*, Philosophical Library, New York, 1954.

Cook, Francis Dojun, *How to Raise an Ox*, Center Publications, Los Angeles, 1978.

Coomaraswamy, Ananda K., *The Buddha and the Gospel of Buddhism*, G. P. Putnam's Sons, New York, 1916.

David-Neel, Alexandra, *Buddhism: Its Doctrines and Its Methods*, Avon Books, New York, 1979.

De Spelder, Lynne Ann, and Albert Strickland, *The Last Dance: Encountering Death and Dying*, Mayfield Publishing Co., Palo Alto, Calif., 1983.

Dossey, Larry, M.D., *Beyond Illness*, New Science Library, Shambhala, Boston, 1984.

Editors of Consumer Reports, *Funerals: Consumers' Last Rights,* W. W. Norton & Co., Inc., New York, 1977.

Elias, Norbert, *The Loneliness of the Dying,* Basil Blackwell, Oxford and New York, 1985.

Engel, George, "Pain," in *MacBryde's Signs and Symptoms,* ed. Robert S. Blacklow, J. B. Lippincott Co., Philadelphia, 1983.

Evans-Wentz, W. Y., *Tibetan Yoga and Secret Doctrines,* 2nd edition, Oxford University Press, London, 1958.

———, ed., *The Tibetan Book of the Great Liberation,* Oxford University Press, London, 1954.

———, trans., *The Tibetan Book of the Dead,* 3rd edition, Oxford University Press, London, 1957.

Fairley, Peter, *The Conquest of Pain,* Charles Scribner's Sons, New York, 1978.

Ford, Charles V., M.D., *The Somatizing Disorders: Illness as a Way of Life,* Elsevier Biomedical, New York.

Frazer, Sir James, *The Golden Bough,* abridged edition, The Macmillan Co., New York, 1945.

Fremantle, Francesca, and Chogyam Trungpa, trans., *The Tibetan Book of the Dead,* Shambhala, Berkeley, Calif., 1975.

Fromm, Eric, *The Heart of Man,* 2nd edition, Perennial Library, Harper & Row, New York, 1980.

Fulton, Robert, Eric Markusen, Greg Owen, and Jane L. Scheiber, eds., *Death and Dying,* Addison-Wesley Publishing Co., Reading, Mass., 1978.

Giles, Herbert A., trans., *Chuang Tzu,* George Allen & Unwin, Ltd., London, 1961.

Govinda, Lama Anagarika, *Creative Meditation and Multidimensional Consciousness,* The Theosophical Publishing House, Wheaton, Ill., 1978.

———, *Foundations of Tibetan Mysticism,* E. P. Dutton, New York, 1960.

Gray, J. Glenn, *The Warriors,* Harper Colophon Books, New York, 1970.

Grollman, Earl, *When Your Loved One Is Dying,* Beacon Press, Boston, 1980.

———, ed., *Concerning Death: A Practical Guide for the Living,* Beacon Press, Boston, 1974.

Gunaratna, V. F., *Buddhist Reflections on Death,* The Wheel Publication No. 102/103, Buddhist Publication Society, Kandy, Sri Lanka, 1966.

Hampton, Charles, *The Transition Called Death,* The Theosophical Publishing House, Wheaton, Ill., 1979.

Harmer, Ruth Mulvey, *The High Cost of Dying,* Collier Books, New York, 1963.

Hastings, James, ed., *Encyclopedia of Religion and Ethics,* Vol. 12, Charles Scribner's Sons, New York, 1951.

Hodson, Geoffrey, *Through the Gateway of Death,* The Theosophical Publishing House, London, 1976.

Humphrey, Derek, and Ann Wickett, *The Right to Die: Understanding Euthanasia,* Harper & Row, New York, 1986.

James, P. T., *Cover Her Face,* Warner Books, New York, 1982.

Jung, C. G., *The Undiscovered Self,* The New American Library of World Literature, Inc., New York, 1958.

Kamath, M. V., *Philosophy of Death and Dying,* Himalayan International Institute of Yoga Science and Philosophy, Honesdale, Pa., 1978.

Kapleau, Philip, *The Wheel of Death,* George Allen & Unwin, Ltd., London, 1972.

Kierkegaard, Søren, "The Decisiveness of Death: At the Side of a Grave," in *Thoughts on Crucial Situations: Three Discourses on Imagined Occasions,* trans. David F. Swenson, 2nd edition, Augsburg Publishing House, Minneapolis, 1941.

Kothari, Manu L., and Lopa A. Mehta, *Death: A New Perspective on the Phenomena of Disease and Dying,* Marion Boyars, London and New York, 1986.

Kübler-Ross, Elisabeth, *Death: The Final Stage of Growth,* Simon & Schuster, New York, 1986.

———, and Mal Warshaw, *To Live Until We Say Goodbye,* Prentice-Hall, Inc., Englewood Cliffs, N.J., 1978.

Ladd, John, ed., *Ethical Issues Relating to Life and Death,* Oxford University Press, New York, 1979.

Lee, Jung Young, *Death and Beyond in the Eastern Perspective,* Gordon & Breach, New York, 1974.

Lepp, Ignace, *Death and Its Mysteries,* trans. Bernard Murchland, The Macmillan Co., New York, 1968.

Levine, Stephen, *Who Dies?* Anchor Press/Doubleday, Garden City, N.Y., 1982.

Lewis, C. S., *The Problem of Pain,* Collins/Fontana Books, London, 1959.

Lifton, Robert Jay, and Eric Olson, *Living and Dying,* Praeger Publishers, New York, 1974.

Lipp, Martin R., M.D., *Respectful Treatment: A Practical Handbook of Patient Care,* 2nd edition, Elsevier, New York.

Little, Deborah Whiting, *Home Care for the Dying,* Dial Press/Doubleday, Garden City, N.Y., 1985.

Longaker, Christine, *Facing Death and Finding Hope: A Guide to the Emotional and Spiritual Care of the Dying,* Doubleday, New York, 1997.

Lunceford, Ron and Judy, *Attitudes on Death and Dying,* Hwong Publishing Co., Los Alamitos, Calif., 1976.

Lusseyran, Jacques, *And There Was Light,* trans. Elizabeth R. Cameron, Parabola Books, New York, 1987.

———, *The Blind in Society* and *Blindness, A New Seeing of the World,* Proceedings No. 27, The Myrin Institute, New York.

Maguire, Daniel, *Death by Choice,* Image Books/Doubleday, Garden City, N.Y., 1984.

Maslow, Abraham H., *Toward a Psychology of Being,* D. Van Nostrand Co., Inc., Princeton, N.J., 1962.

Maximov, Vladimir, et al., eds., *Kontinent* 2, Anchor Press/Doubleday, Garden City, N.Y., 1976.

May, Rollo, *Love and Will,* Dell, New York, 1969.

Melter, Milton, *Never to Forget: The Jews of the Holocaust,* Harper & Row, New York, 1976.

Meltzer, David, ed., *Death,* North Point Press, San Francisco, 1984.

Melzack, Ronald, and Patrick D. Wall, *The Challenge of Pain,* revised edition, Basic Books, Inc., New York, 1983.

Morgan, Ernest, *A Manual of Death Education and Simple Burial,* 11th edition, Celo Press, Burnsville, N.C., 1988.

Mullin, Glenn H., *Death and Dying: The Tibetan Tradition,* Arkana, Boston, 1986.

Museo Universitario, Universidad Nacional Autonoma de México, *La Muerte: Expresiones Mexicanas de un Enigma,* (Death: Mexican Expressions of an Enigma), Mexico City, 1975.

Neale, Robert E., ed., *The Art of Dying,* Harper & Row, New York, 1973.

Nelson, Leonard J., ed., *The Death Decision,* Servant Books, Ann Arbor, Mich., 1984.

Osborne, Arthur, *Ramana Maharshi and the Path of Self-knowledge,* Rider & Company, London, 1963.

Paramananda, Swami, *The Problem of Life and Death,* 2nd edition, The Vedanta Centre, Boston, 1917.

Parrish-Harra, Carol W., *A New Age Handbook on Death and Dying,* De Vorss & Co., Marina del Rey, Calif., 1982.

Pelgrin, Mark, *And a Time to Die,* ed. Sheila Moon and Elizabeth B. Howes, The Theosophical Publishing House, Wheaton, Ill., 1962.

Porath, Samuel, *Life Beyond the Final Curtain,* KTAV Publishing House, Inc., Hoboken, N.J., 1985.

Rachels, James, *The End of Life: Euthanasia and Morality,* Oxford University Press, New York, 1986.

Rawlings, Maurice, M.D., *Beyond Death's Door,* Bantam Books, New York, 1978.

Ring, Kenneth, *Life at Death,* Quill, New York, 1982.

Sabom, Michael B., M.D., *Recollections of Death,* Harper & Row, New York, 1982.

Sahler, Olle Jane Z., M.D., ed., *The Child and Death,* The C. V. Mosby Co., St. Louis, 1978.

Saunders, Cicely, M.D., and Mary Baines, M.D., *Living with Dying: The Management of Terminal Disease,* Oxford University Press, Oxford and New York, 1989.

Saunders, Dame Cicely, M.D., "Pain and Impending Death," in *Textbook of Pain,* ed. Patrick D. Wall and Ronald Melzack, Churchill Livingstone, London, 1984.

Schwiebert, Pat, R.N., and Paul Kirk, M.D., *When Hello Means Goodbye,* University of Oregon Health Sciences Center, Portland, Ore., 1981.

Shibayama, Zenkei, *Zen Comments on the Mumonkan,* Harper & Row, New York, 1974.

Shibles, Warren, *Death: An Interdisciplinary Analysis,* The Language Press, Whitewater, Wis., 1974.

Silverman, Morris, ed., *High Holiday Prayer Book,* Prayer Book Press, Hartford, Conn., 1939.

Simonton, O. Carl, M.D., Stephanie Matthews-Simonton, and James Creighton, *Getting Well Again,* J. P. Tarcher, Inc., Los Angeles, 1978.

Simpson, Keith, consultant, *The Mysteries of Life and Death,* ed. Martin Schultz, Crescent 1980 edition, Crown Publishers, Inc., New York.

Singh, Kirpal, *The Mystery of Death,* Ruhani Satsang, Delhi, India, 1968.

Smith, Huston, *The Religions of Man,* Harper & Row, New York, 1958.

Snellgrove, D. L., *Four Lamas of Dolpo,* Harvard University Press, Cambridge, Mass., 1967.

Spiro, Howard M., M.D., *Doctors, Patients, and Placebos,* Yale University Press, New Haven, Conn.

Stoddard, Sandol, *The Hospice Movement: A Better Way to Care for the Dying,* Vintage Books, New York, 1978.

Strain, James J., M.D., and Stanley Grossman, M.D., *Psychological Care of the Medically Ill,* Appleton-Century-Crofts, New York.

Strauss, Maurice B., M.D., ed., *Familiar Medical Quotations,* Little, Brown and Co., Boston, 1968.

Sumangalo, Ven., *Buddhist Stories for Young and Old,* Poh Ern Monastery, Singapore, 1980.

Toynbee, Arnold, and Daisaku Ikeda, *Choose Life,* ed. Richard L. Gage, Oxford University Press, London, 1976.

Twycross, Robert G., and Sylvia A. Lack, *Symptom Control in Far Advanced Cancer: Pain Relief,* Pitman, London.

von Franz, Marie-Louise, *On Dreams and Death,* Shambhala, Berkeley, Calif., 1986.

Walshe, M. O'C., *Buddhism and Death,* English Sangha Trust Ltd., London, 1970.

Ward, Milton, *The Brilliant Function of Pain,* Optimus Books, New York, 1977.

Watson, Lyall, *The Romeo Error: A Matter of Life and Death,* Anchor Press/ Doubleday, Garden City, N.Y., 1975.

Zaleski, Carol, *Otherworld Journeys,* Oxford University Press, New York, 1987.

The following books and articles are recommended under the topic of moral philosophy and medical ethics:

Dyck, Arthur J., *On Human Care,* Abingdon Press, Nashville, Tenn., 1977.

Frankena, William K., *Ethics,* 2nd edition, Prentice Hall, Englewood Cliffs, N.J., 1973.

Kohl, Marvin, "Understanding the Case for Beneficent Euthanasia," *Science, Medicine and Man,* Vol. 1, 1973.

Reiser, Stanley, Arthur J. Dyck, and William Curran, eds., *Ethics in Medicine,* MIT Press, Cambridge, Mass., 1977.

Karma and Rebirth

Articles, Pamphlets, Reports

"Goblins and Bad Girls," *New York Times Book Review,* April 3, 1988.

Gunaratna, V. F., *Rebirth Explained,* The Wheel Publications No. 167/169, Buddhist Publication Society, Kandy, Sri Lanka, 1971.

Jayatilleke, K. N., *Survival and Karma in Buddhist Perspective,* The Wheel Publications No. 141/142/143, Buddhist Publication Society, Kandy, Sri Lanka, 1969.

Nyanatiloka, Mahathera, *Karma and Rebirth,* The Wheel Publication No. 9, Buddhist Publication Society, Kandy, Sri Lanka, 1964.

"Reincarnation and Renewed Chances," *The Christian Agnostic,* Abingdon Press, Nashville, Tenn., 1965.

Rosellini, Lynn, "Learning to Live Again," *Reader's Digest,* May 1986.

Smith, Susan J., "Kidney Dialysis: Learning to Accept a Life of Limitations," *Times-Union,* Rochester, N.Y., October 29, 1986.

Stevenson, Ian, M.D., *The Evidence for Survival from Claimed Memories of Former Incarnations,* M. C. Peto, Tadworth, Surrey, England, 1961.

Bibliography

Story, Francis, *The Case for Rebirth*, The Wheel Publications No. 12/13, Buddhist Publication Society, Kandy, Sri Lanka, 1959.

———, "Rebirth and the Western Thinker," *Light of the Dhamma*, Vol. 5, No. 2, April 1958.

Weatherhead, Leslie D., *The Case for Reincarnation*, reprint of a lecture given to the City Temple Literary Society, New York, 1957.

Yamamoto, Kosho, "Karma," *Young East: Japanese Buddhist Quarterly*, Summer 1956.

Books

Abhedananda, Swami, *Doctrine of Karma*, 4th edition, Ramakrishna Vedanta Math, Calcutta, India, 1965.

———, *Reincarnation*, Ramakrishna Vedanta Math, Calcutta, India; distributed by Vedanta Press, Hollywood, Calif.

Aurobindo, Sri, *The Problem of Rebirth*, Sri Aurobindo Ashram, Pondicherry, India, 1952.

Blackman, Sushila, ed., *Graceful Exits: How Great Beings Die—Death Stories of Tibetan, Hindu & Zen Masters*, Weatherhill, New York, 1997.

Blofeld, John, *The Wheel of Life*, Shambala, Berkeley, Calif., 1972.

Borowski, Tadeusz, "The Death of Schillinger," in *In a Dark Time*, ed. Robert Jay Lifton and Nicholas Humphrey, Harvard University Press, Cambridge, Mass., 1984.

Carse, James P., *Death and Existence*, John Wiley & Sons, New York, 1980.

Carus, Paul, *The Dharma*, The Open Court Publishing Co., La Salle, Ill., 1943.

———, *Karma/Nirvana*, The Open Court Publishing Co., La Salle, Ill., 1973.

Cerminara, Gina, *Many Lives, Many Loves*, William Sloane Associates, Inc., New York, 1963.

———, *Many Mansions*, William Sloane Associates, Inc., New York, 1950.

Chang, Garma C. C., *The Buddhist Teaching of Totality*, Pennsylvania State University Press, University Park, Pa., and London, 1977.

Ch'en, Kenneth K. S., *Buddhism: The Light of Asia*, Barron's Educational Series, Inc., Woodbury, N.Y., 1968.

Conze, Edward, ed., *Buddhist Texts Through the Ages*, Philosophical Library, New York, 1954.

Davids, T. W. Rhys, trans., *The Questions of King Milinda*, Part 1, Dover Publications, New York, 1963.

Evans-Wentz, W. Y., trans., *The Tibetan Book of the Dead*, 3rd edition, Oxford University Press, London, 1957.

Fisher, Joe, *The Case for Reincarnation,* Bantam Books, New York, 1985.

Frazer, Sir James, *Belief in Immortality,* The Macmillan Co., New York, 1913.

Fremantle, Francesca, and Chogyam Trungpa, trans., "The First Six Days of the Bardo of Dharmata," *LOKA, a Journal of the Naropa Institute,* Anchor Press/Doubleday, New York, 1975.

———, trans., *The Tibetan Book of the Dead,* Shambhala, Berkeley, Calif., 1975.

Gallup, George, Jr., with William Proctor, *Adventures in Immortality,* McGraw-Hill Book Co., New York, 1982.

Gaster, Rabbi Moses, ed., *Encyclopedia of Religion and Ethics,* Vol. 12, Scribner's Sons, Hames Hasting, N.Y., 1955.

Govinda, Lama Anagarika, *The Psychological Attitude of Early Buddhist Philosophy,* Rider & Company, London, 1961.

Hall, Manly P., *From Death to Rebirth,* The Philosophical Research Society Inc., Los Angeles, 1972.

Hanson, Virginia, and Rosemarie Stewart, *Karma: The Universal Law of Harmony,* 2nd edition, The Theosophical Publishing House, Wheaton, Ill., 1981.

Harrison, Gavin, *In the Lap of the Buddha,* Shambhala, Boston, 1994.

Head, Joseph, and S. L. Cranston, eds., *Reincarnation: The Phoenix Fire Mystery,* Julian Press/Crown Publishers, Inc., New York, 1977.

Humphreys, Christmas, *Karma and Rebirth,* The Theosophical Publishing House, Wheaton, Ill., 1983.

Jastrow, Robert, *God and the Astronomers,* Warner Books, New York, 1980.

Jung, C. G., *Memories, Dreams, Reflections,* ed. Aniela Jaffe, trans. Richard and Clara Winston, Pantheon Books/Random House, New York, 1963.

Kapleau, Philip, *The Three Pillars of Zen,* Anchor Press/Doubleday, Garden City, N.Y., 1980.

———, *Zen: Merging of East and West,* Anchor Press/Doubleday, Garden City, N.Y., 1980.

Kelsey, Denys, and Joan Grant, *Many Lifetimes,* Doubleday & Company, Inc., Garden City, N.Y., 1967.

Küng, Hans, *Eternal Life?* trans. Edward Quinn, Doubleday & Company, Inc., Garden City, N.Y., 1984.

Langley, Noel, ed., *The Hidden History of Reincarnation,* A. R. E. Press, Virginia Beach, Va., 1965.

MacGregor, Geddes, *The Christening of Karma,* The Theosophical Publishing House, Wheaton, Ill., 1984.

———, *Reincarnation in Christianity,* The Theosophical Publishing House, Wheaton, Ill., 1978.

Moody, Raymond A., Jr., M.D., *Life After Life,* Bantam Books, New York, 1976.

Mullin, Glenn H., *Death and Dying: The Tibetan Tradition,* Arkana, Boston, 1986.

Narada Thera, trans., *The Dhammapada,* Varjirarama, Colombo, Sri Lanka, 1972.

Neufeldt, Ronald W., *Karma and Rebirth: Post Classical Developments,* State University of New York Press, Albany, N.Y., 1986.

Paramananda, Swami, *Reincarnation and Immortality,* The Vedanta Centre, Cohasset, Mass., 1961.

Perkins, James C., *Through Death to Rebirth,* The Theosophical Publishing House, Wheaton, Ill., 1961.

Prabhavananda, Swami, *The Spiritual Heritage of India,* Doubleday & Company, Inc., Garden City, N.Y., 1963.

Rahula, Walpola, *What the Buddha Taught,* Grove Press, New York, 1959.

Rastrapal Bhikshu, *An Exposition of Kamma and Rebirth,* Buddhist Research and Publication Society of India, 1965.

Rinpoche, Sogyal, *The Tibetan Book of Living and Dying,* HarperCollins, San Francisco, 1992.

Sangharakshita, *The Three Jewels,* Rider & Company, London, 1967.

Schilpp, Paul Arthur, ed., *The Philosophy of Sarvepalli Radhakrishnan,* Tudor Publishing Co., New York, 1952.

Stevenson, Ian, M.D., "Twenty Cases Suggestive of Reincarnation," *Proceedings of the American Society for Psychical Research,* Vol. 26, September 1966.

Suzuki, D. T., *Essays in Zen Buddhism, First Series,* Grove Press, Inc., New York, 1961.

Takakusu, Junjiro, *The Essentials of Buddhist Philosophy,* ed. Wingtsit Chan and Charles A. Moore, 3rd edition, Office Appliance Co., Ltd., Honolulu, 1956.

Tatz, Mark, and Jody Kent, *Rebirth: The Tibetan Game of Liberation,* Anchor Press/Doubleday, Garden City, N.Y., 1977.

Toynbee, Arnold, et al., *Life After Death,* Weidenfeld & Nicholson, London, 1976.

Trungpa, Chogyam, *Cutting Through Spiritual Materialism,* Shambhala, Berkeley, Calif., 1973.

Warren, Henry Clarke, *Buddhism in Translations,* Harvard Oriental Series, Vol. 3, No. 9, Harvard University Press, Cambridge, Mass., 1947.

Yasutani, Hakuun, *Eight Bases of Beliefs in Buddhism,* trans. Eido Tai Shimano, Youval Tal Ltd., Jerusalem, 1966.

Zukav, Gary, *The Dancing Wu Li Masters: An Overview of the New Physics,* Bantam Books, New York, 1980.

INDEX